*This book is dedicated to the
fond memory of my parents*

Acknowledgements

This is to express my gratitude to the
following persons who made this publication
possible:

Jonel Kho, Bienvenido Luna, Joseph Tuazon
Alfonso Cancio, Jr., Rodolfo Mabazza, Jr.
Medel Esponilla, Roderick Callueng
and
Jesus Relles

In this expanded edition,
special thanks to
Mr. Mark Viduya for editing the book
and also to Ms. Merlina Merton,
my former associate, who
edited the addendum.

PREFACE

The purpose of this book is to impart the basic knowledge of *Feng Shui* to those who would like to improve their condition in life. It can be used by those who have a basic knowledge in *Feng Shui* as a reference work or as a primer for those who are as yet unaware of the subject.

Originally *Feng Shui* was used by the emperors and nobles in China to perpetuate their reign, to assure their hold and authority over the public and to increase their tribe. This was achieved mostly by employing the services of *Feng Shui* experts *(Geomancers)* to select the best burial site for their deceased parents and for themselves. The *geomancers* were sometimes tasked to destroy the *Feng Shui* of the burial site of prospective contenders and enemies. This type of *Feng Shui* concerning burial sites is called *Yin Feng Shui* or *Feng Shui* for the Dead.

The principle of *Yin Feng Shui* is that a well-chosen burial site with strong and beneficial energy or *chi* emanating from the surrounding mountains, called Dragons, will nourish the skeleton buried there and act on the RNA and DNA molecules (which control heredity). This will in turn transmit to its descendants, in a mysterious way, the beneficial *chi* of the site.

One of the important aspects of *Yin Feng Shui* is choosing the most auspicious date and time for burial as this will trigger or activate the floodgate of the beneficial *chi* of the site to work on the remains/corpse.

The *geomancers* also help in the design of the houses of the nobles to ensure the accumulation of fortune and the continuous growth of their tribes. This is called *Yang Feng Shui* or *Feng Shui* for the Living. This aspect of *Feng Shui* is the subject of this book.

It was during the Tang Dynasty (A.D. 618 - A.D. 907) that *Feng Shui* was propagated to the masses. This was due to the persecution of *geomancers* by the Emperors and the ruling classes because many *geomancers* refused to misuse their arts. This knowledge was handed down from generation to generation up to the present day.

There are many *Feng Shui* schools which are classified into two main branches, these are the Form and the Compass Schools. Some of the more popular branches of compass school are: the Ba-Gua school, Three *Yuan* school, Three Harmony, Nine Moving Stars and *Xuan Kong* Moving Stars. The Form School of *Feng Shui* is considered as the basic course to all the above-mentioned compass schools.

The compass school especially the Nine Moving Stars, *Xuan Kong* Moving Stars and the Three *Yuan* Schools are able to predict and forecast events. The violations of the Form School often serve as the triggering factors for these events. Hence, it is of primary importance to have a genuine awareness of the violations of the Form School of *Feng Shui* and understand its underlying principles.

The author has studied and researched for many years and has synthesized the knowledge gained from the different schools of *Feng Shui* and has validated the proven and effective cures for *Feng Shui* violations. These cures are updated and adapted to suit the modern way of life. Many of the cures are given in this book.

It is because of the author's desire to make learning *Feng Shui* easy and fun for everybody, that it took three years to prepare the almost 200 illustrations finely drawn by architects in the modern context. The principles behind the *Feng Shui* violations are thoroughly explained with their corresponding cures given so that the readers will be able to administer the cures in their own homes should any *Feng Shui* principles be violated. It is the author's wish that every reader would be able to improve their lives and make this world a better and more enjoyable place to live in.

The presentation of the book takes the form of a *Feng Shui* 'tour' wherein the author takes the readers through a step-by-step procedure on how to conduct a *Feng Shui* assessment and reveals all the possible violations as well as their cures as the journey unfolds. The author guides the readers from the outside of a house to the inside, as that is the way you would tour a real house.

Should the readers be interested to go deeper into the study of *Feng Shui,* the author has arranged a three-level correspondence course, comprised of 72 lessons called *'Applied Feng Shui for Modern Living.'* This is to help the readers absorb, understand and apply the principles of the Compass Schools in order to achieve success and lead a more fruitful life. The three-level course is easy to read and understand and the lessons are programmed so that the readers will be able, by the end of the course, to be fully equipped with the knowledge of applied *Feng Shui.* In the first Level, four quarterly bonus lessons of a complete system of *Qi-Gong* or Chinese *chi* exercises will be included. In Level II, the Three Yuan school will be thoroughly examined. Problem solving will be the focus of this level. In Level III, the prosperity aspects of *Feng Shui* for business and offices will be taught.

CONTENTS

I	The History of the Plot	1
II	Outside Factor = Topography	10
III	'Backing' = Essential Condition of Good Feng Shui	16
IV	The Terrain = Four Basic Conditions of Feng Shui	30
V	Streets and Waterways Affect Your Fortune	41
VI	Outside *'Sha'* (Harmful *Chi*) Hidden Arrows	54
VII	Trees = *Chi* Indicator	66
VIII	*'Sha'* (Harmful *Chi*) at Your Doorstep I	71
IX	*'Sha'* (Harmful *Chi*) at Your Doorstep II	86
X	Gates and Walls	96
XI	Shapes	106
XII	Size of a House	117
XIII	Main Door = Mouth of the House	123
XIV	Floors = Channel of *Chi*	144
XV	Ceilings	150
XVI	Stairs = Conduits of *Chi*	154
XVII	Center (Heart) of a House	165
XVIII	Toilet = Source of *Yin Chi*	172
XIX	Kitchen	182
XX	Well	198
XXI	Bedrooms	206
XXII	Altars	240
Addendum	22 Most Frequently Asked Questions About Feng Shui	256
	Index	279

CHAPTER I

THE HISTORY OF THE PLOT

The purpose of this book is to let the reader not only acquire a good understanding of the basic tenets of *Feng Shui*, but also have the vicarious experience of conducting *Feng Shui* sitings with a *geomancer* (the author) through hundreds of finely drawn illustrations and in the process learn how to adjust or prescribe remedies for situations that violate *Feng Shui* principles.

The basic principles of *Yang Feng Shui* are:

(1) To preserve the beneficial *chi* (intrinsic energy or Life Force) of a site,

(2) How to bring in good *chi* from the outside into your place,

(3) How to chart the energy grid of the house to achieve a balanced and harmonious distribution of *chi* that can have a beneficial effect on the occupants. This will foster harmonious interaction between them.

It will also promote good health, increasing their efficiency in whatever endeavor they set out to achieve, thus improving the family fortune.

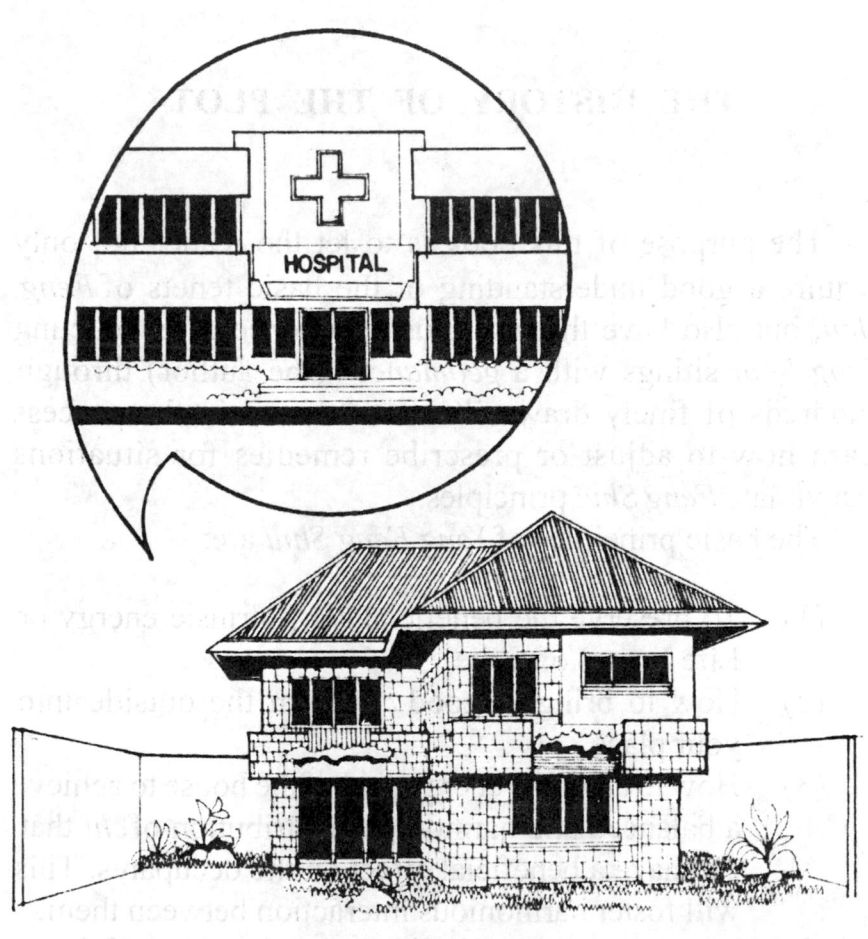

(Fig. 1) A house built on the former site of a hospital.

(Fig. 2) A house built on the former site of a funeral parlor.

All Chinese esoteric studies evolved from the principle of *Yin* and *Yang* or the principle of polarity. *Yin* pertains to female, darkness, dead, steady and water and *yang* pertains to male, light, living, moving and fire. It is the interaction of these two energies that creates the universe.

In *Yang Feng Shui* or *Feng Shui* for the living, the predominance of the *yang chi* is of utmost importance, as it brings 'life and activity' to a place.

So the first item in our *Feng Shui* checklist is to know the history of the plot. We should avoid a place that used to be the former site of:

(1) A hospital (Fig. 1) for it holds the frequency or energy of the sick and the dead,

(2) A funeral parlor (Fig. 2) for the energy of grief still hangs around it,

(3) A cemetery (Fig. 3) which could cause haunting,

(4) A slaughter house (Fig. 4) for it holds the energy of fright and despair,

(5) A temple or a church (Fig. 5) for the energy of the spiritual world is *yin* and incidents of ghostly manifestations are very likely to occur, and

(6) A police station (Fig. 6) where the energy of suffering and anxiety prevail.

(Fig. 3) A house built on the former site of a cemetery.

(Fig. 4) A house built on the former site of a slaughter house.

All of the above 'carry' or 'hold' the negative or *yin chi* that was associated and generated by the previous activities of the place. This *yin chi* can adversely affect the health and fortune of the occupants.

It is also not advisable to immediately build a structure on a property that was burned to the ground, as whatever energy pattern was associated with the plot was destroyed by the fire. To rectify or resurrect the energy pattern of the plot, one has to remove one meter of the top soil and replace it with new filling from a 'good' source that does not hold negative *chi*.

For those living near an earthquake belt, it is not a bad idea to check with the local geodetic authority regarding the location of fault lines. This is to avoid selecting a property that sits on a fault line as this could spell disaster to the occupants whenever an earthquake occurs.

Before embarking on our *Feng Shui* 'tour,' there are some basic precepts of *Feng Shui* you should be acquainted with in order to appreciate the art.

ℵᚈℵᚈℵᚈℵᚈℵᚈ

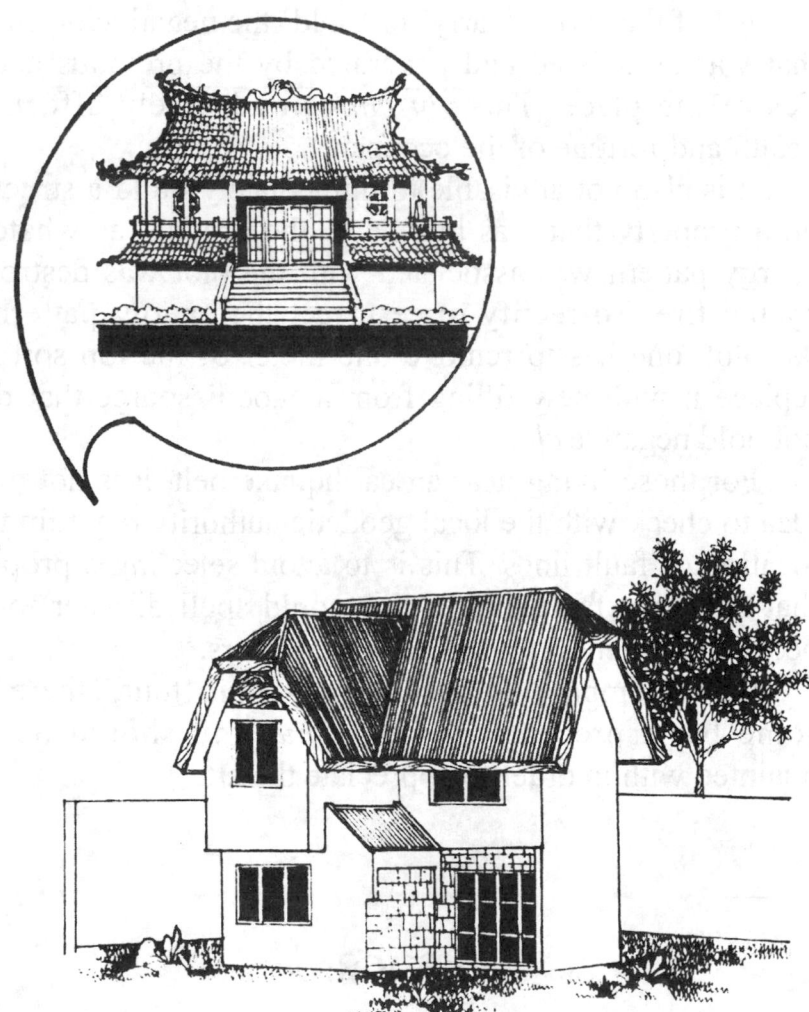

(Fig. 5) A house built on the former site of a temple.

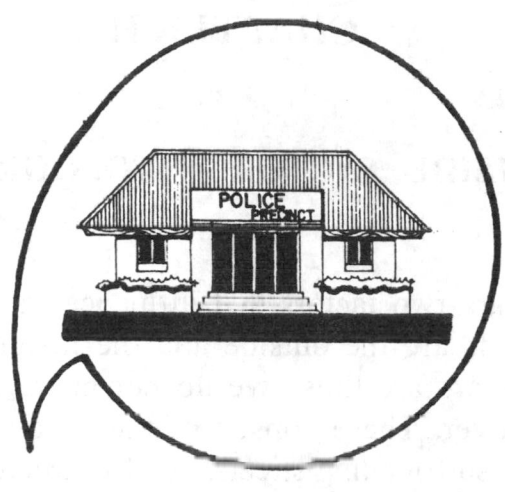

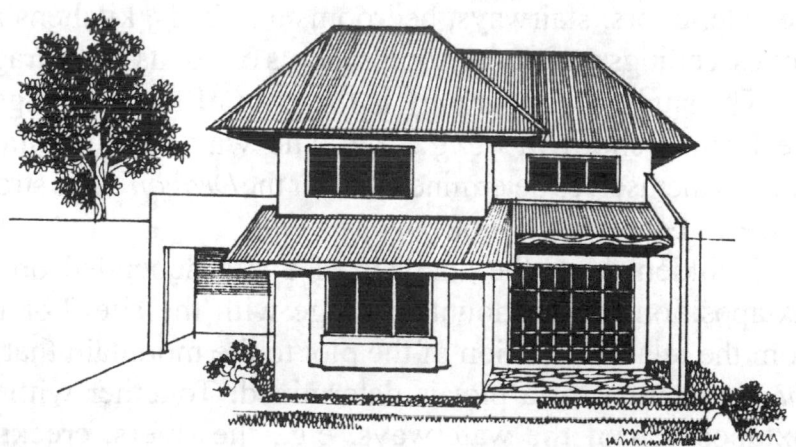

(Fig. 6) A house built on the former site of a police station.

CHAPTER II

OUTSIDE FACTOR = TOPOGRAPHY

There are two factors that influence the *Feng Shui* of a plot. These are the outside and the inside factors. The outside factors are those we do not have any control or influence over. These consist of the topography, terrain, waterways, surrounding streets, nearby structures or trees.

The inside factors are those which we have an influence over and these are: the shape of the house, the placement of the gate, doors, stairways, bedrooms and beds, kitchens and stoves, ceilings and floors, toilets, pools or ponds and garages.

The study of topography is the crux of the teachings of the Form School of *Feng Shui*. The way the mountains extends themselves determine whether the *Dragon chi* is strong or weak, beneficial or not.

In olden days, the analysis of a site depended on the juxtaposition of the mountain range with the site. For it is from the relative position of the plot to the mountain that the *chi* or element of a plot is determined. Together with the juxtaposition of the waterways, e.g., the rivers, creeks or streams in the area, that freeze the *chi* emanating from the mountain.

(Fig. 7) A house built on the highest portion of an area.

In modern days, the mountain or *Dragon chi* is interpreted as high ground, buildings, tall tress or high walls and the streets pertain to waterways.

The topography of a region molds the type of *chi* that covers the area, hence an area with a mountain range at the rear that extends to embrace both the left and the right side is considered as having good *Feng Shui* as it has 'backing' or support of the mountain at the rear and is being protected by higher ground on its left and right flanks. The connotation is that people inhabiting the area will receive the support or 'backing' from all sectors in their undertakings and will have helpful friends or colleagues. It also connotes stability likened to an emperor's throne with all the officials and army providing protection and 'backing.'

This condition when coupled with a wide expanse in front, that serves as the *'Ming Tang'* is considered to have most favorable *Feng Shui*. A wide expanse in front inculcates a wide perspective in one's outlook and foresees no obstacle in one's undertakings. Thus the essential condition of good *Feng Shui* of a plot is to have higher ground at the rear, if possible also to have high ground to its left and right sides and lower ground or no obstruction in front.

(Fig. 8) A house at the edge of high ground.

If you have built your house on the highest part of a site (Fig. 7), then it does not have good *Feng Shui* for the following reasons:

(A) It does not have protection from natural calamities such as typhoons and thunderstorms.

(B) It has no 'backing' which means that in all your undertaking, brinkmanship is the game you will play (Fig. 8).

(C) The place cannot hold or accumulate *chi* as the wind readily disperses it.

Conversely, if your house is built at the lowest portion of an area (Fig. 9) especially if it is below street level, then all the *chi* in the area will be accumulated in front of your house; this could lead to the stagnation of *chi*. Congested *chi* is not a favorable feature in *Feng Shui,* besides your house will be prone to floods during rainy days.

ଊଔଊଔଊଔଊଔଊଔ

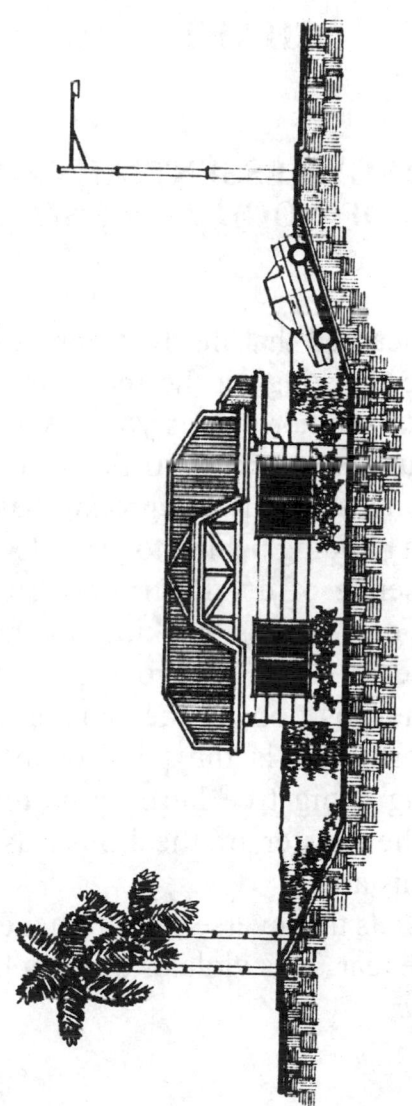

(Fig. 9) A house at the lowest portion of an area.

CHAPTER III

'BACKING' = ESSENTIAL CONDITION OF GOOD *FENG SHUI*

You have learned that the first condition of good *Feng Shui* is to have 'backing' at the rear. Let us start our *Feng Shui* 'tour' as the author guides you in choosing a place for a client to set up his residence, office or commercial outlet. In Fig. 10, the house in the foreground has good *Feng Shui* because it has a building behind to provide 'backing.'

In the absence of a tall structure, a big tree at the rear of a house could act as 'backing' as shown in Fig. 11.

A big tree in the northwest of a house (Fig. 12) strengthens the position of the master of the house. In *Feng Shui,* northwest is the position of authority (Fig. 13) and having a big tree here connotes support to the authority of the master of the house as the tree brings up the *chi* of this area.

Fig. 14 depicts the reverse condition, i.e., no mountain or 'backing' at the rear. This violates the first basic condition of good *Feng Shui*.

(Fig. 10) A tall building behind a house.

BIG
TREE

R O A D

(Fig. 11) A big tree at the rear of a house.

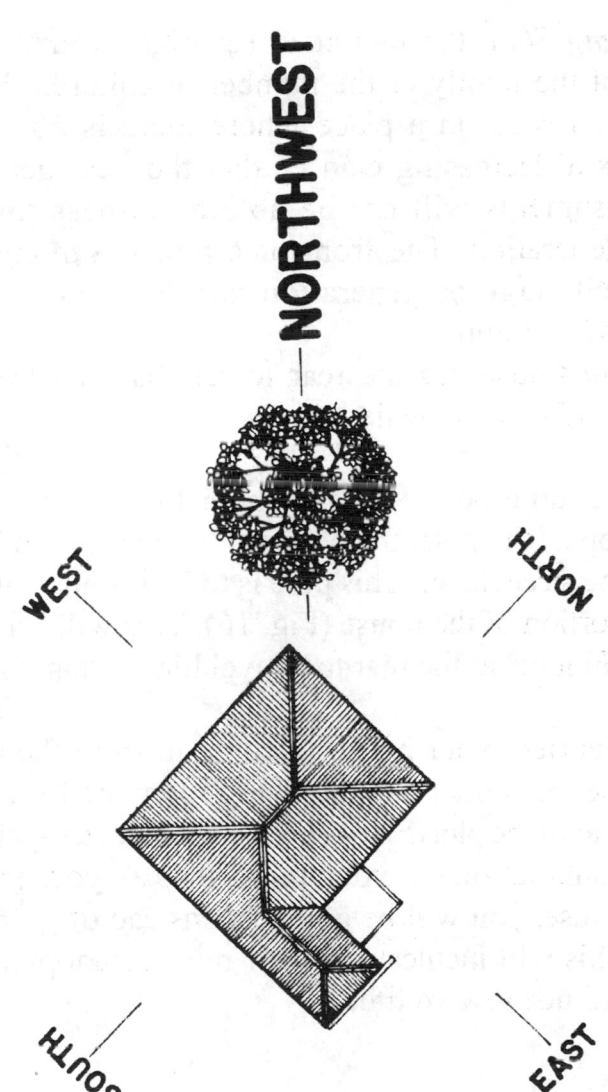

(Fig. 12) A tree in the northwest of a house.

In *Feng Shui,* the mountain (or high ground) governs the size of the family or the number of children the family will have. Living in a place where there is no 'backing' insinuates a decreasing clan or that the next generation's accomplishments will not be able to surpass that of the present generation. The front of a plot is synonymous to the present stage or generation and the rear of the plot represents the future.

If your house has the rear lower than the front street level (Fig. 15), the remedies are:

(1) Set up a pole with a 24-hour low wattage lamp on top of the pole, the height of which should be above the street level. This pole is to be installed at the rear portion of the house (Fig. 16). This will bring up the *chi* level at the rear to a level higher than the front.

(2) Reorient your house to come in from the rear, i.e., the main door and the living room are located at the rear of the plot (Fig. 17). This will have a psychological connotation on your mind that as you enter your house, you will be going up instead of going down. This will inculcate in your mind to adopt a positive attitude toward life.

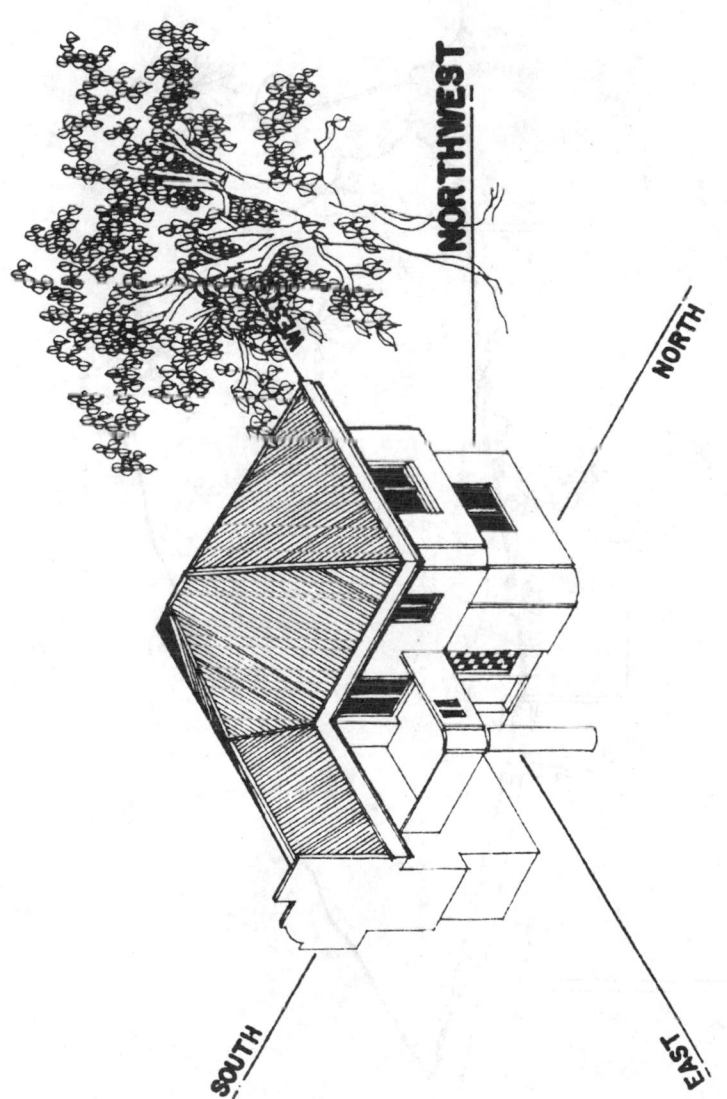

(Fig. 13) A big tree in the northwest

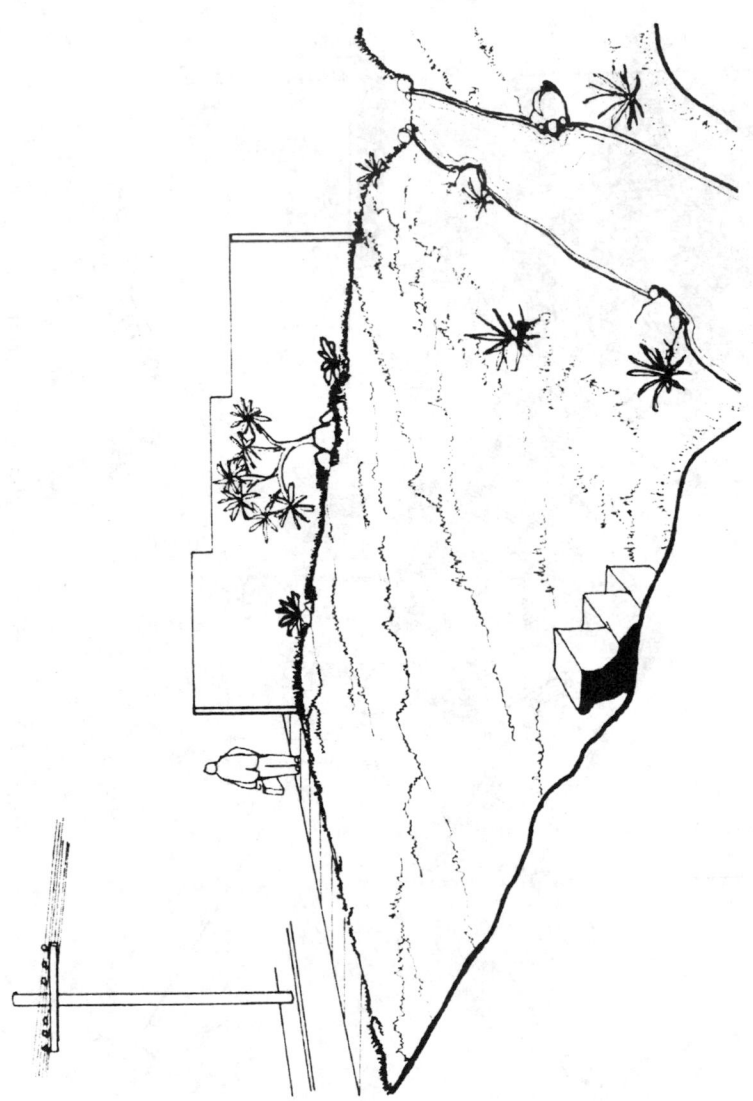

(Fig. 14) A plot sloping toward the rear.

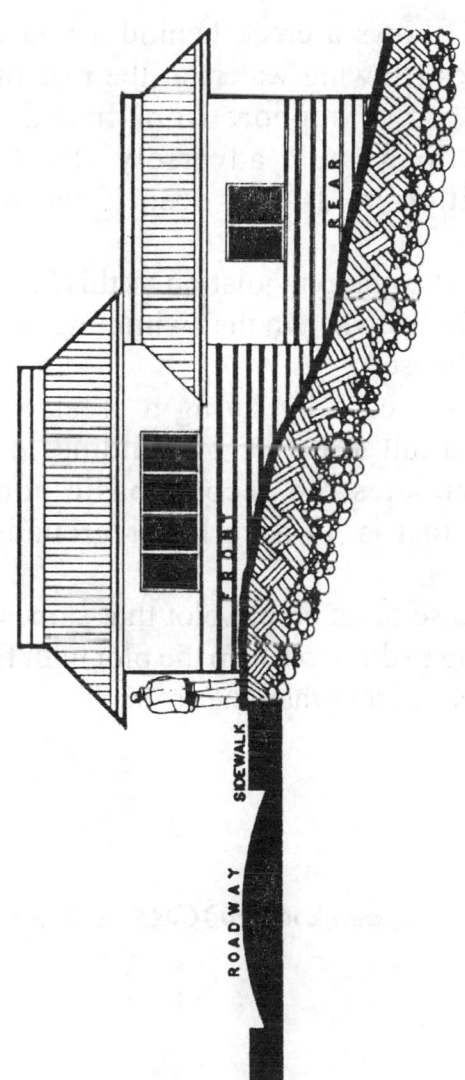

(Fig. 15) The rear of the house lower than the street.

Fig. 18 shows a creek behind a house. Here we have moving lines (flowing water) at the rear of the house. This connotes loss of support from friends and household members which could adversely affect family fortune. This condition holds true even if the plot has an even elevation.

The most common violation to this *Feng Shui* concept is shown in Fig. 19 wherein the swimming pool is located right behind the house.

The worst case is having a creek at the rear of the house and a tall structure or building in front of it (Fig. 20) This violates the second basic condition of good *Feng Shui,* that is, to have lower grounds in front of the plot.

In the case of an empty plot that slopes towards its rear, the best thing to do is to fill up the plot with filling materials to make the rear higher than the front.

ഇൻഇൻഇ ൻ ഇൻഇൻ

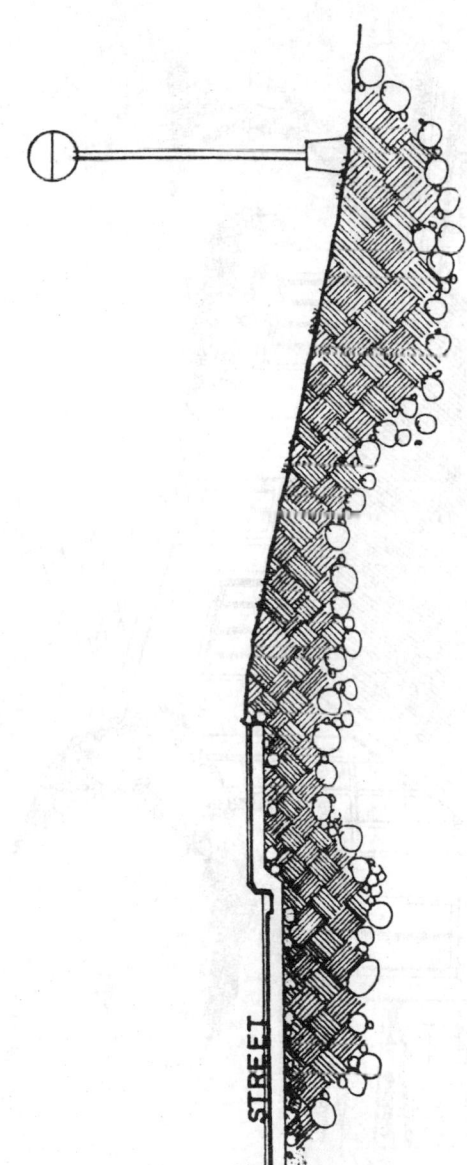

(Fig. 16) Remedy for a plot that slopes toward the rear.

(Fig. 17) Reorienting the house to come from the rear.

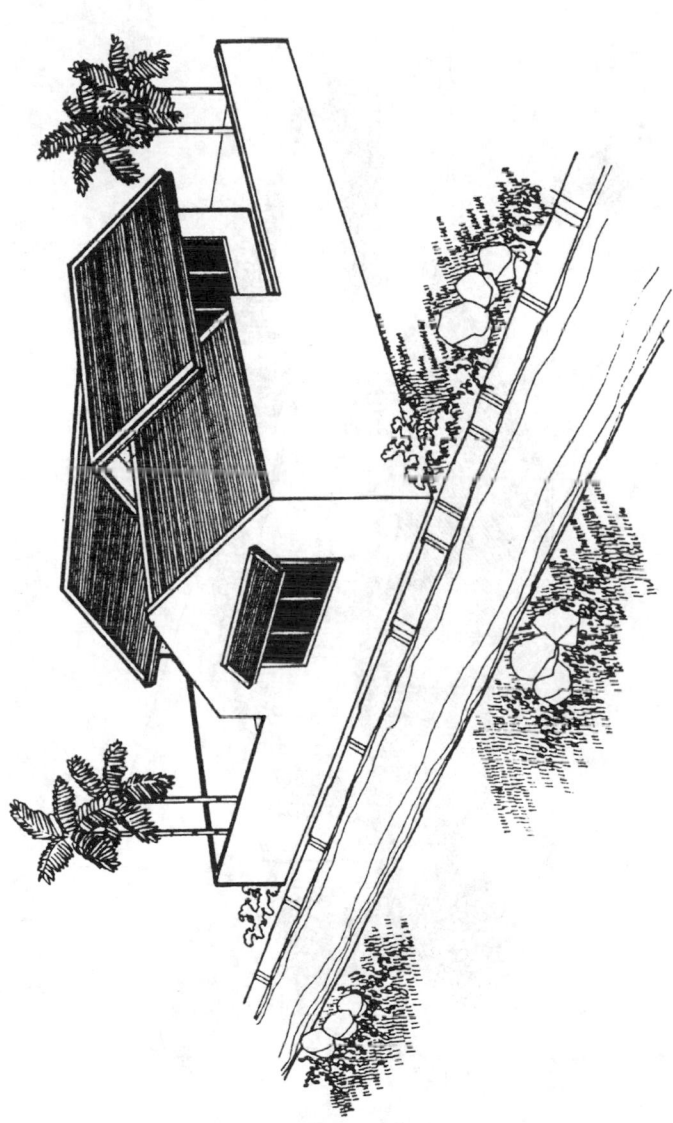

(Fig. 18) a creek behind a house.

(Fig. 19) A swimming pool at the back of a house.

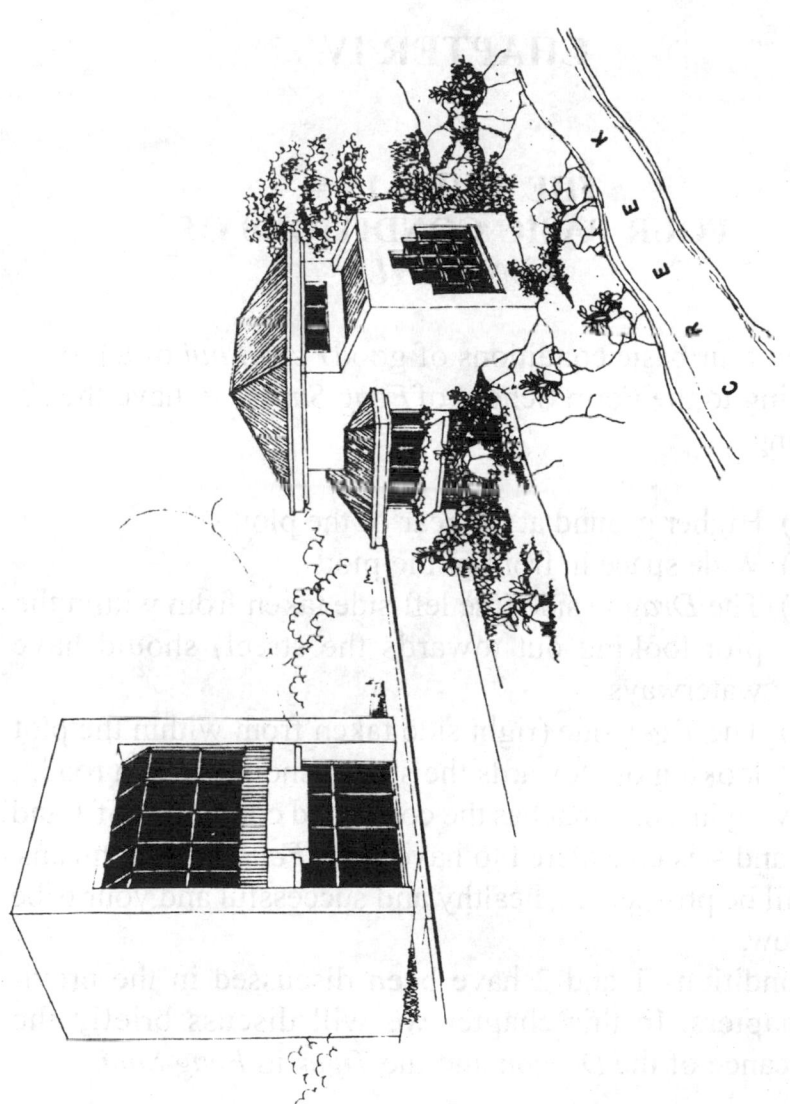

(Fig. 20) A house with a building in front and creek behind.

CHAPTER IV

THE TERRAIN =
FOUR BASIC CONDITIONS OF
FENG SHUI

The four basic conditions of good *Feng Shui* of a plot according to the Form School of *Feng Shui* is to have the following:

(1) Higher ground at the rear of the plot,
(2) Wide space in front of the plot,
(3) The *Dragon* side (the left side taken from within the plot looking out towards the street) should have waterways.
(4) The *Tiger* side (right side taken from within the plot looking out towards the street) should have a road.

Living in a plot that has the combined conditions of 1 and 2 or 3 and 4 is considered to have good *Feng Shui*. It means you will be prosperous, healthy and successful and your tribe will grow.

Conditions 1 and 2 have been discussed in the previous chapters. In this chapter we will discuss briefly the significance of the *Dragon* and the *Tiger* in *Feng Shui*.

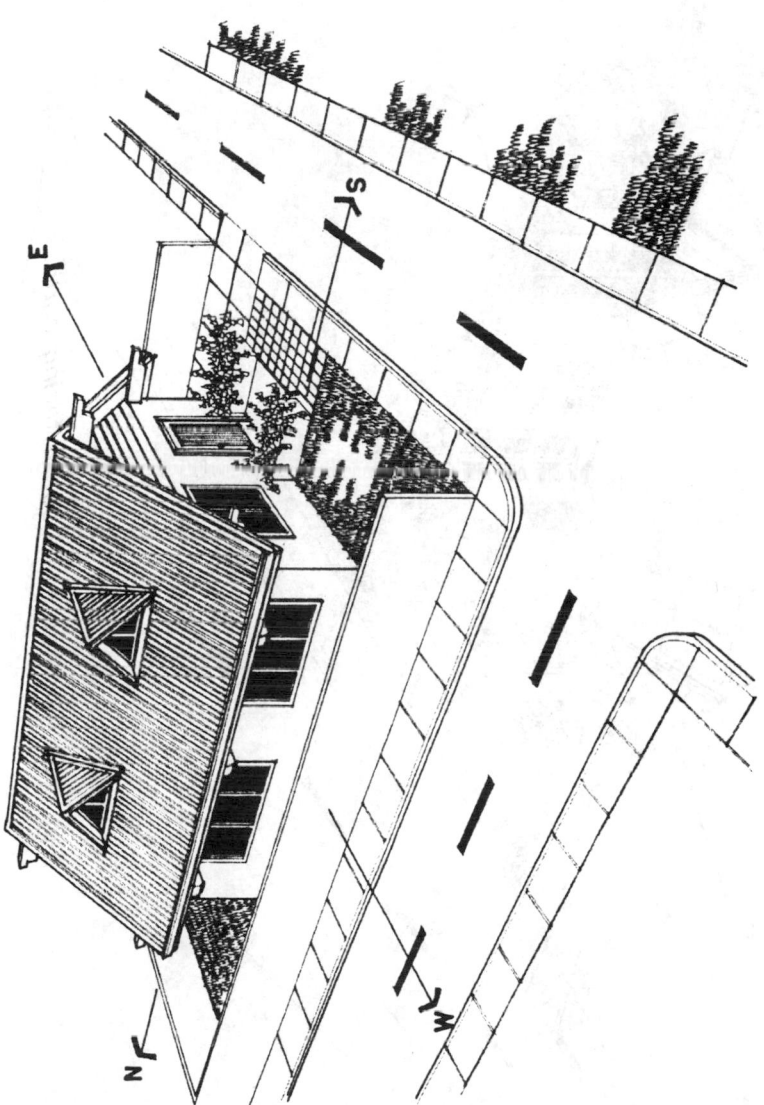

(Fig. 21) A house sited north facing south.

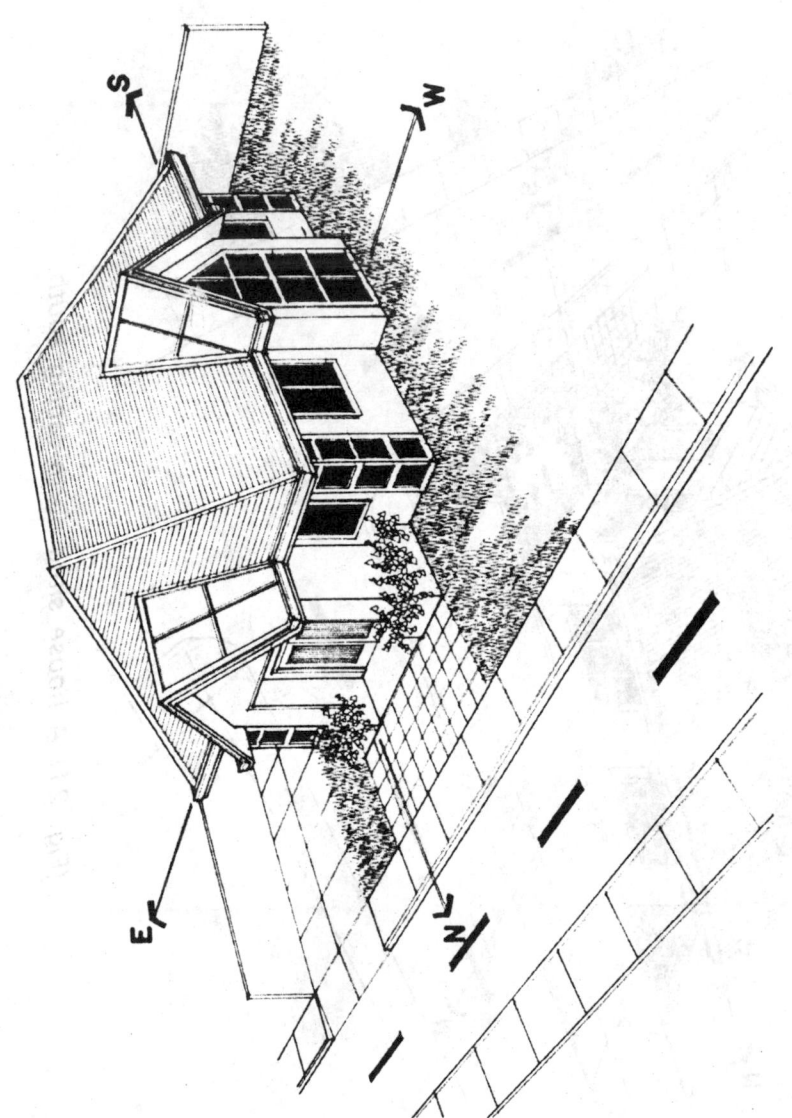

(Fig. 22) A house sited south facing north.

The *Dragon* is an auspicious animal. It is revered by the Chinese for it connotes activity and prosperity. While the *Tiger* is considered as a harmful and vicious animal that is feared and venerated. Hence, keeping the Tiger (the right side from within the property facing the street) passive or inactive is advisable as activity on this side will provoke the Tiger that might cause harm to the tenants of the house.

In China, cold winds blow from the north during winter, it is the rule of thumb to have the house sited with its back to the north and the door opening to the south as Fig. 21; this satisfies the four basic conditions.

Houses sited south facing north (Fig. 22) are considered unfavorable because the cold wind will enter the house every time the door is opened and this can cause sickness in the family. This rule only applies to countries in the northern hemisphere but not to countries in the southern hemisphere or tropical zones. This is misunderstood by many to mean that a door that opens to face the north is a *Feng Shui* violation.

The ideal siting of a house is sited west facing east where the rising sun greets you with its vibrant energy when you open the door of your house every day. Letting sunlight come into your house is a sure way of eliminating harmful germs and bacteria and to usher in *yang chi.*

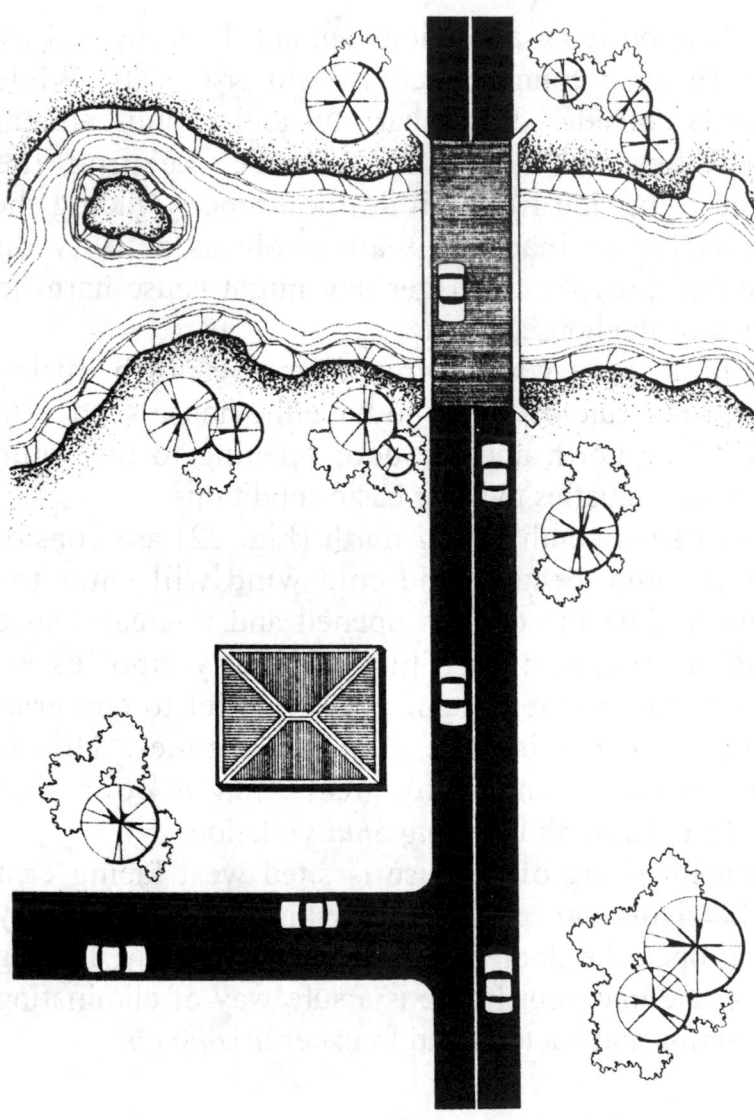

(Fig. 23) Top view of house satisfying the Four Basic Conditions of Feng Shui.

(Fig. 24) A driveway on the Dragon side of a house.

A bird's eye view of a house satisfying the four basic conditions is shown in Fig. 23. Here we have a river on the *Dragon* side and a road on the *Tiger* side, lower ground in front and higher ground and trees at the rear.

Since it is not easy to have waterways to the left of the plot, a driveway on the *Dragon* side will serve the purpose (Fig. 24).

Corner lots with a road on the *Tiger* side and a driveway on the *Tiger* side is bad *Feng Shui* (Fig. 25) because the *Tiger* is being unduly activated.

A garage in the northeast section (Fig. 26) of the house is not favorable as the northeast is called the *'Devil's Gate'* in *Feng Shui*. This will bring in *'bad' chi* to the house. This topic will be discussed in detail in Level I of the *Applied Feng Shui for Modern Living* course.

In the animal kingdom the Dragon ranks higher than the Tiger, hence the *Dragon's* position should be higher than the position of the *Tiger*. (In the Compass School of *Feng Shui*, the position of the *Tiger* and *Dragon* could alter based on the orientation or siting of the house.)

To continue our *Feng Shui* 'tour,' let's say that we are now on a rolling landscape in an elevated area where the plots along both sides of the street have different levels of *Tiger* and *Dragon*. This is especially true if the house is being built to conform with the terrain.

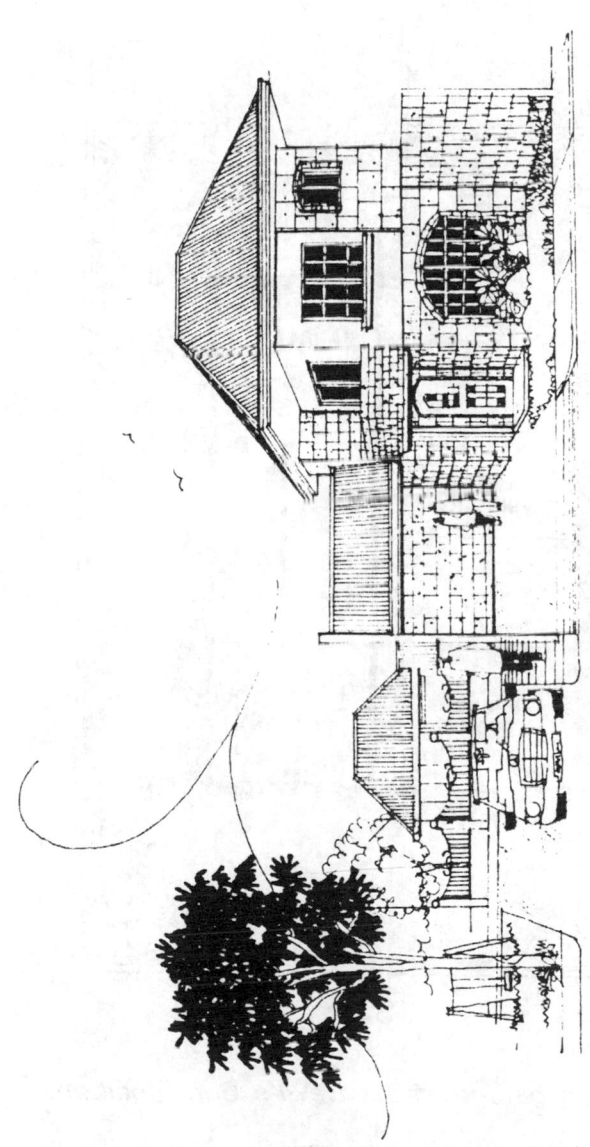

(Fig. 25) A road and a driveway on the Tiger side of a house.

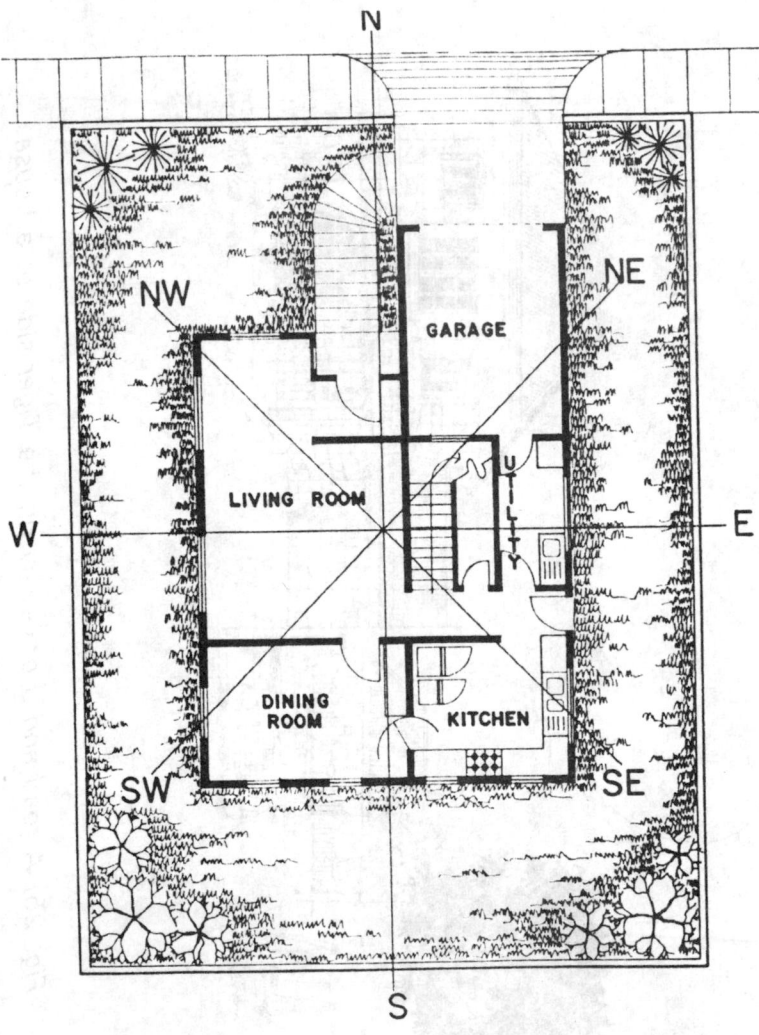

(Fig. 26) A garage in the Devil's Gate position.

Fig. 27 shows the *Tiger* side higher than the *Dragon* which connotes not having helpful friends in your undertakings. It is advisable to select a plot where the *Dragon* side (left from within) is higher than the *Tiger* side.

In a relatively flat area, the garage and the entrance to the house should be placed on the *Dragon* side. This combines the conditions 3 and 4 of the four basic conditions of good *Feng Shui*.

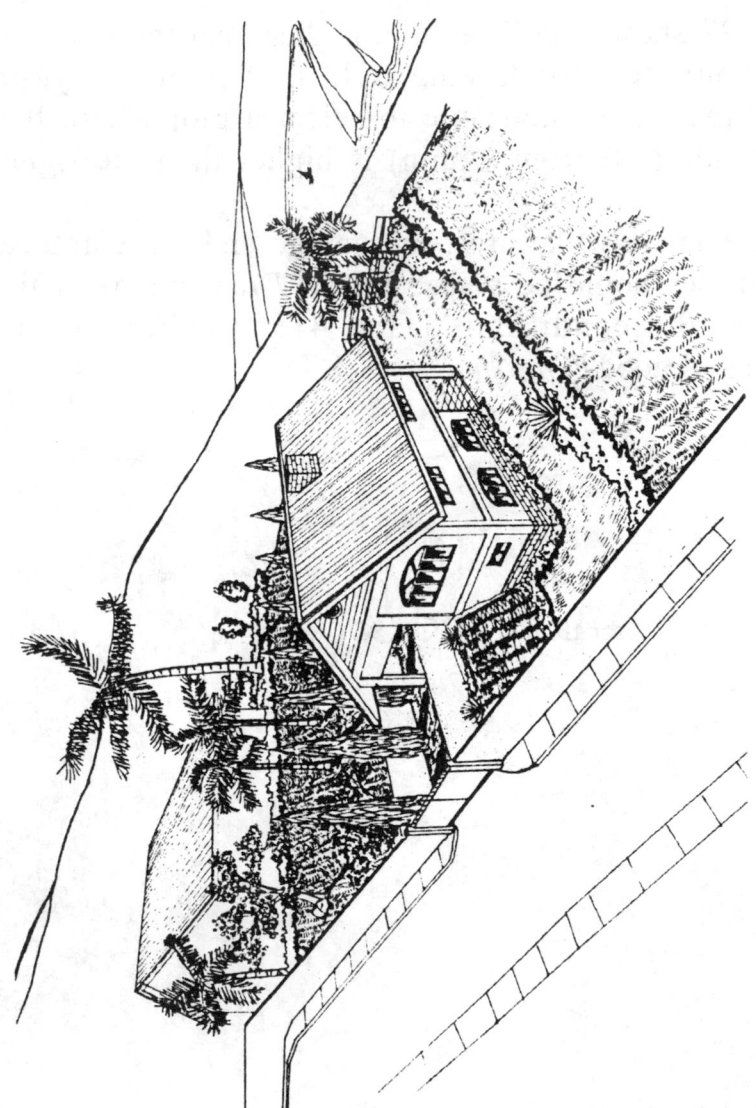

(Fig. 27) A house with the Tiger side higher than the Dragon side.

CHAPTER V

STREETS AND WATERWAYS AFFECT YOUR FORTUNE

Waterways play an important role in *Feng Shui* for it freezes the *chi* emanating from the mountain. Its juxtaposition in relation to the plot determines the fortune of the occupants of a property. In *Feng Shui*, streets are considered to be quasi-waterways. There are two types of water, beneficial water and harmful water.

Beneficial water or streets, are streets that gently cascade in a meandering manner towards the property (Fig. 28) where the *chi* generated by the water flow or by the traffic is neither strong nor destructive. Waterways or streets that embrace the property bring fortune to its occupants (Fig. 29).

Harmful water or streets, are streets that rush strongly towards the plot and turn abruptly at an angle (Fig. 30) to the plot. The momentum of the energy propelled by the sudden turn of direction still continues to travel and hit the plot. The strong *sha* can 'trigger' accidents and mishaps in the household.

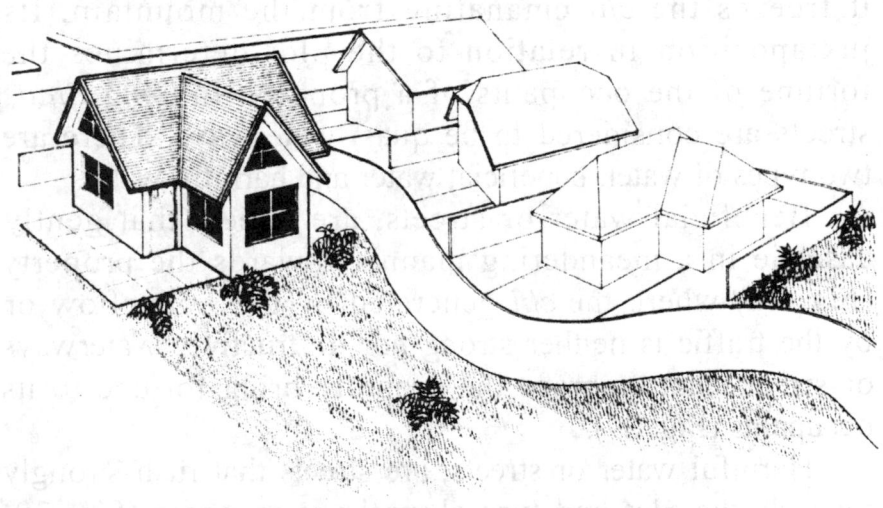

(Fig. 28) A house on a meandering street.

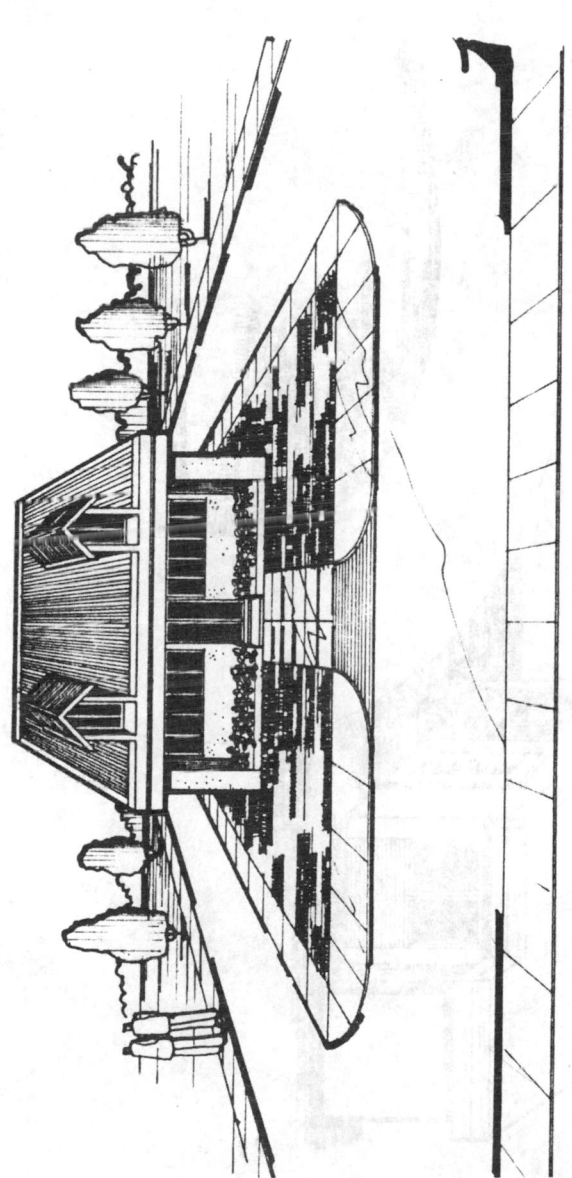

(Fig. 29) A house embraced by a street.

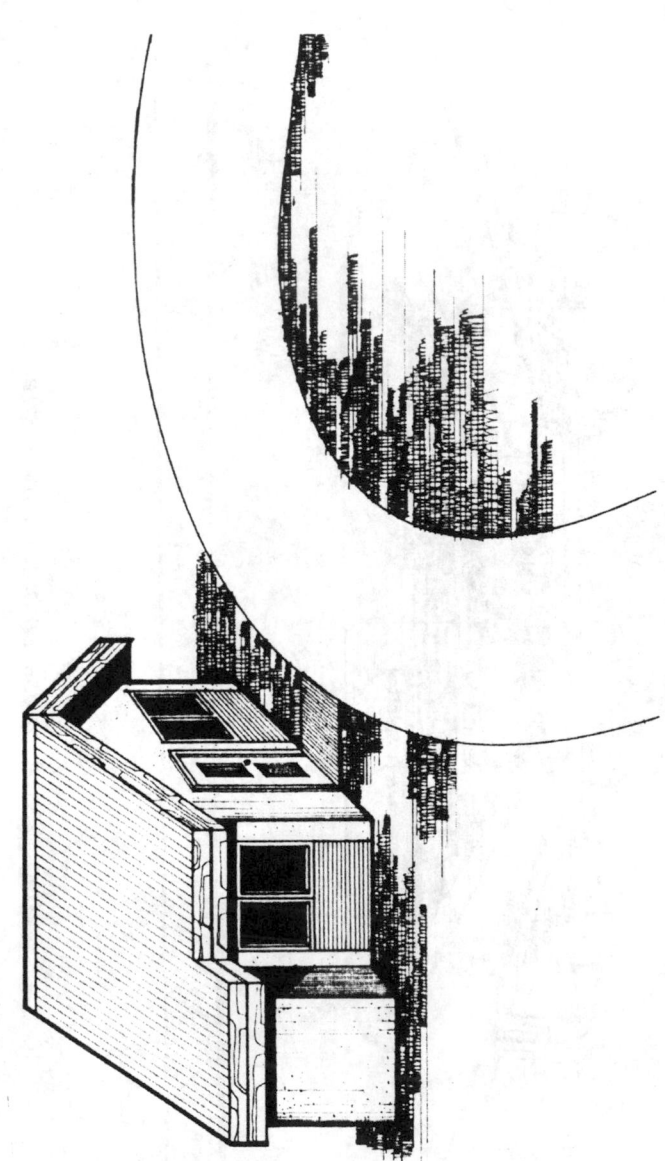

(Fig. 30) A house on the cutting edge of a street.

In Level III of the *Applied Feng Shui for Modern Living* course, you will learn to predict what year an accident or mishap will most likely occur and which member of the family will be affected.

The house (Fig. 31) on the left bears the brunt of the cutting *chi* of the river that could adversely affect the fortune of its tenants. The house on the right is being embraced by the river, this feature can facilitate the accumulation of wealth by its tenants.

In modern days this is translated in Fig. 32. The building in the foreground is embraced by the flyover, hence it will be easier for the tenants of this building to accumulate wealth. The building across the flyover in the background suffers from the cutting *chi* generated by the traffic flow. It is believed that the tenants of this building will encounter difficulty with their finances.

Another type of harmful water or street is a straight road leading to a house at a T-junction (Fig. 33). The strong and harmful *chi* generated by the traffic could cause loss of business opportunities and family disintegration this type of *sha* is called a *'chiong.'*

The remedy is to relocate the door so as not to be directly facing the road and in its stead put up a wall to block the *sha*. If this is not possible tall shrubs planted in front of the door can soften the *'chiong.'*

(Fig. 31) A river cutting one house and embracing another.

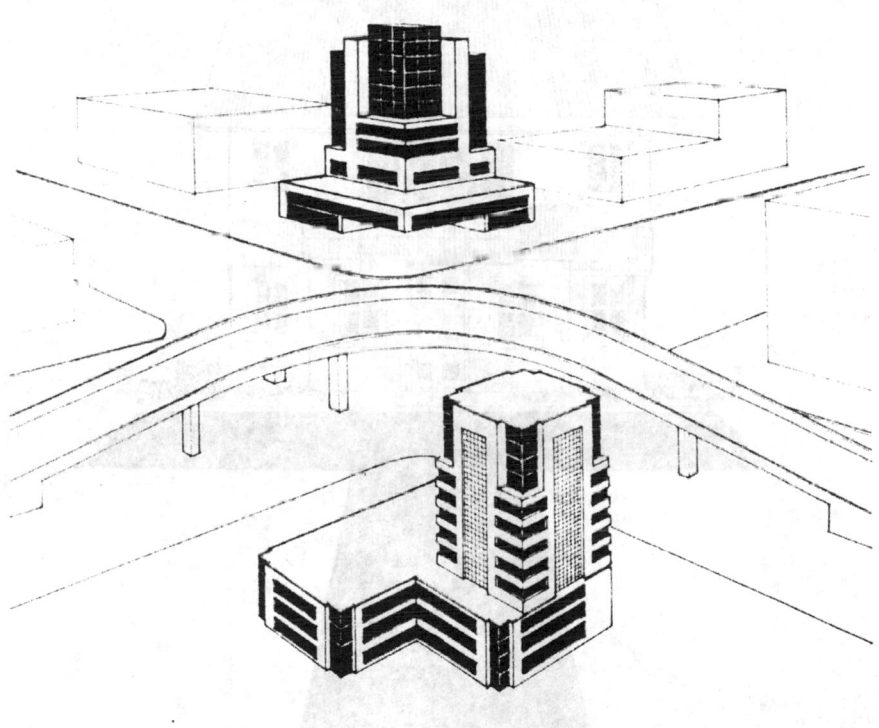

*(Fig. 32) A flyover embracing one building
and cutting another.*

(Fig. 33) A house at a T-junction.

A flowing fountain installed in front of the door could also disperse the *sha*. Hang a hexagram *Ba-gua* (see attached cutout) and a convex mirror on top of the door to deflect the *sha* when any or all of the above-mentioned cures are not possible to implement.

A house that is situated at the dead end of an inverted T-junction (Fig. 34) connotes that its tenants will suffer undue financial expenditures. This is due to the depleting*chi* generated by the traffic on the main thoroughfare that continues to 'siphon' the *chi* from the house. The cure is to install a concave mirror on top of the door.

Avoid selecting a house that faces the entrance of a residential subdivision (Fig. 35). The house is being subjected to two different types of *sha* generated by the oncoming and outgoing traffic. One is a stabbing*sha* (oncoming traffic) and the other a depleting (outgoing traffic). The energy pattern of the house is aberrant and does not enhance family unity and fortune. The remedy is to transfer the main door to the side of the house and plant shrubs to act as a buffer to the*sha*.

People residing in a house located at a Y-junction (Fig. 36) suffer the same consequences as that on a T-junction. The cures are also the same.

Fig. 37 illustrates a river in front of a house. This is considered to be beneficial if the water is clean, free flowing and not noisy. If the water is stagnant or foul smelling and noisy it becomes harmful water.

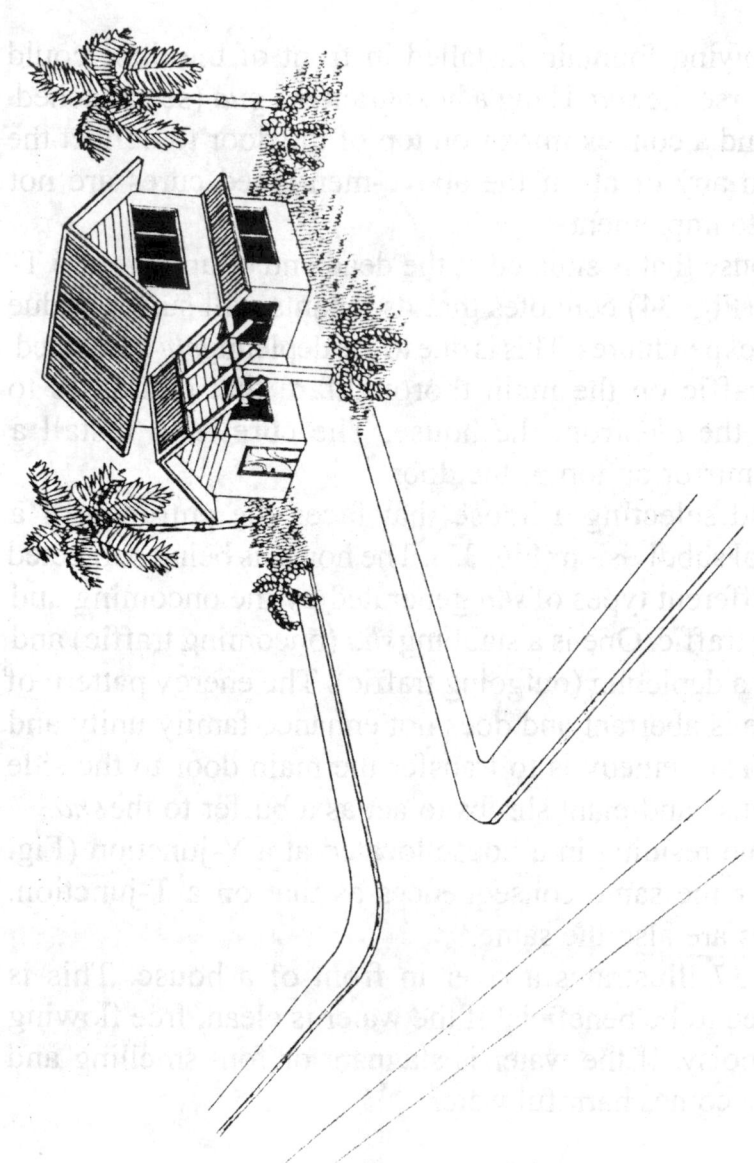

(Fig. 34) A house at an inverted T-junction.

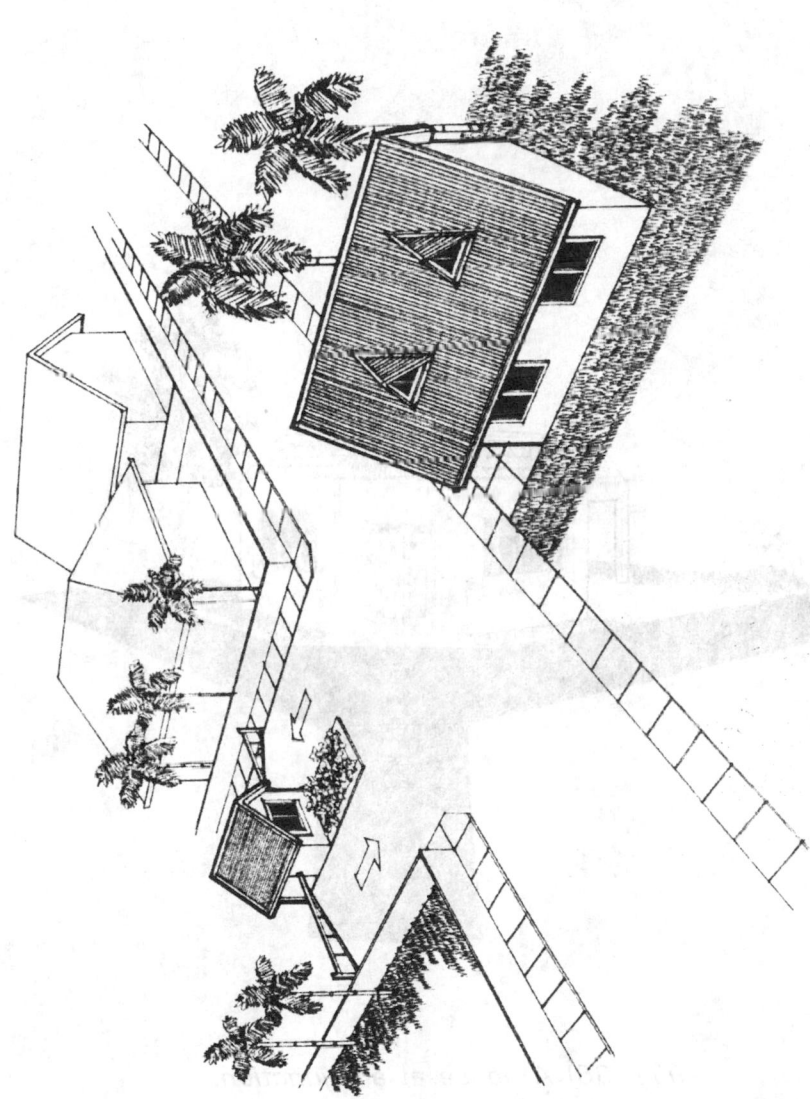

(Fig. 35) A house that faces the entrance of a subdivision.

(Fig. 36) A house at a Y-junction.

(Fig. 37) A river in front of a house.

CHAPTER VI

OUTSIDE *'SHA'* (HARMFUL *CHI)* = HIDDEN ARROWS

After knowing the topographical conditions of an area, we can determine whether the area has positive and 'protective' *chi*. Having considered the terrain based on the four basic conditions of good *Feng Shui* we have more or less selected a place with favorable *Feng Shui* features. The next aspect to consider is the *sha* coming from outside factors of the immediate surroundings; these are structures, buildings, trees or objects within sight that can affect the energy field of the property.

These harmful *chi* are known as hidden arrows and can exert a psychological influence on the minds of the occupants of the site which in turn can affect their outlook in life. Here are some frequently encountered *'sha'*:

(1) A property that is located near an electrical sub-station (Fig. 38) will adversely affect the health of the occupants of the house because the electro-magnetic frequencies generated by the sub-station are known to cause cancer-related illness to people living nearby.

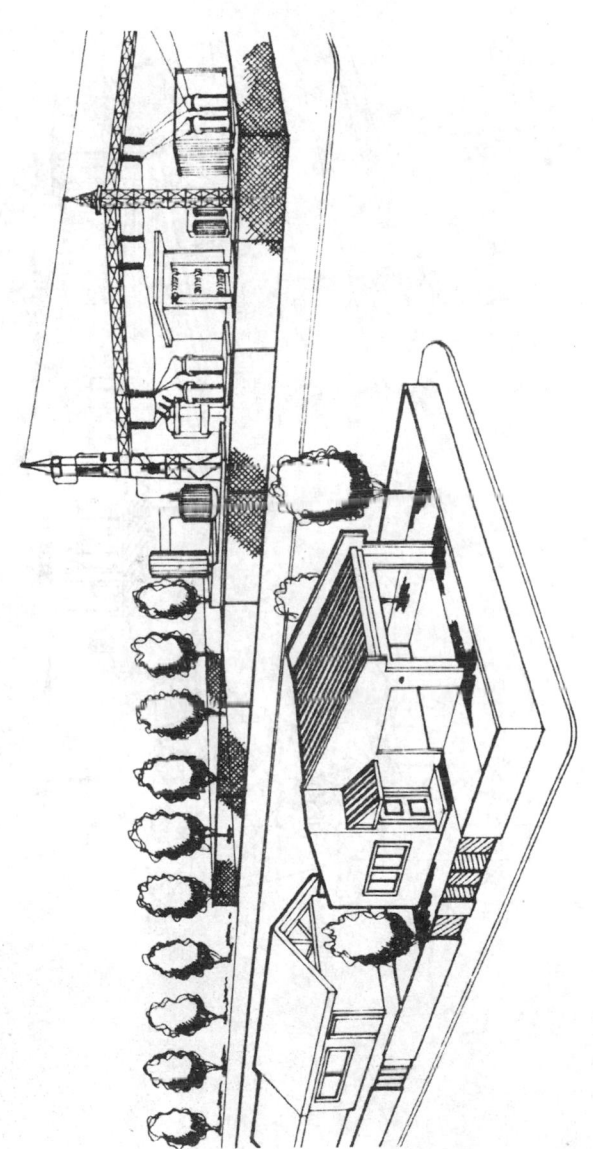

(Fig. 38) A house near an electrical sub-station.

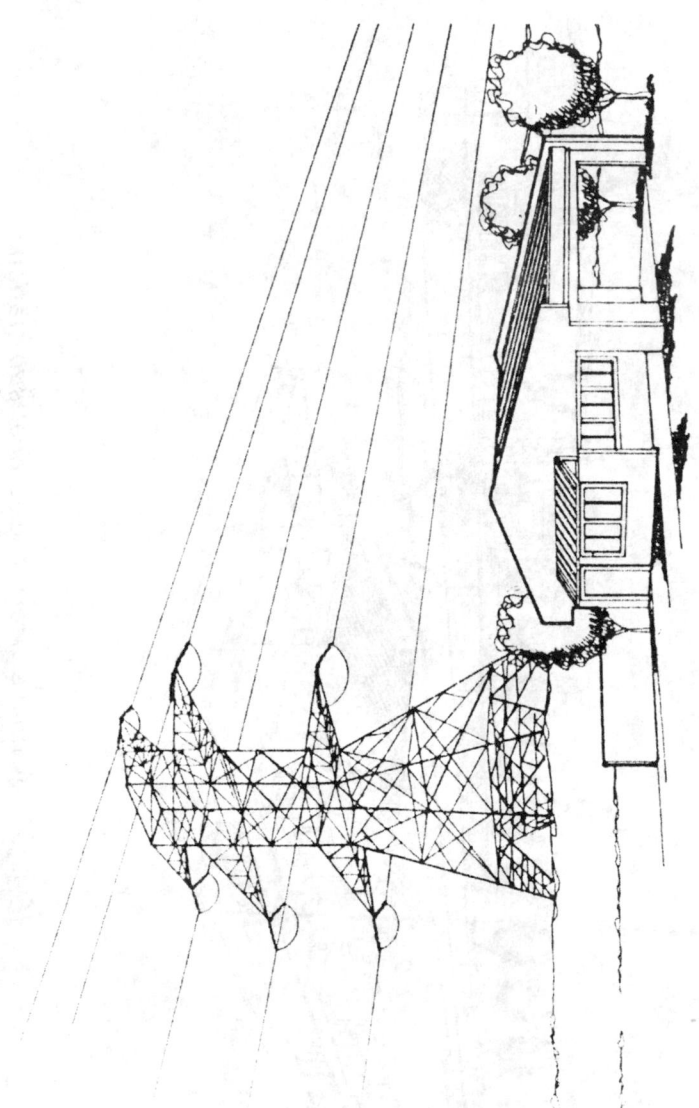

(Fig. 39) A house near a high voltage electrical tower.

The effect will be exacerbated should the main door be situated directly opposite it.

(2) A house located near a high voltage electrical tower (Fig. 39) is not as bad as the preceding case but the high frequency emitted can cause misalignment of one's magnetic field that can cause emotional upset or illness.

(3) The transmission tower of a communication station (Fig. 40) can affect the nervous system of the people living nearby. This will reduce their efficiency and can affect their family fortune.

(4) A house that is located in an industrial zone (Fig. 41) will have an adverse effect on the occupants' health especially their respiratory system. This is due to the pollutants emitted by the factories. The best way to get out of this situation is to transfer to a regulated residential area.

(5) Fig. 42 illustrates the worst *sha* to be encountered when your house is directly opposite two narrowly-spaced high rise buildings. This is known as the 'wind tunnel' *sha* as the wind funnels through the narrow clearance between the two buildings can create a 'cutting' *chi* that will hit the house with an impact similar to that of a sword. This cuts the house energy field in half; which can cause accidents, fire hazards and mishaps to occur. It is wise to avoid living in a house

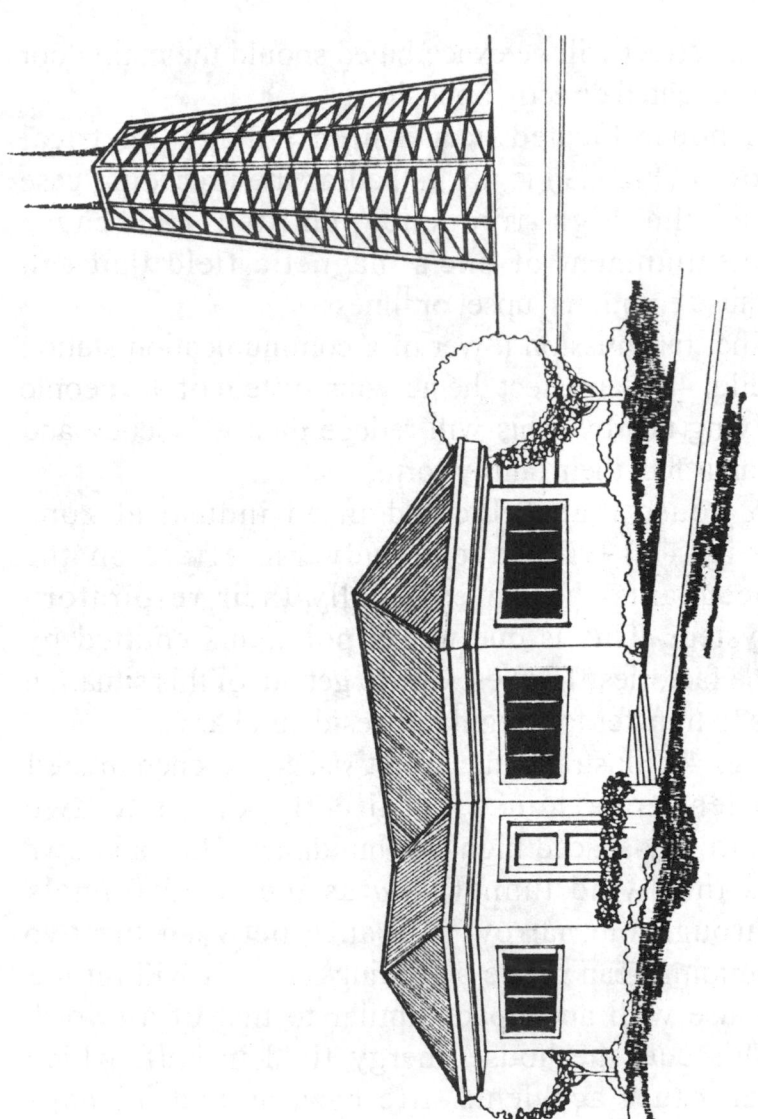

(Fig. 40) A house near a trasmission tower.

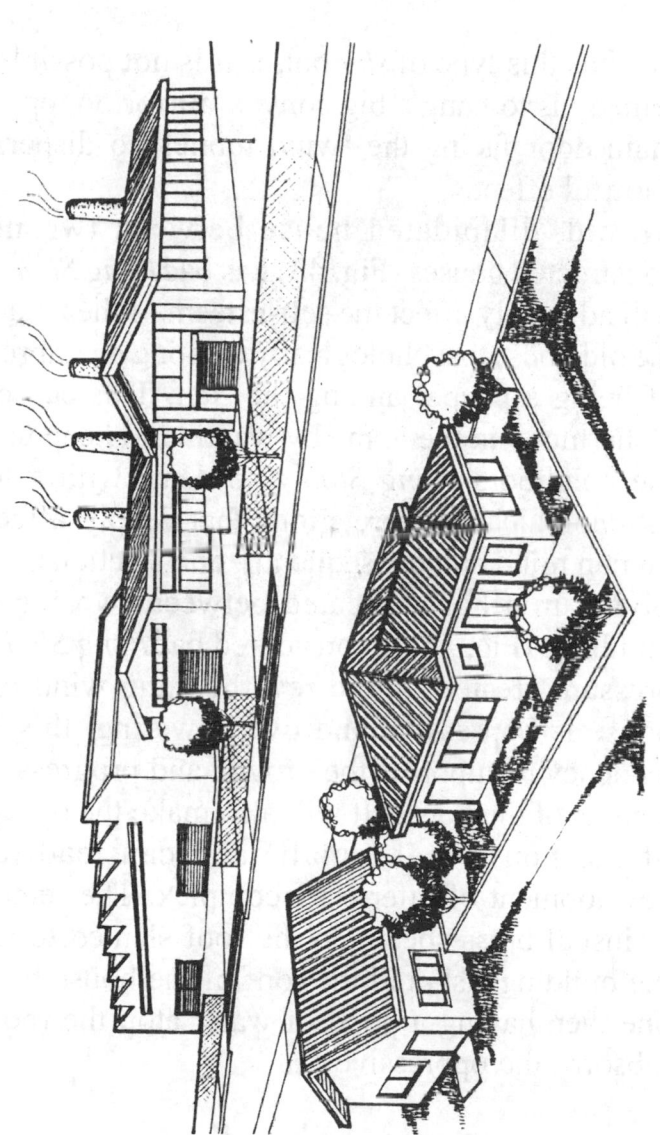

(Fig. 41) A house in an industrial complex.

that has this type of *sha* but, if it is not possible, the remedy is to hang a big convex mirror on top of the main door facing the 'wind tunnel' to disperse its harmful effect.

(6) An old, dilapidated house between two newly constructed houses (Fig. 43) has bad *Feng Shui*. This will adversely affect the self-esteem of the tenants of the old house, psychologically creating an impression of being a pauper among the rich. This can create disharmony in the home by wanting to keep up with the neighbors. *Feng Shui* also deals with a lot of psychological interpretations that deeply affect the human mind and consequently one's actions.

(7) Living in a house located between two high rise buildings (Fig. 44) is considered bad *Feng Shui*. The pressure created by the reverberating wind on the house is oppressive and overpowering, this has a tendency to suppress the growth and progress of the tenants of the house. It will also make the occupants of the house feel 'small' and can lead to the development of inferiority complex. The remedy is to install brass sheets on the roof slanted to reflect the buildings; should the roof of the house be a flat one then having a pond of water atop the roof will 'absorb' the oppressive *chi*.

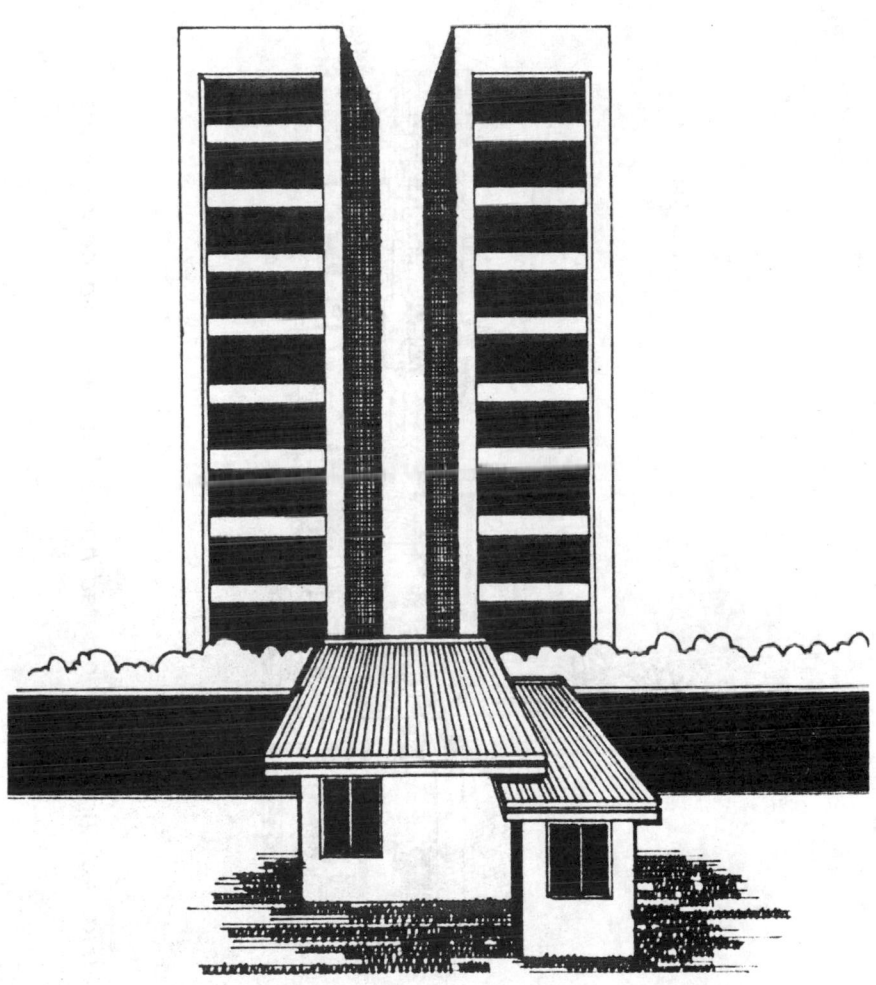

(Fig. 42) A house with a 'wind tunnel' sha.

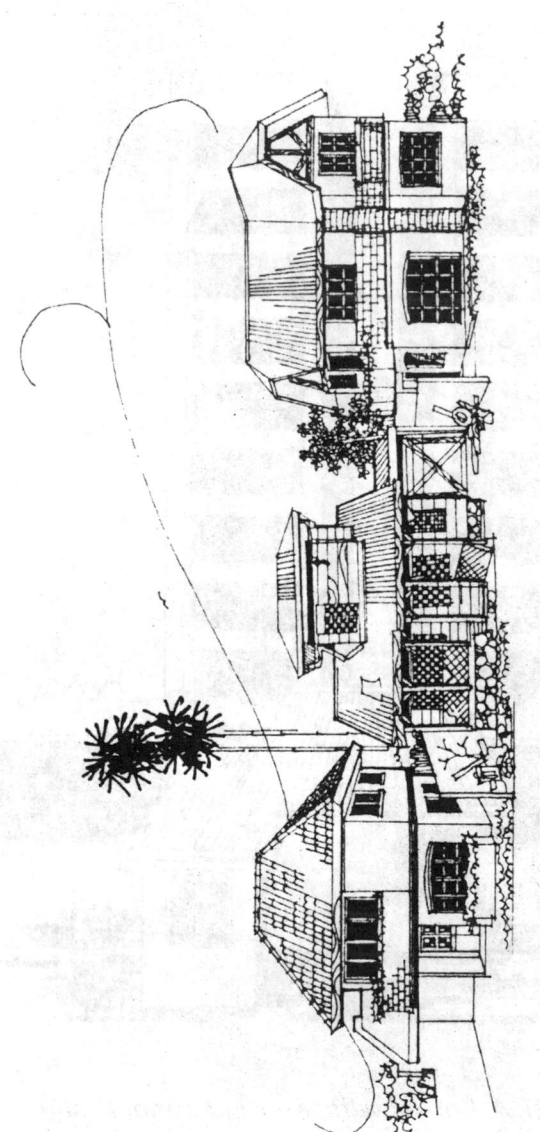

(Fig. 43) An old dilapidated house between two new houses.

Modern zoning is the best safeguard against high rise buildings being built in a residential zone as the maximum height for structures to be built in the area is fixed.

(8) The tallest building (Fig. 45) in the vicinity when the building juts out excessively from the skyline of the area possesses bad *Feng Shui* features for the following reasons:

(A) The building has no 'backing.'

(B) The levels of the building above the rest of the neighboring structures are being exposed to the wind all day and will not be able to accumulate *chi.*

(C) Despite being 'outstanding' the building 'pierces' through the *chi* or energy field of the surrounding area and is out of sync with the area's energy pattern. This does not augur well for the fortune of the occupants of this building, because the *chi* that flows into the building will not be consistent and tends to be aberrant.

(D) The tenants occupying the top floors will develop a tendency not to be 'grounded' and at times could be 'out-of-touch' with the rest of the world.

(E) It is definitely not enviable, try to imagine how the occupants will react if a fire breaks out on a lower floor.

(Fig. 44) A small house between two high rise buildings.

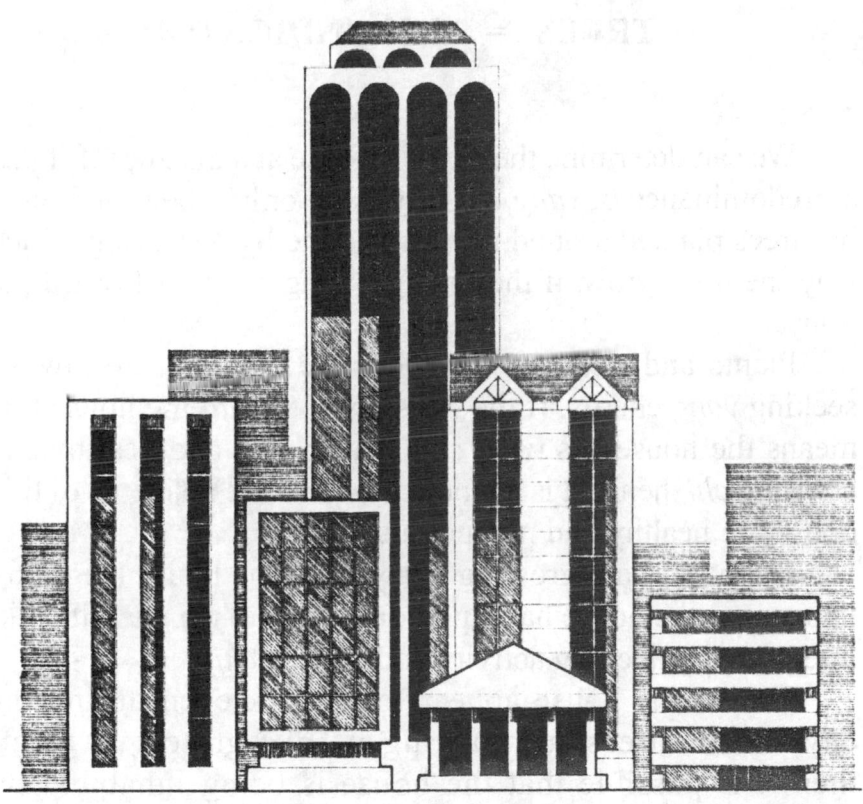

(Fig. 45) The tallest structure in the area.

CHAPTER VII

TREES = *CHI* INDICATOR

We can determine the *chi* of a house at a distance if it has a predominance of *yang chi* or *yin chi* only when the house has trees planted around it. This is done by observing which way the trees grow, if they are growing away or toward the house.

Plants and trees grow toward the sun and are always seeking *yang* energy. If the trees grow toward the house this means the house has *yang chi*. Fortune *chi* and healthy *chi* are *yang chi,* hence it is an indication that the residents of this house are healthy and prosperous.

If the trees are growing away from the house (Fig. 46), this means the house has a predominance of *yin chi* which is interpreted as lacking activity and healthy *chi*.

Should the house appear to be dark even during the day and the trees surrounding it have grotesque forms then it is possible that the house is being inhabited by elemental energies or unseen forces.

A house is considered to be lucky if it is planted with bamboo around it (Fig. 47). Bamboo was used to trumpet good news in the olden days, but too much bamboo that

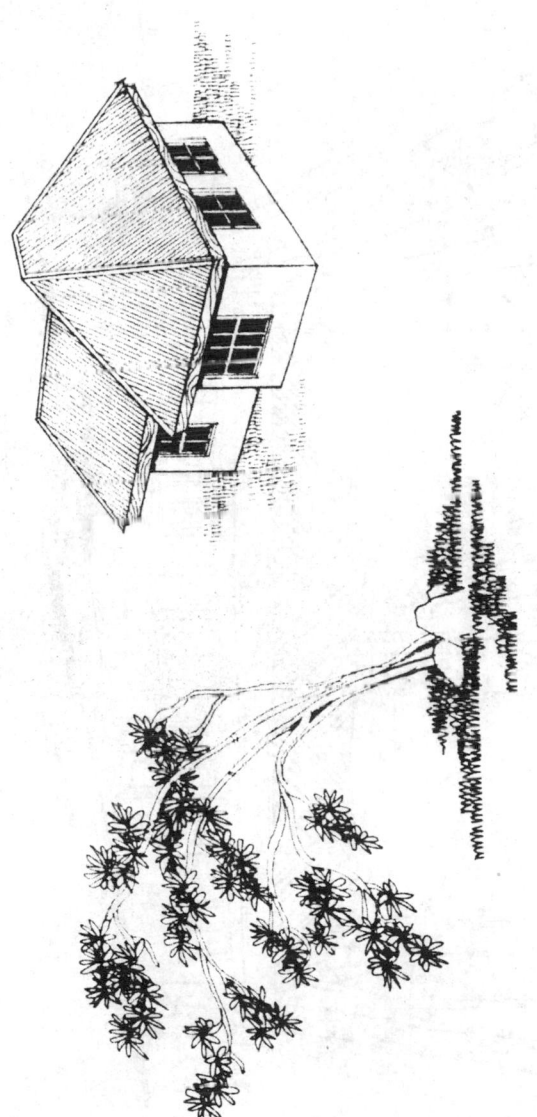

(Fig. 46) Trees growing away from the house.

(Fig. 47) A house planted with bamboo.

blocks sunlight from entering the house could also cause manifestations of elemental energies.

It is of utmost importance in *Feng Shui* to have good ventilation and to let as much sunshine into the house as possible. This will encourage *yang chi* to permeate the house.

A tree that grows very close to the house is not a good feature in *Feng Shui* (Fig. 48). The roots of the tree will insidiously encroach onto the foundation of the house as the tree grows taller and bigger. This will threaten the stability of the foundation of the house and could also affect the stability of a happy home.

හිශ්ෂිශ්හිශ්යිශ්ෂිශ්

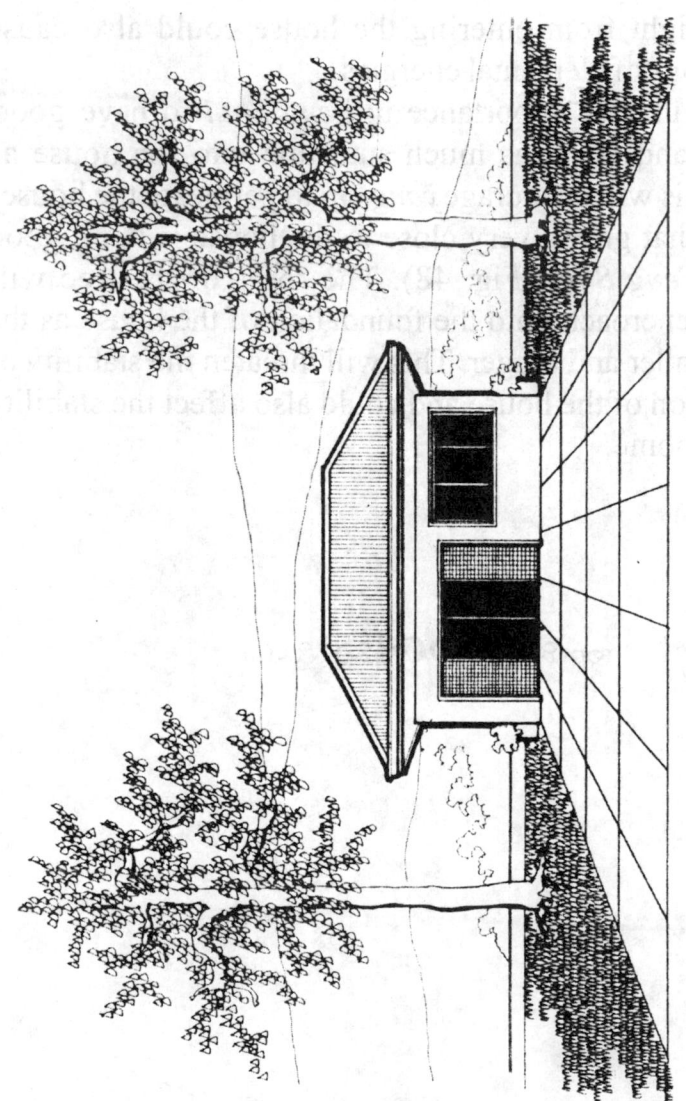

(Fig. 48) Trees very close to a house.

CHAPTER VIII

'*SHA*' = (HARMFUL *CHI*) AT YOUR DOORSTEP I

The primary objective of *Feng Shui* is to bring in good *yang chi* into the house or plot. This is achieved by the correct placement of the gate. In the Form School of *Feng Shui,* the *Dragon* (left from within the plot) gate is the first choice and the centrally located gate is the second choice, the *Tiger* gate is the last choice.

In Level III of the *Applied Feng Shui for Modern Living* course, this rule does not apply as different orientations have different favorable door placements.

The gate or the main door is considered to be the 'mouth' of the plot or the house. The gate ushers outside *chi* into the property, hence the quality of the *chi* the gate brings into the property is of utmost importance as this can affect the health and fortune of the occupants. We are going to deal with several situations where the *sha* is just right outside the main entrance.

The first case is a property which has a pile of garbage (Fig. 49) in front of its gate. The health of the occupants will be adversely compromised and the family fortune or business will be difficult to come by. The cure to this situation is to have the garbage removed.

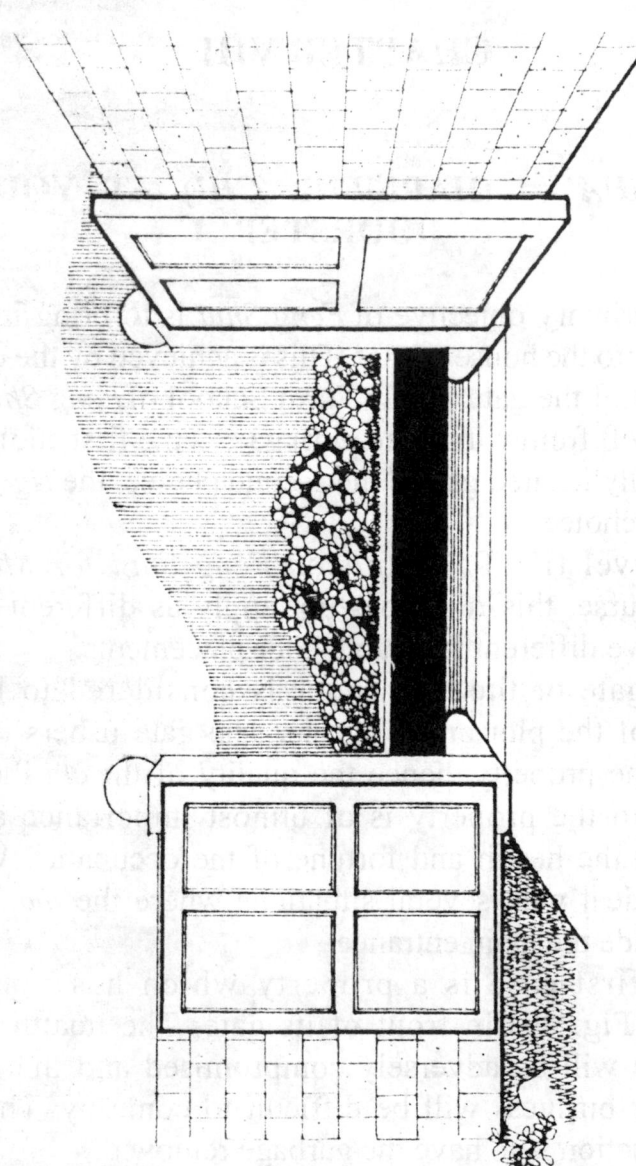

(Fig. 49) A pile of garbage in front of a gate.

(Fig. 50) a chimney stack fronting the main door.

(Fig. 51) An air conditioning exhaust fronting the main door.

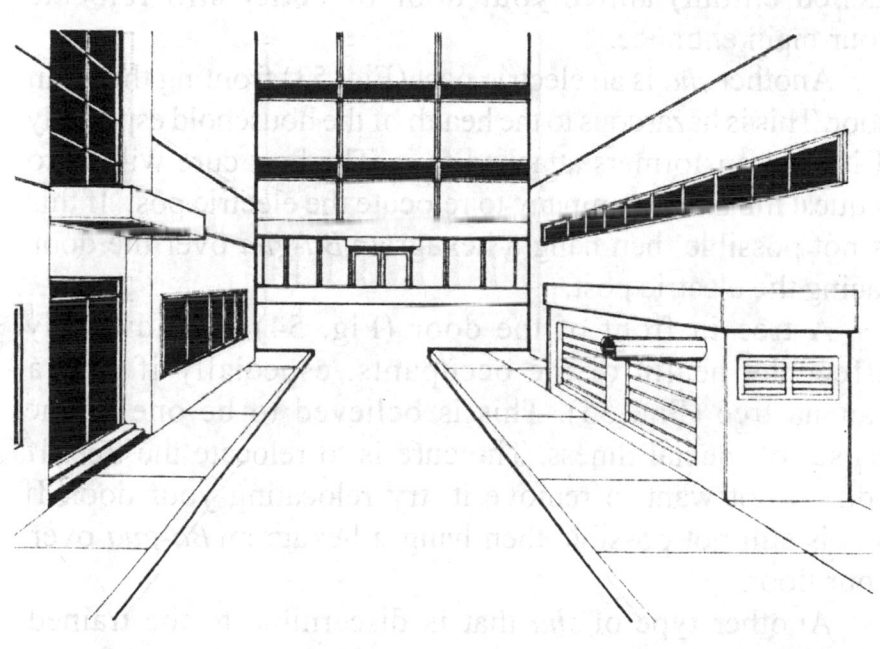

(Fig. 52) A generator exhaust fronting the main door.

Next we have the situation where a chimney stack is fronting the main door (Fig. 50), worse if we have the exhaust of an air conditioning system (Fig. 51) or that of a generator (Fig. 52) facing the front door. This is considered a *sha* that forbodes death or illness. The cure is to hang a convex mirror and a hexagram *Ba-gua* (attached cutout) above your door or better still relocate your main entrance.

Another *sha* is an electric post (Fig. 53) fronting the main door. This is hazardous to the health of the household especially if it has transformers attached to it. The best cure will be to request the utility company to relocate the electric post. If this is not possible then hang a hexagram *Ba-gua* over the door facing the electric post.

A tree in front of the door (Fig. 54) can adversely affect the health of the occupants, especially if it is a banana tree (Fig. 55). This is believed to be one of the causes of mental illness. The cure is to relocate the tree. If you do not want to remove it, try relocating your door. If this is still not possible then hang a hexagram *Ba-gua* over your door.

Another type of *sha* that is discernible to the trained eyes of a *geomancer* is *sha* emitted from the gables or ridges of neighboring houses or buildings (Fig. 56). These are known as *'hidden arrows,'* the *sha* can be directed towards your door or window. It is the health and fortune

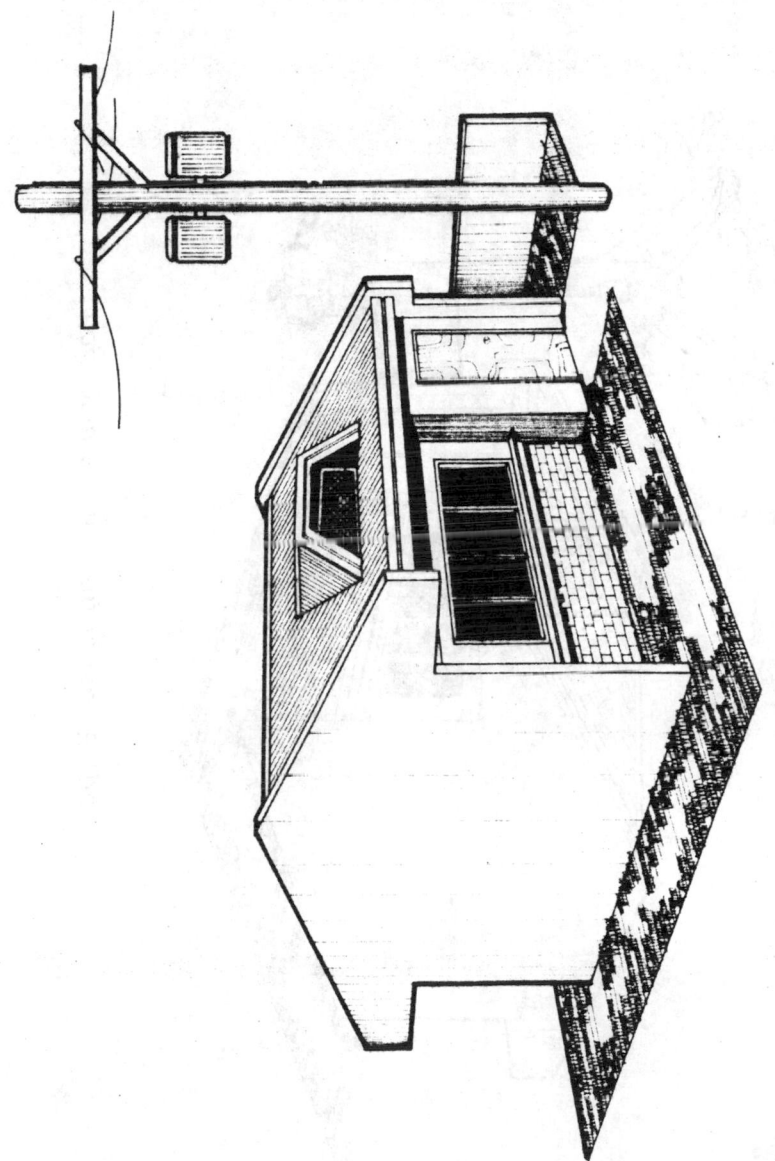

(Fig. 53) An electric post in front of the main door.

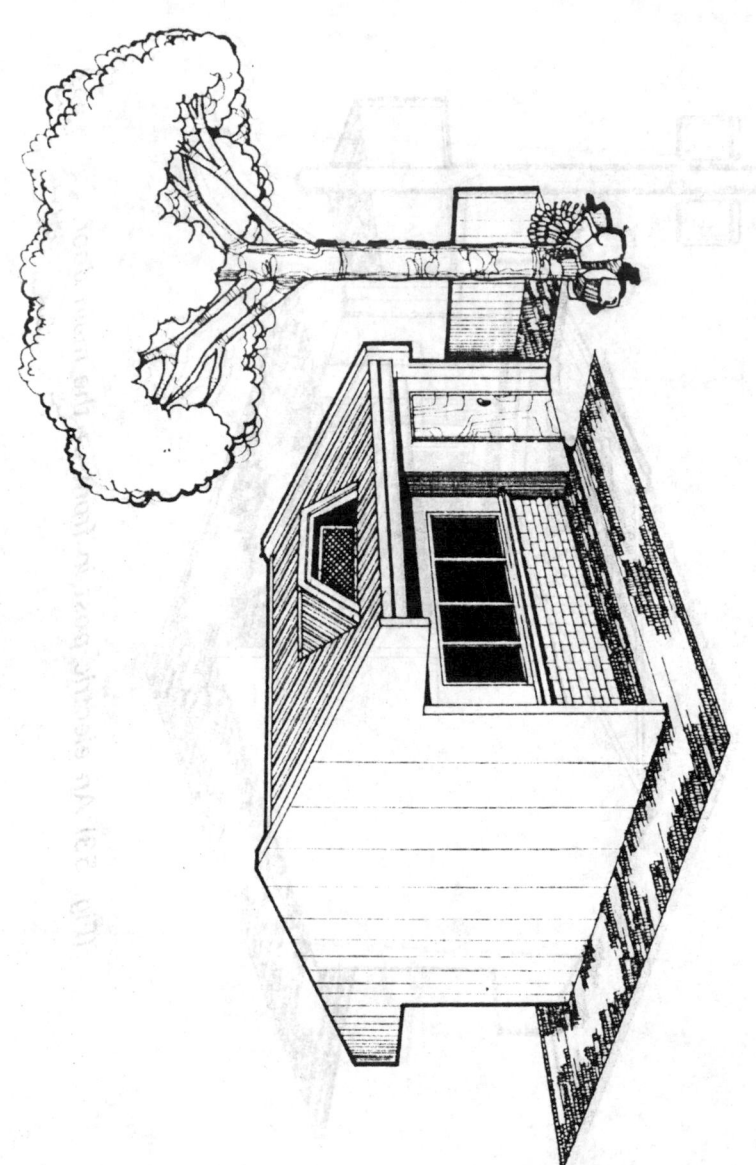

(Fig. 54) A tree in front at the main door.

(Fig. 55) A banana tree in front of the main door.

(Fig. 56) Neighbor's gable pointing to the main door.

of the occupants that will be jeopardized. The cure is to hang a convex mirror and a hexagram *Ba-gua* (attached cutout) above your door or window.

Figs. 57 & 58 illustrate the common *sha* in the city. The *sha* from the street sign and lamp post could be dispersed with a convex mirror hung on top of the door facing the source of *sha.*

The most obvious *sha* found in urban living is shown in Fig. 59 where the neighbor's gate across the street is opposite your door. The function of the gate, considered to be the 'mouth' of a property in *Feng Shui,* is to draw in fortune. The house with the bigger gate will be able to 'suck' in more *chi* or fortune from the street than the house with a smaller gate. It will be more logical for both parties to place their gates in different directions than to outdo each other by installing bigger gates. If your gate is the smaller one and there is no way to transfer it hang a hexagram *Ba-gua* on the gate post.

When the driveway of your neighbor is in line with your main door (Fig. 60) this constitutes a *'chiong'* (opposing *sha)* akin to being hit by traffic on a T-junction. This could result in the loss of business opportunity because the *'chiong'* disperses *chi* from entering your house. The cure is to hang a convex mirror and a hexagram *Ba-gua* on top of your door.

(Fig. 57) A street lamp in front of the main door.

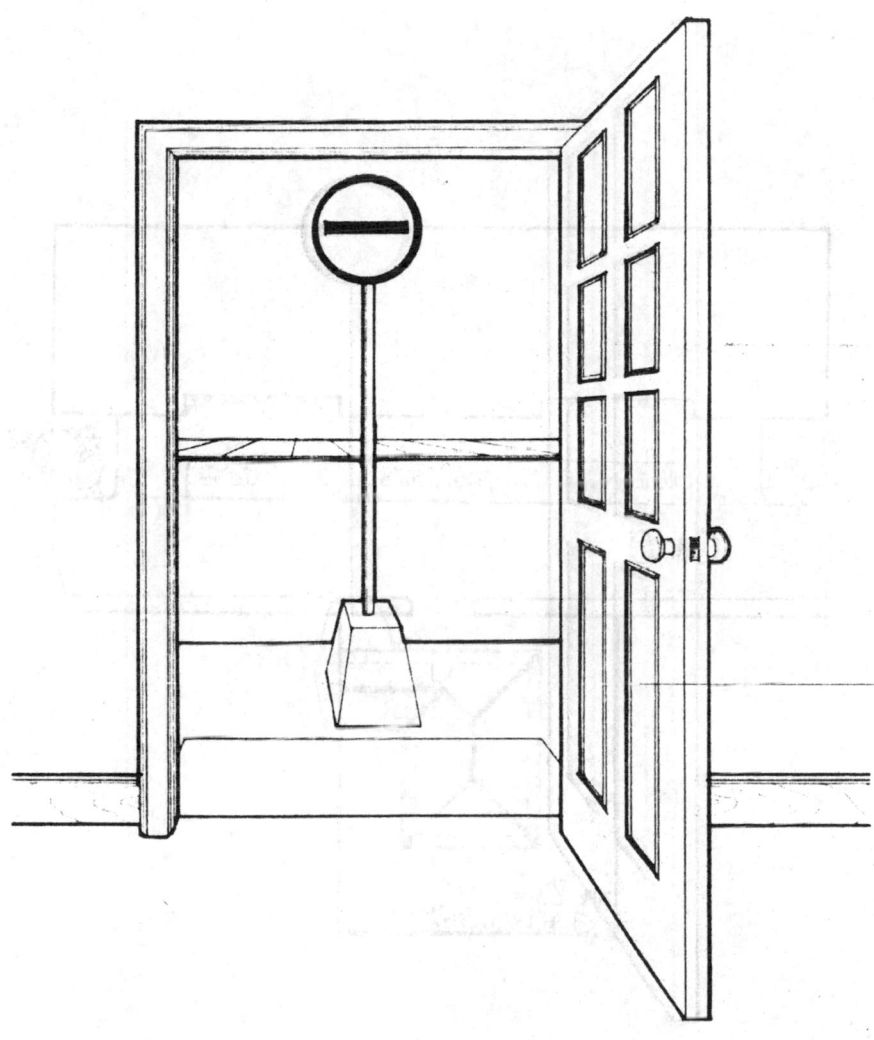

(Fig. 58) A street sign in front of the main door.

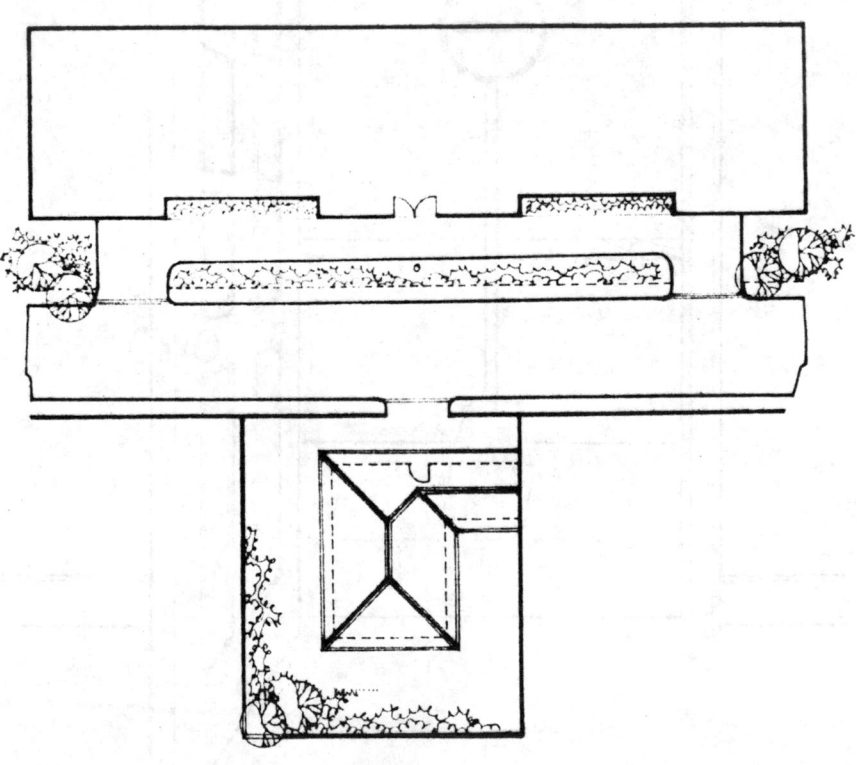

(Fig. 59) Two gates facing each other.

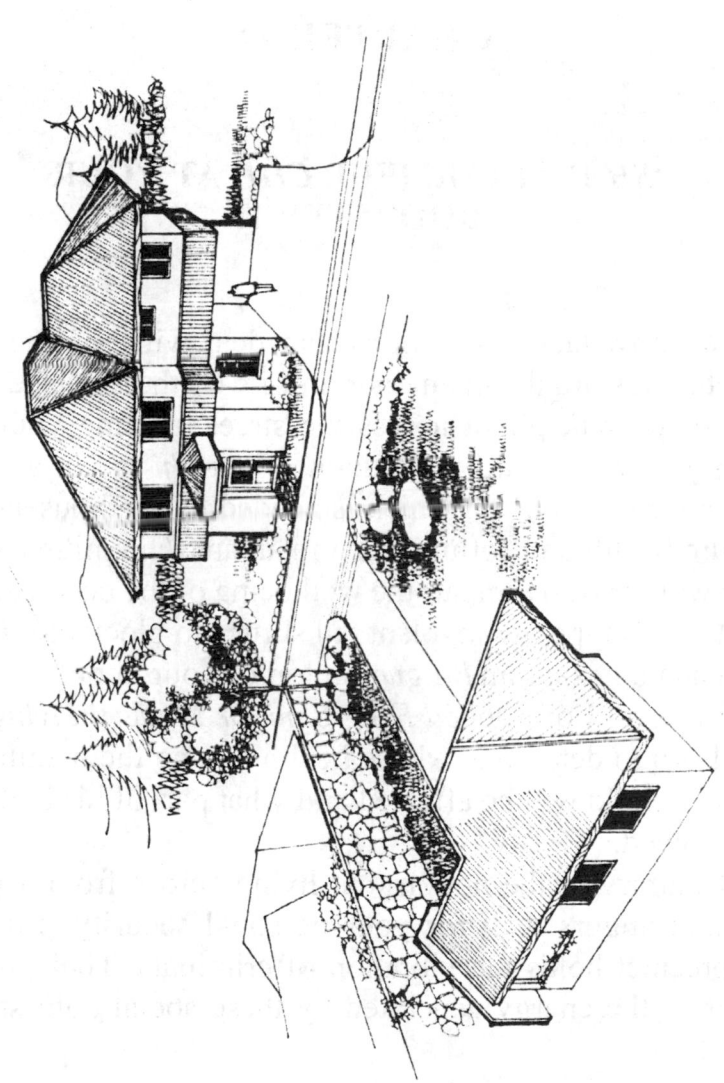

(Fig. 60) A driveway opposite a main door.

CHAPTER IX

'SHA' = (HARMFUL CHI) AT YOUR DOORSTEP II

We now tackle situations that deal with pure *yin sha* directing toward the main door. In Fig. 61 the elevated water tank of your neighbor across the street fronting your door emits *yin sha* toward your door. Water *chi* is *yin* and can neutralize the *yang chi* which is needed by the household to nurture health and fortune. The resultant *sha* emitted to the door will seriously impair the well being of the occupants. To counter this type of *sha,* plant tall shrubs to block the *yin sha* and hang a hexagram *Ba-gua* on top of your door.

In Level I of *Applied Feng Shui for Modern Living* you will learn to determine whose health among the members of the household will be affected and what part of his body will be involved.

Contrary to the notion that living across from a police precinct augurs well for your personal security (Fig. 62), the precinct holds the vibration of criminals. Their thought forms or the energy generated by these social outcasts will

(Fig. 61) A water tank fronting the main door.

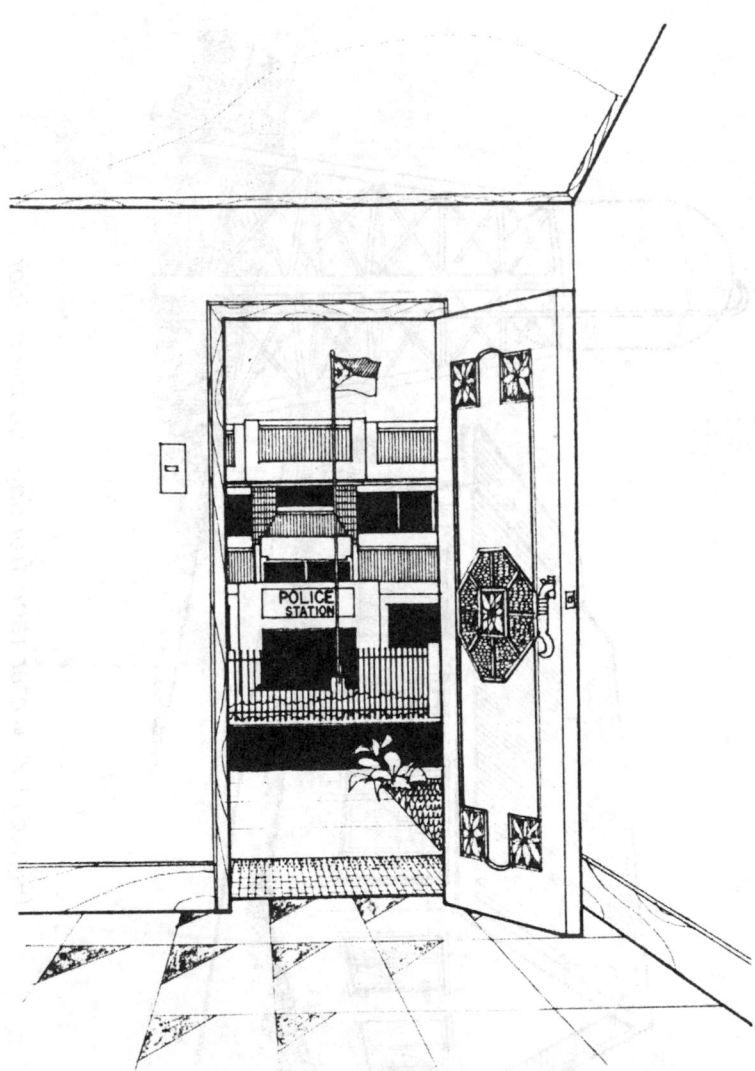

(Fig. 62) A police station opposite the main door.

be drawn into the house through the door. This will have a discordant effect that works against the unity and harmony of the family.

A funeral parlor fronting a house (Fig. 63) is most unfortunate. The funeral parlor 'holds' the *yin chi* associated with grief and the dead. This energy will be 'drawn' into the house through the door and can trigger nervous breakdowns, apparitions and sickness. The best solution is to transfer to another area; if this is not possible then relocate the front door to a position not directly facing the funeral parlor. If this still is not possible, hang a hexagram *Ba-gua* and a convex mirror on top of your door.

It could be reassuring to some to live close to a hospital, especially in case of emergencies. But living across from a hospital gives *sha* to the house (Fig. 64). The hospital, a source of *yin chi*, confines the sick and incidence of death is almost an every day occurrence. The door of the house fronting the hospital will draw in these *yin* energies. The cure is the same as the house facing the funeral parlor.

To be religious is a virtue but to be living opposite a church or a temple is not conforming to good *Feng Shui* rules (Fig. 65). Churches or temples belong to the spiritual world. The energy associated with a church or temple is also *yin* and at times the ritual for the dead is

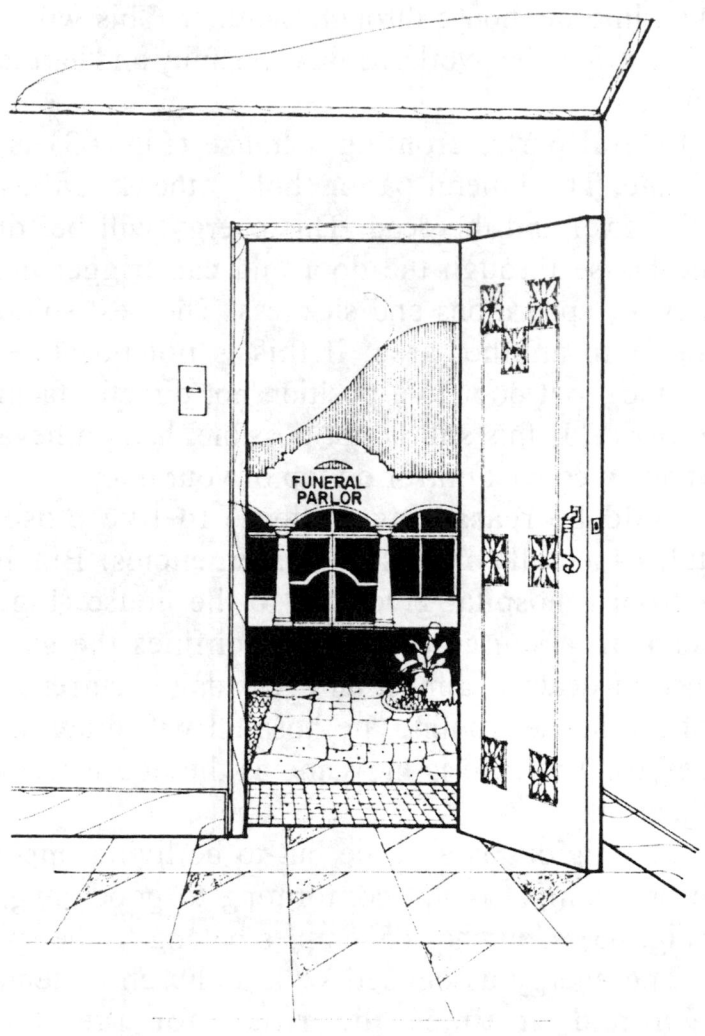

(Fig. 63) A funeral parlor fronting the main door.

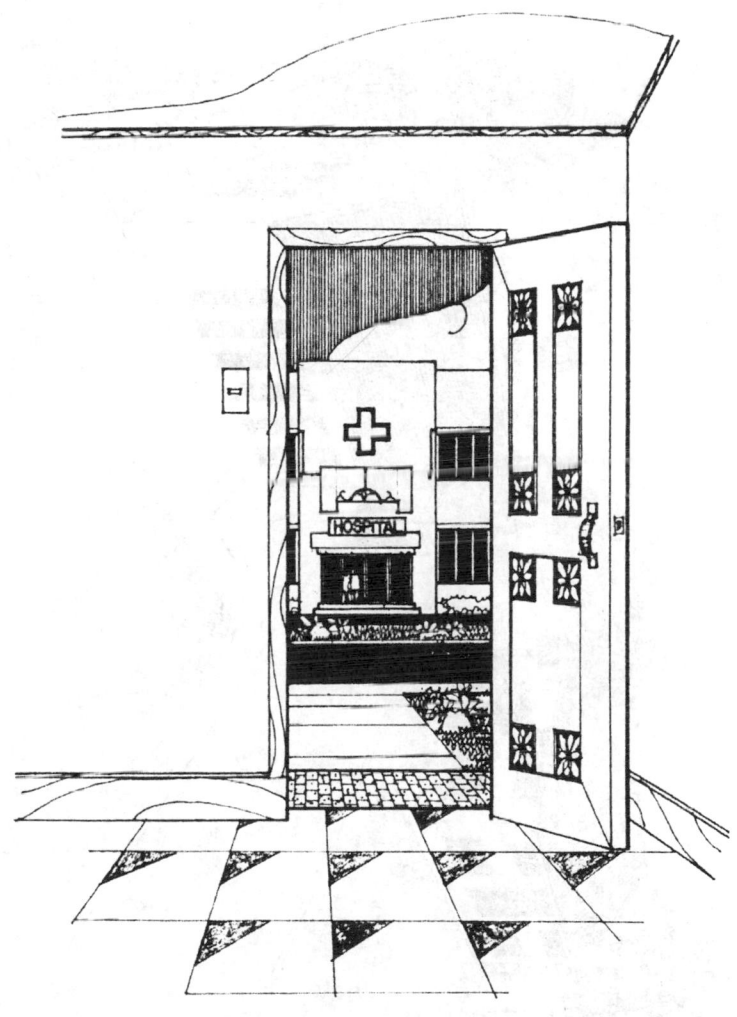

(Fig. 64) A hospital in front of the main door.

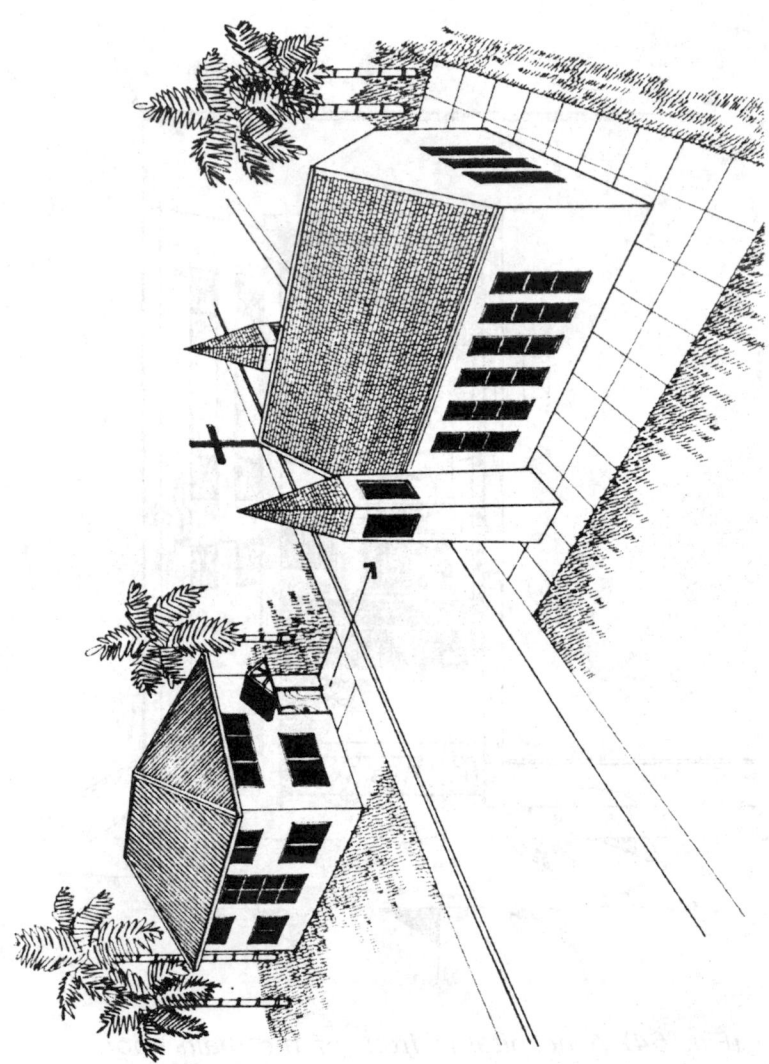

(Fig. 65) A church in front of a house.

performed there. Drawing this type of energy into the house may cause sickness and *yin* manifestations. A church behind a house (Fig. 66) is not as bad as being in front. But it should nonetheless be avoided.

The last type of *sha* is found at the outskirts of a community where the cemetery is located. A house fronting the cemetery (Fig. 67) will certainly bring in the pure *yin chi* associated with it. It is observed that family fortune will go down. Sickness and strange happenings will manifest. A hexagram *Ba-gua* hung over the door facing the cemetery and a 24-hour, low wattage lamp on the door will ameliorate the situation. The same cure can be applied to the house that faces a church or a temple.

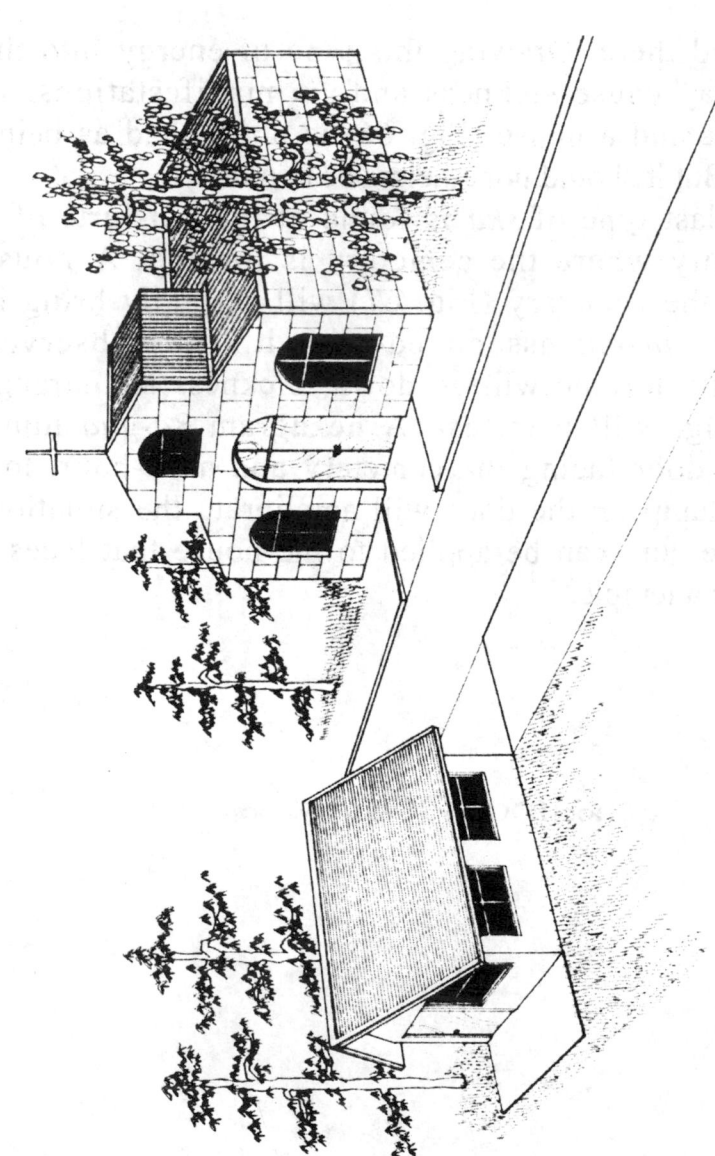

(Fig. 66) A church behind a house.

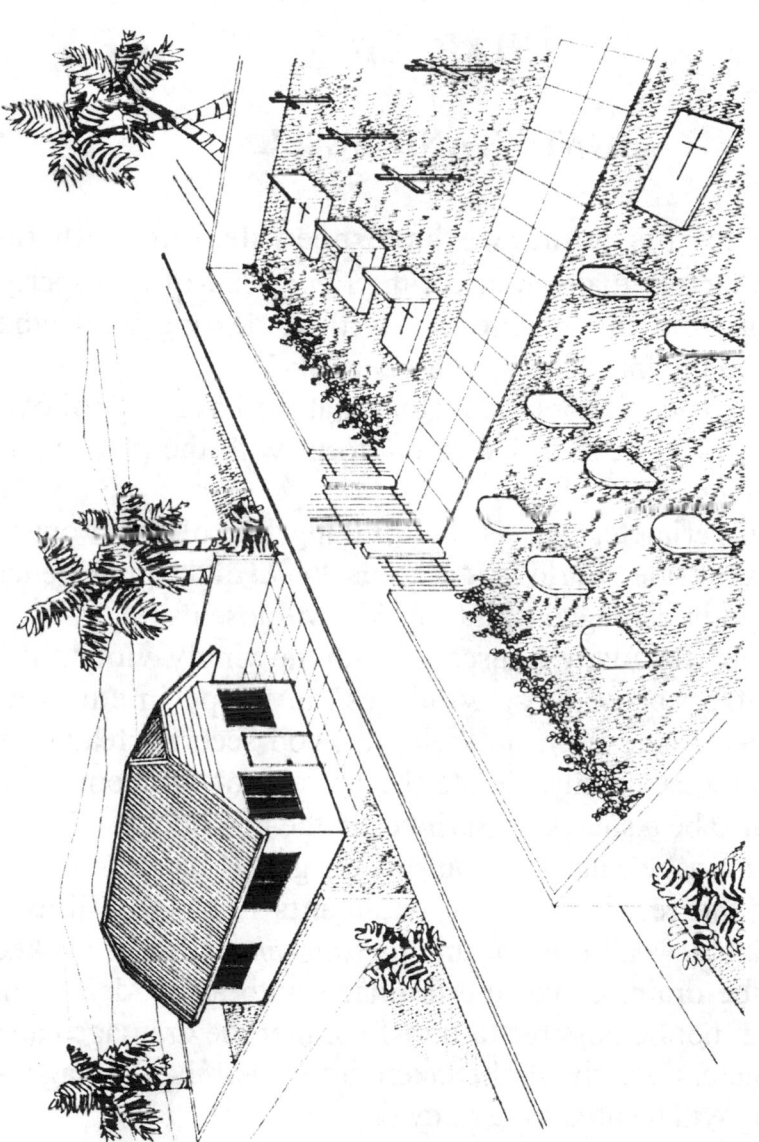

(Fig. 67) A cemetery opposite a house.

CHAPTER X

GATES AND WALLS

Up to this point, we have been dealing with the outside factors that can affect the *Feng Shui* of a property. Starting from this chapter we will be dealing with what are called the inside factors of *Feng Shui*.

The inside factors are factors that we have control over and these can be rectified to conform with the precepts of good *Feng Shui*.

The perimeter wall is the dividing line of the property with the outside 'world' and it holds the *chi* of the plot. Hence a cracked or damaged wall (Fig. 68) will lose its *chi*.

There are many houses that unknowingly violate this concept by providing 'windows' in its perimeter wall (Fig. 69). Aside from not being a good security feature as passers-by can easily violate the privacy of the home, this could also be a source of intrigues in the neighborhood.

A drainage canal right outside the gate (Fig. 70) could be one of the reasons for the occupants not being able to accumulate wealth or fortune as *yang chi* is being sucked down the drain. Cover the drainage with a wooden plank should it not be possible to transfer either the drainage canal or the gate. Care should be taken not to seal the drainage or flooding will result during rainy days.

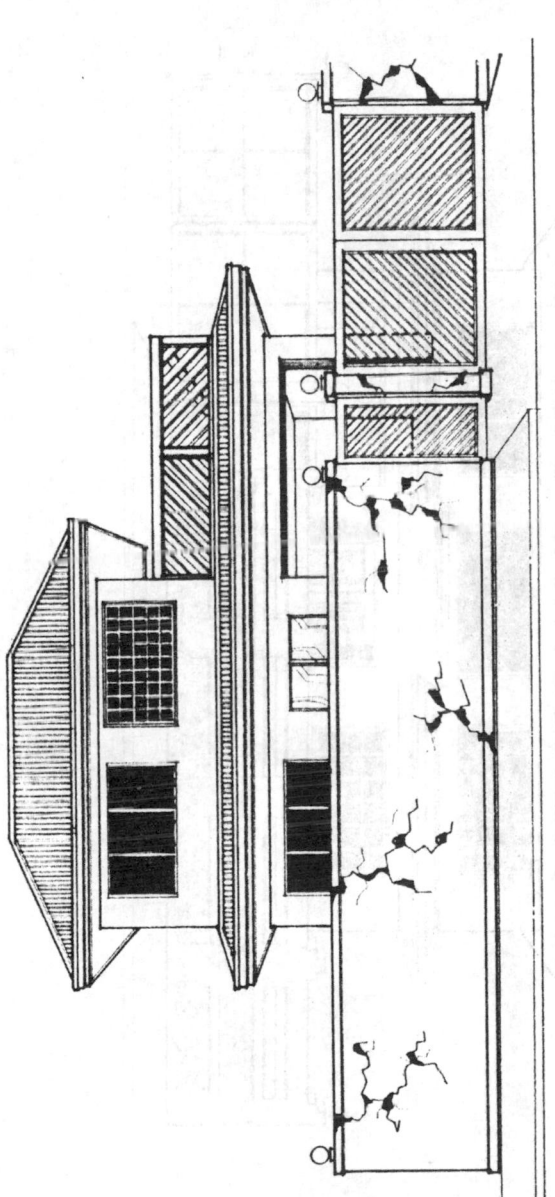

(Fig. 68) Walls with cracks.

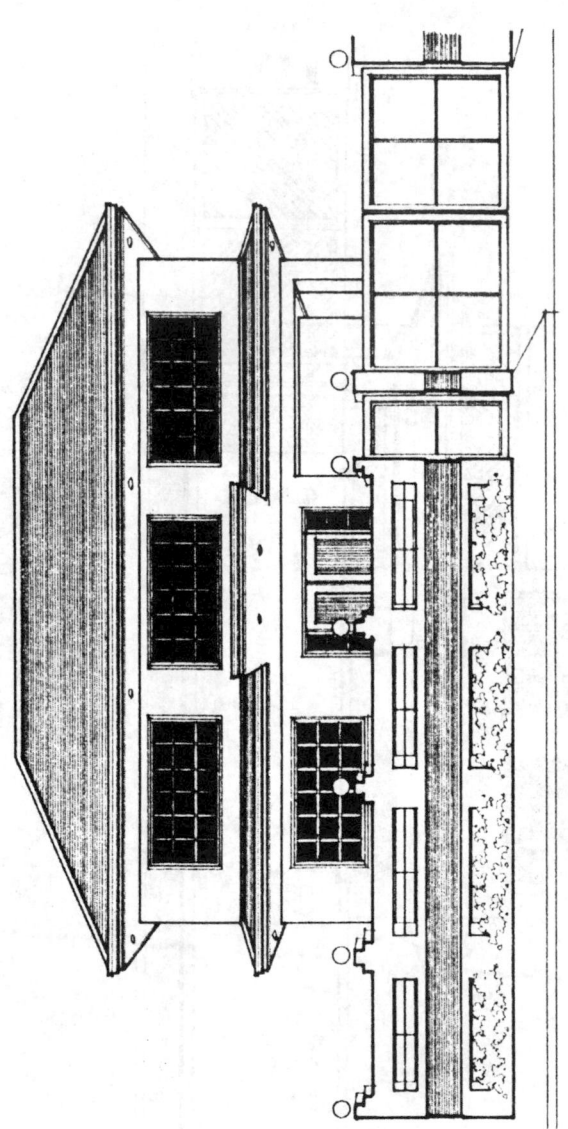

(Fig. 69) Windows in the walls.

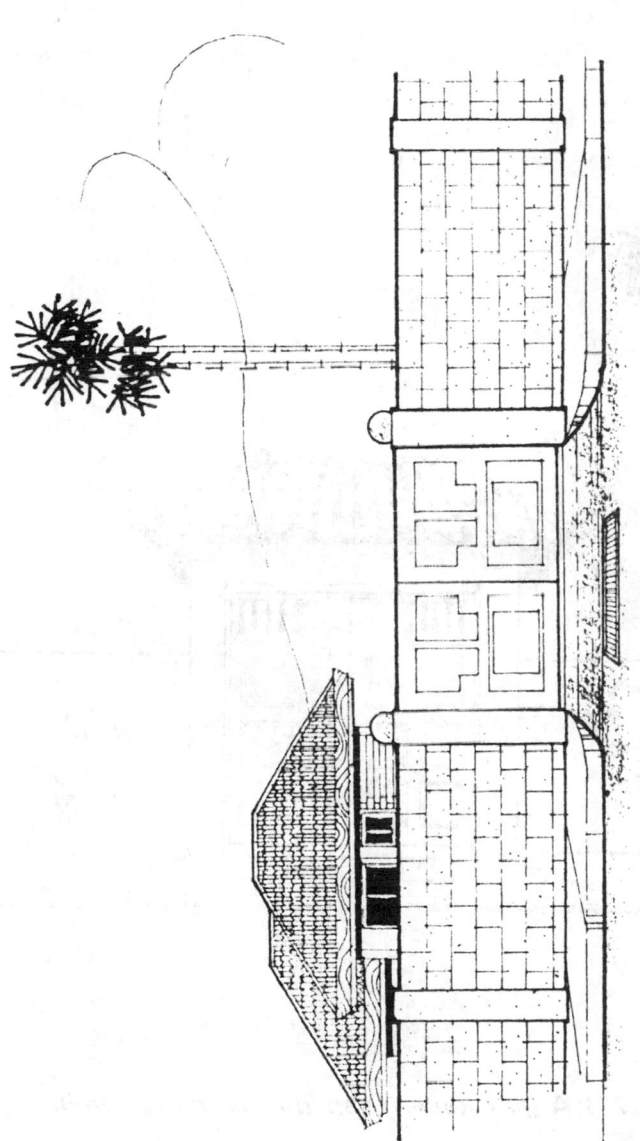

(Fig. 70) A drainage canal in front of the gate.

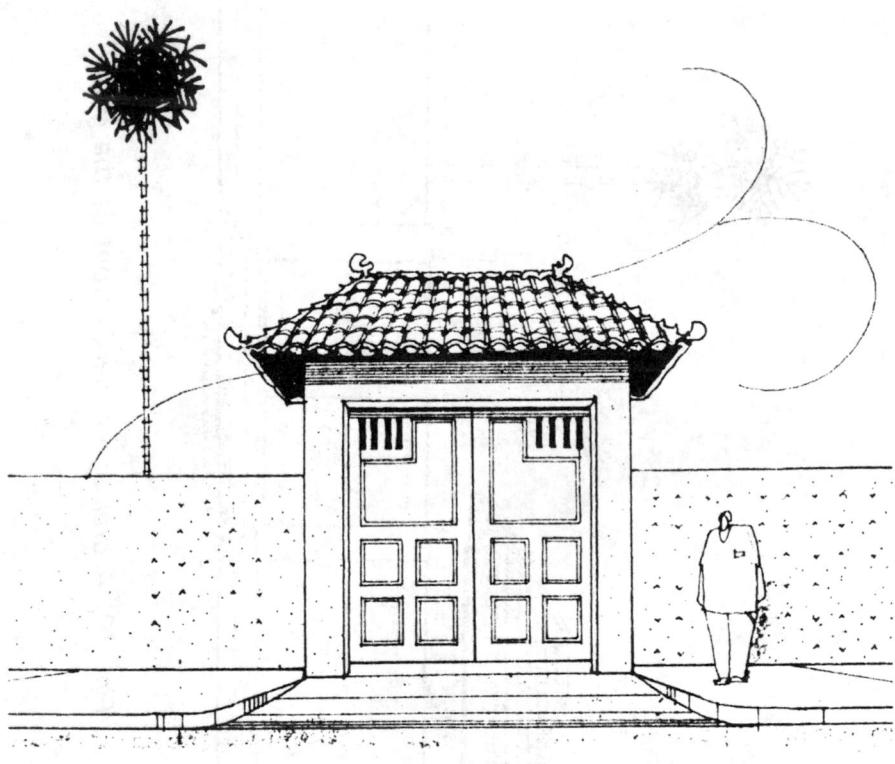

(Fig. 71) A gate taller than the perimeter wall.

The gate should, as a rule of thumb, be of uniform height to the wall. Tall gates (Fig. 71) are found in government offices where the symbols of power and authority are indirectly impressed upon people entering the premises.

Avoid having a massive gate with a roof design that has the shape of a coffin.

The gate should be centrally located between the supporting gate posts. Avoid (Fig. 72) installing a lopsided gate where one panel of the gate is bigger than the other. In *Feng Shui* depending on which side of the gate is smaller connotes either the master of the house (left) or the wife (right) will die early.

It is taboo in *Feng Shui* to have two gates on a wall (Fig. 73) as it suggests insubordination within the family resulting from altercation between the master of the house and his offspring. This arrangement could also pose a problem to the security of the premises.

A house that is dilapidated (Fig. 74) can not hold the *chi*. This does not augur well for family unity as it gives the impression of a house that is crumbling or disintegrating.

Roofs that have leaks and cracks (Fig. 75) are not a good feature in *Feng Shui*. This connotes the family is always in financial difficulty. Fix the roof and the family fortune will improve.

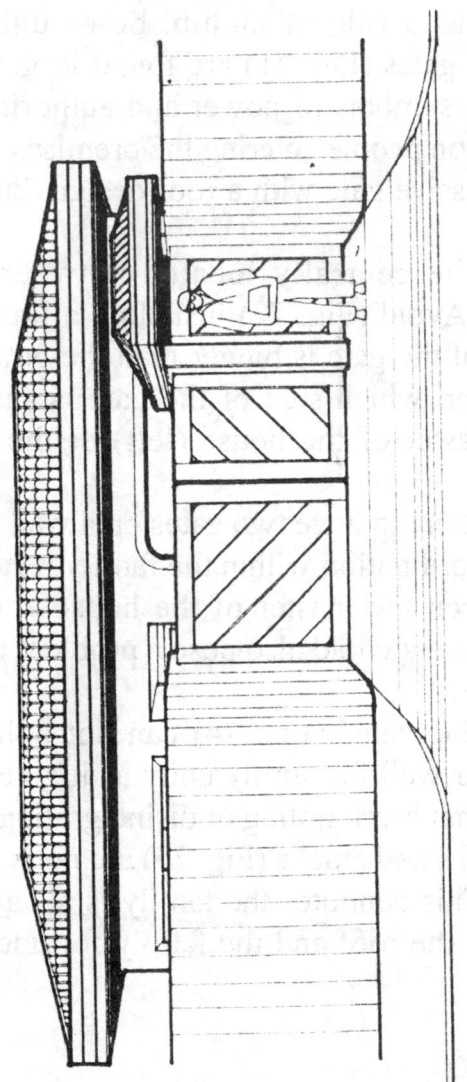

(Fig. 72) One panel of a gate larger than the other.

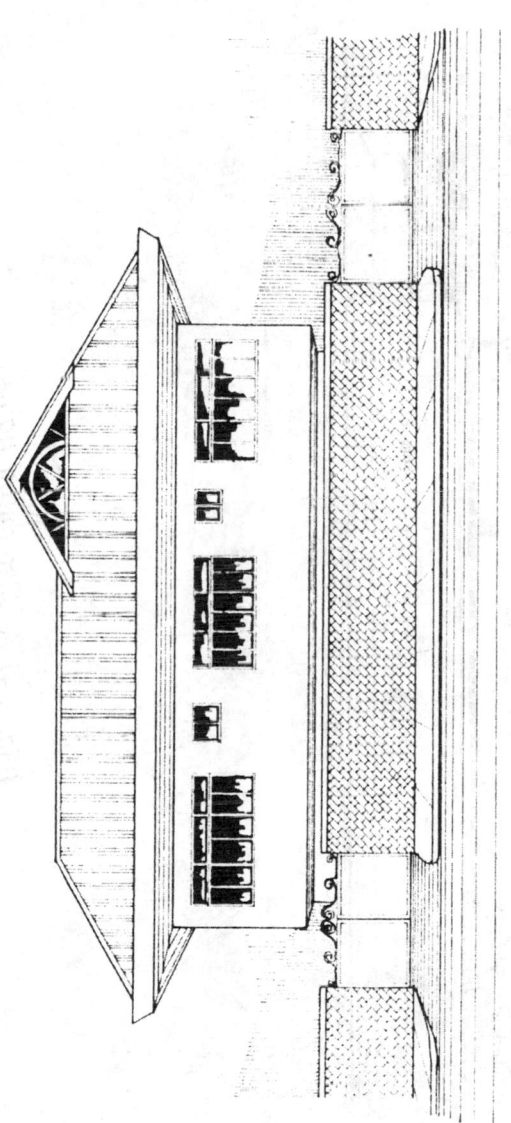

(Fig. 73) Two gates on the same wall.

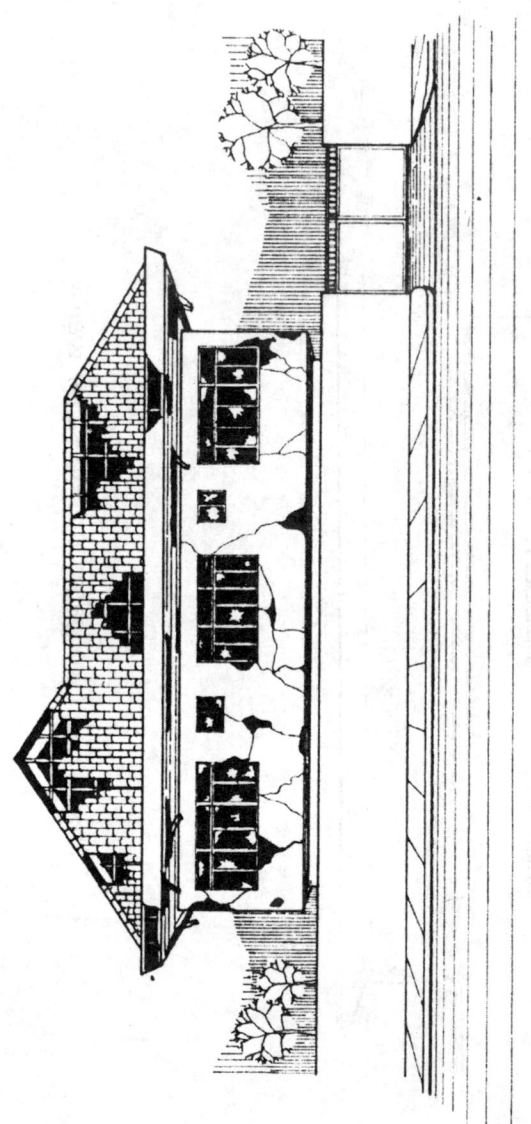

(Fig. 74) A dilapidated house.

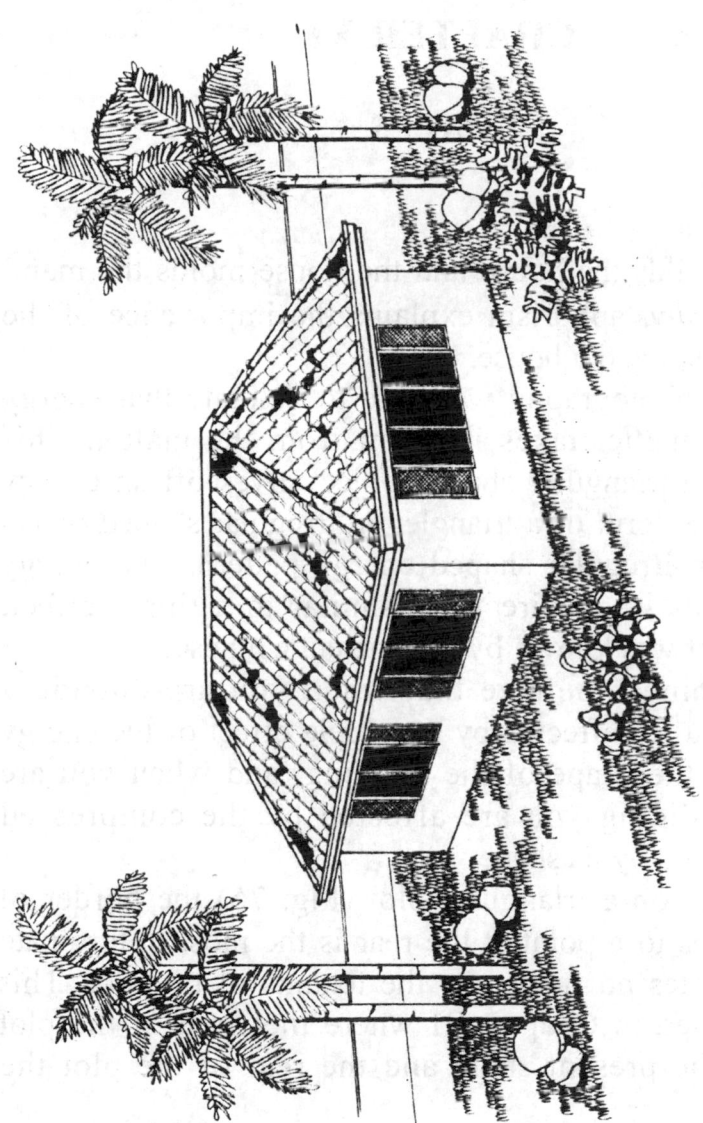

(Fig. 75) The roof of a house with leaks and cracks.

CHAPTER XI

SHAPES

'Man builds the house and the house molds the man.' This *Feng Shui* aphorism explains the importance of the shape of a plot and a house.

Kirlian photography was able to validate that energy emitted by matter takes its form from the matter. This means that a triangular shaped object gives off an energy pattern in the form of a triangle; an irregular shaped object gives off an irregular shaped energy pattern. The energy form extends in all directions similar to a ripple effect. This concept was known by the ancient Chinese.

The Chinese believe that when you are outside a building you are affected by the ripple effect of the energy emitted by the shape of the building; and when you are inside a building you are affected by the compressed energy emitted by its shape.

A house on a triangular plot (Fig. 76) the border of which comes to a point at the rear is the most unfortunate for it connotes no future for the tenants of the plot. This was discussed in Chapter III where the front of the plot indicates the present stage and the rear of the plot the future.

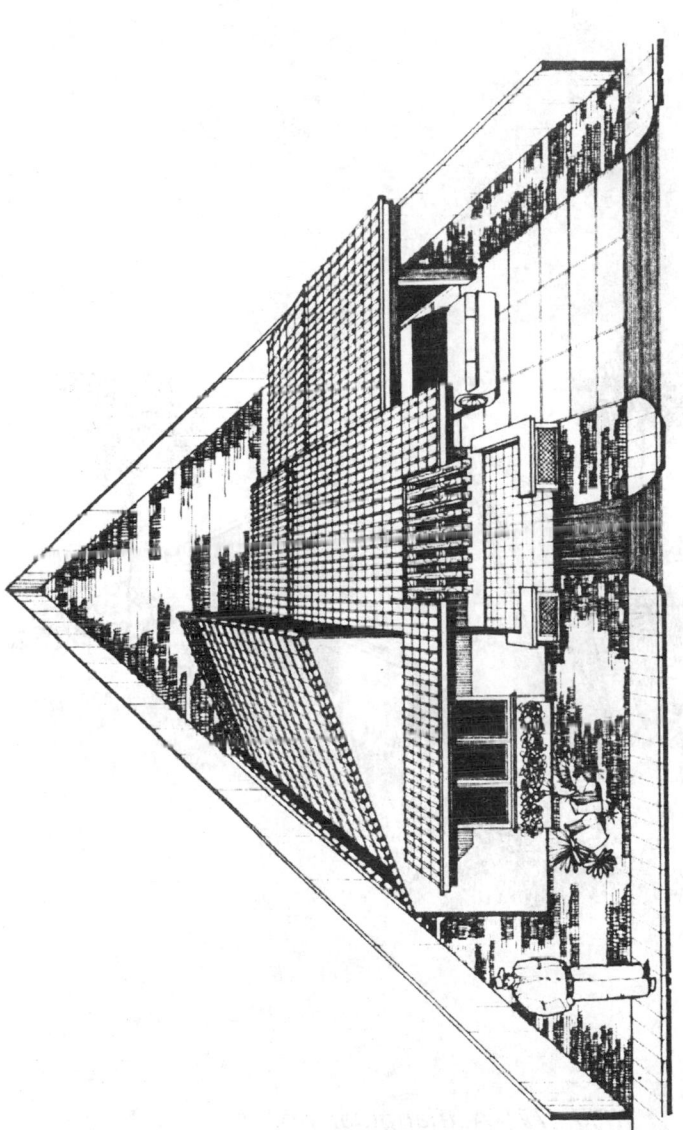

(Fig. 76) A house on a triangular lot.

(Fig. 77) A triangular house.

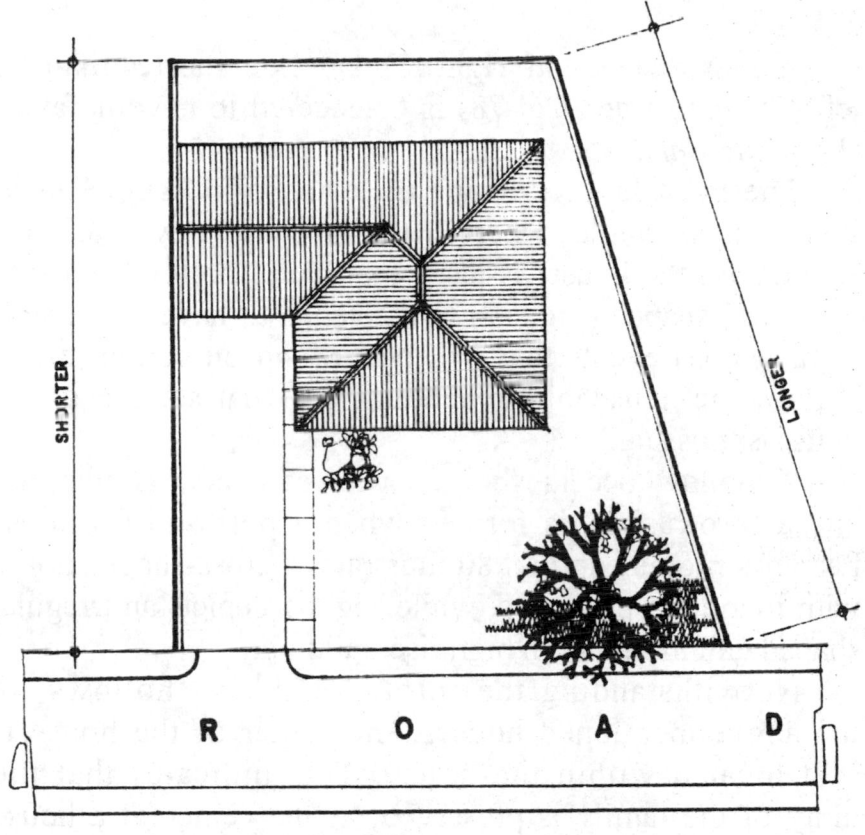

(Fig. 78) The Tiger side of the lot is shorter than the Dragon side.

A triangular shaped house (Fig. 77) also connotes that accidents and mishaps will befall the tenants of the house and some members of the household may encounter personality changes.

A plot that has its right *(Tiger)* side shorter than its left *(Dragon)* side (Fig. 78) is considered to have unfavorable *Feng Shui.*

The most favored shape of a house in *Feng Shui* is that of a rectangle, wherein the *chi* can flow smoothly throughout the house. Houses that have 'hollow' portions like an H-shaped (Fig. 79) house tends to have an adverse influence on events that will occur, and on certain members of the household depending on what section of the house is 'missing.'

A 'hollow' occurs when a portion of a house is 'missing' and a 'protrusion' is formed when a portion of a house becomes prominent. Fig. 80 illustrates a cross-shaped house with four sides protruded, while Fig. 81 depicts an irregular shaped unit in a modern high rise building.

Notwithstanding the 'protrusions' or 'hollows' in the above-mentioned houses, the center of the house is still located within the house. This indicates that the unity of the family is preserved, as the center of a house is considered as the 'heart' of the house.

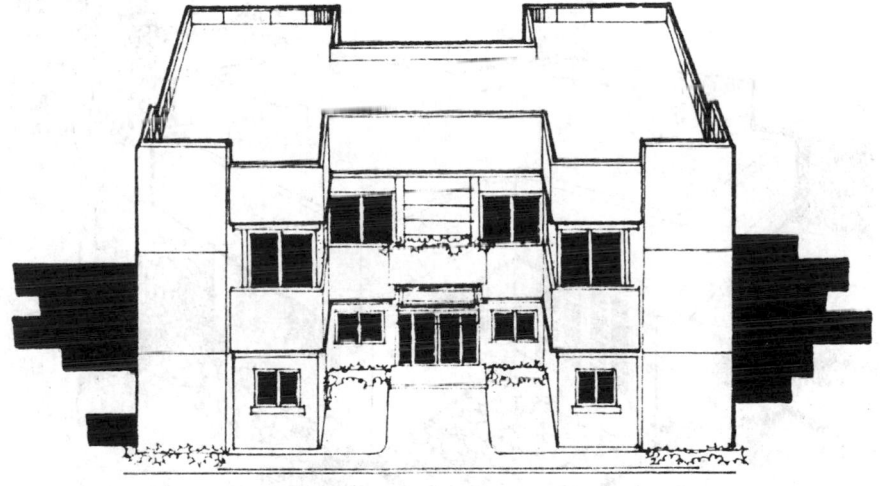

(Fig. 79) An H-shaped house.

(Fig. 80) A cross-shaped house.

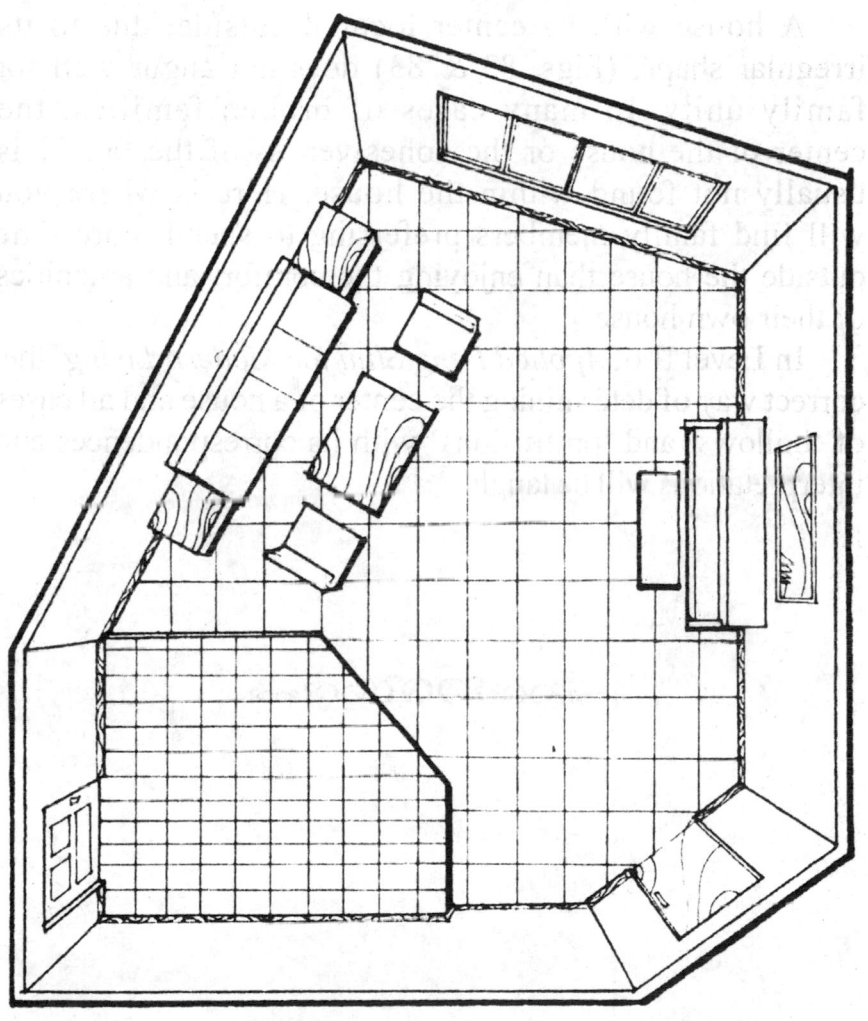

(Fig. 81) An irregular-shaped house.

A house with its center located outside, due to its irregular shape, (Figs. 82 & 83) does not augur well for family unity. In many cases of broken families, the center of the house or the cohesiveness of the family is usually not found within the house. Here is where you will find family members preferring to spend more time outside the house than enjoying the comfort and amenities of their own house.

In Level II of *Applied Feng Shui for Modern Living,* the correct way of determining the center of a house and all cases of 'hollows' and 'protrusions' with its correspondences and interpretations will be taught.

ಐಞ೫ಐ೫೫ಐಞ

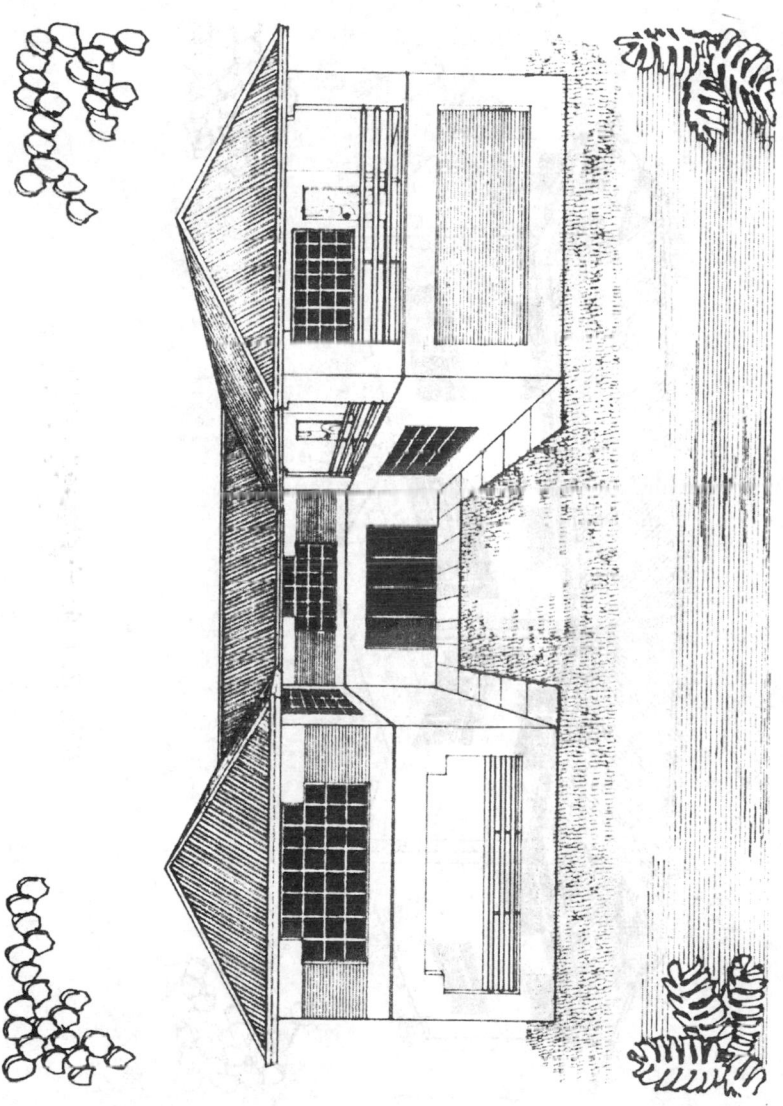

(Fig. 82) A U-shaped house.

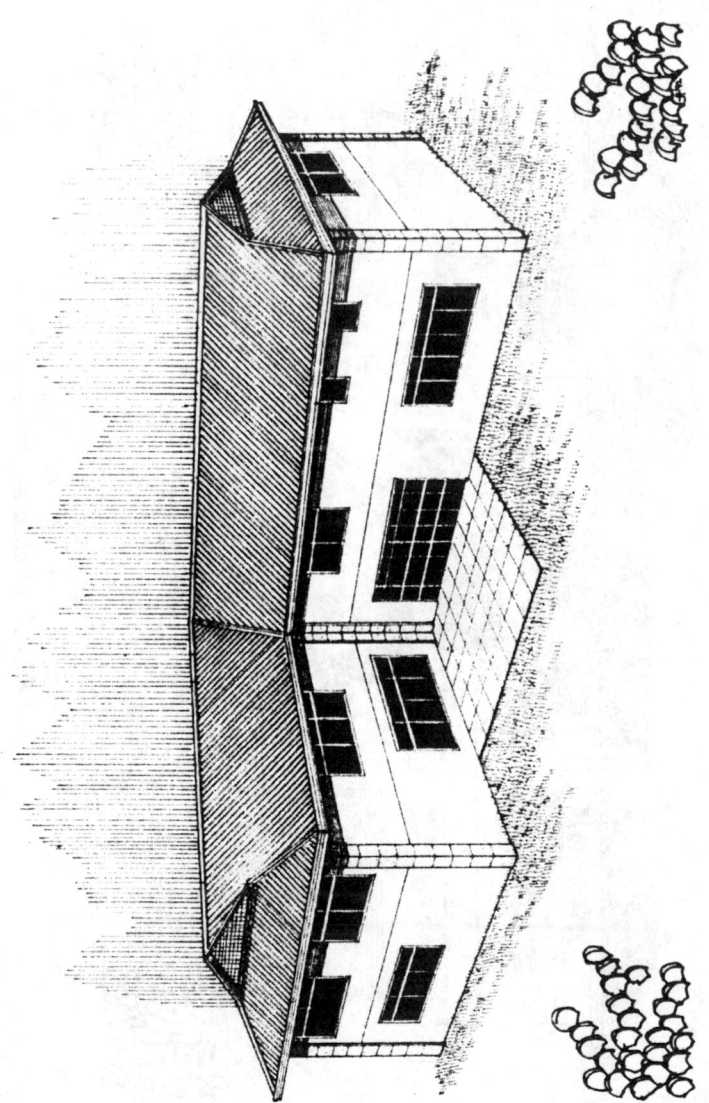

(Fig. 83) An L-shaped house.

CHAPTER XII

SIZE OF A HOUSE

After entering the gate and having looked around the house to determine its shape, we have to take note of the height of the house. If it is a two-storey house (Fig. 84), the height of the upper floor should not exceed that of the ground floor. The two floors can be of equal height.

In *Feng Shui,* the ground floor represents the parents or the master of the house, the second floor represents the children or subordinates. When the height of the upper floor is greater than the ground floor this means that the children will not be filial and will not be able to accord due respect to their parents. This will result in the loss of control of the parents over their children.

Next thing we have to know is the number of people occupying the house in relation to the size of the house. *Feng Shui* emphasizes the balance of the *yin* and the *yang* forces in a house. In *yang Feng Shui* a predominance of *yang chi* is desirable as this enhances the well-being of the occupants. Man belongs to *yang* as he is alive, active and moving while the house is considered *yin* as it is passive and steady.

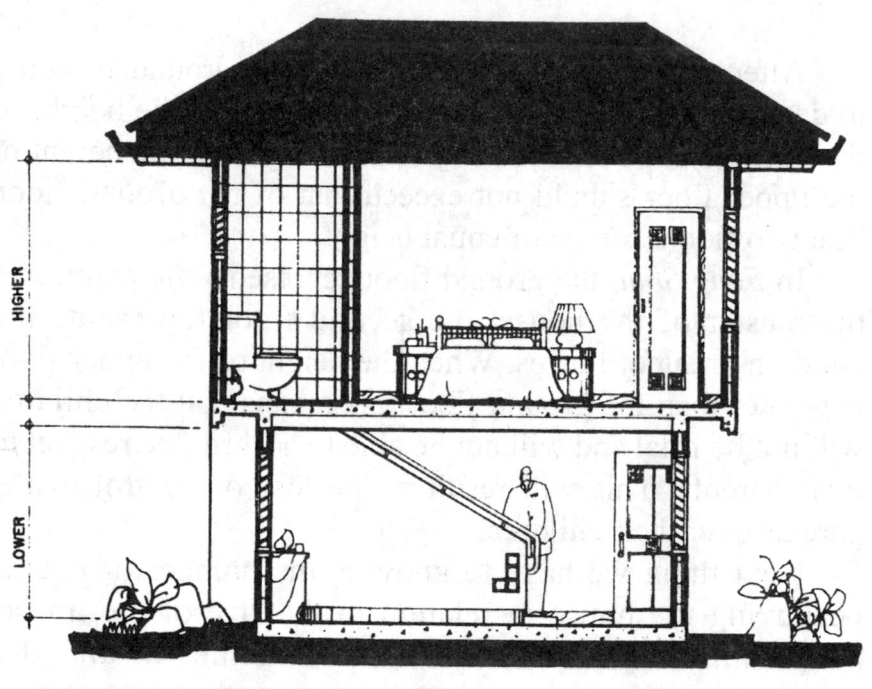

(Fig. 84) A housewith a taller second floor.

(Fig. 85) A big house with few occupants.

A big house with few occupants (Fig. 85) has *yin chi* overpowering the *yang chi.* This will make the house more *yin* or 'cold' and does not nurture the development of a warm, affectionate and close personal relationship among the members of the family.

A small house (Fig. 86) with many occupants has more *yang chi* than *yin chi* in the house. This enhances the development of a closely knit, more personal and affectionate family. This will create a peaceful and harmonious atmosphere in the house which is one of the aims of *Feng Shui.*

In modern living, it is common to have a swimming pool or pond in the house as a landscape feature. The correct placement of a body of water inside a property depends on the orientation of the house and its surrounding terrain. In general a pond or pool should not be placed on the west (Fig. 87) if the house is sited north facing south. This implies that the Tiger, which is the right side of the house looking toward the street from within, has its mouth opened and will cause harm to the household.

In Level III of the *Applied Feng Shui For Modern Living* course, the placement of pools, ponds, wells and water tanks will be taken up in details.

છાલ સળ હ હ હ હ

(Fig. 86) A small house with many occupants.

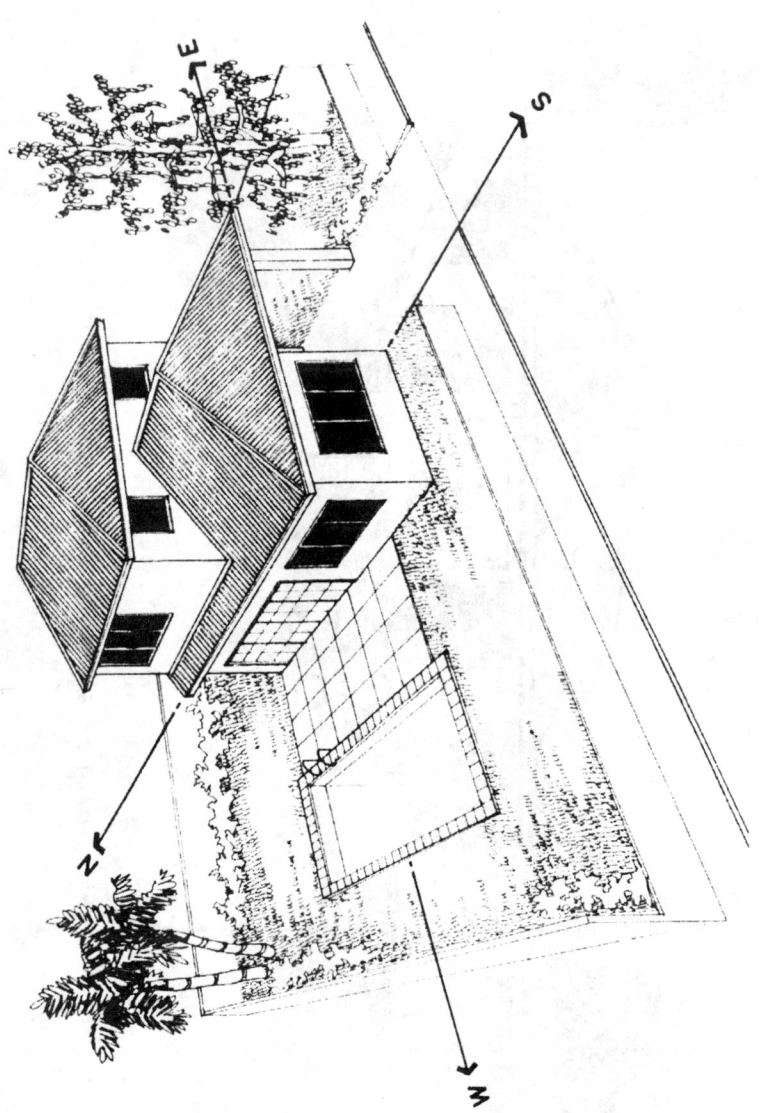

(Fig. 87) A swimming pool at the west of the house.

CHAPTER XIII

MAIN DOOR = MOUTH OF THE HOUSE

We will now tackle the most important feature in *yang Feng Shui* - placement of the main door. The main door is considered as the 'mouth' of the house. The type of *chi* that is brought into the house is distributed throughout and this will have an effect on the health and fortune of the family.

It is of utmost importance to know what type of *chi* or 'nutrients' the door is taking into the house. The *chi* that is brought into the house should be *yang chi* and not *yin chi*.

Figs. 88 and 89 illustrate an external storage room opposite the main door. The storage room has stagnant *chi* which is not considered to be healthy. This is one of the causes of sickness and loss of opportunity to the household. The remedy is to move the door of the storage room to a position not facing the main door.

One of the most frequent violations to the accumulation of family resources is (Fig. 90) having a mirror in line with the front door. The mirror reflects fortune *chi* from entering the house. The cure is to relocate the mirror.

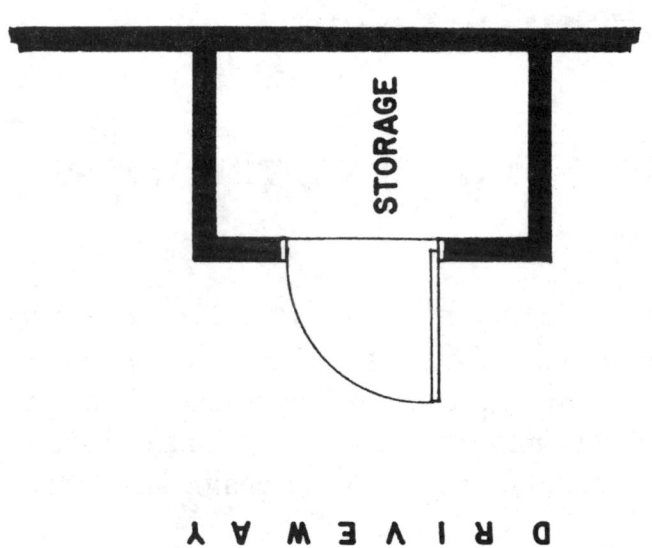

STORAGE

DRIVEWAY

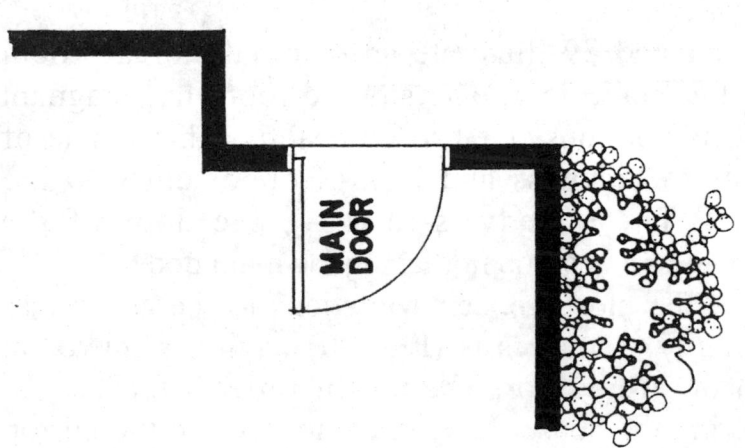

MAIN DOOR

(Fig. 88) The plan of a main door facing a storage door.

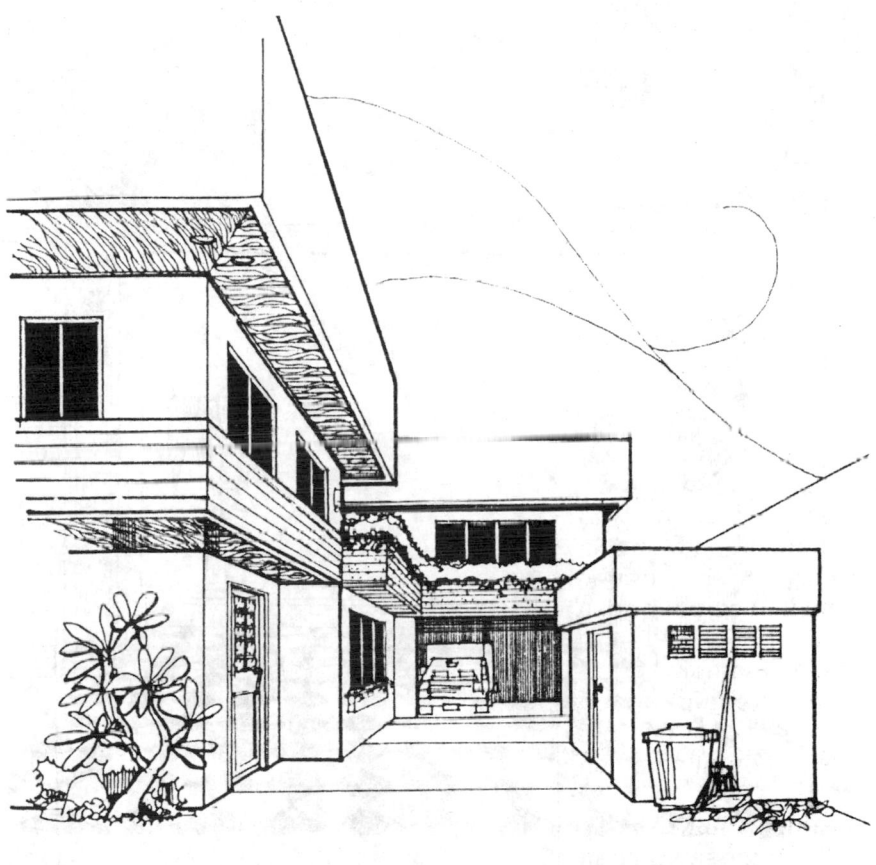

(Fig. 89) The perspective of a storage door opposite the main door.

(Fig. 90) A main door opens to a mirror.

Another arrangement that drains the family resources is shown in Figs. 91 and 92. The front door opens to a window, where the *chi* entering the house does not have a chance to circulate and be distributed around the house. It is immediately passed out through the window. This means fortune in and fortune out. Worse if there is an outside *sha* emitted by the neighbor's gable (Fig. 93). The cure is to install venetian blinds on the window and have the slats closed.

A toilet door facing the front door (Fig. 94) keeps the fortune *(yang) chi* from entering the house as the *yin chi* produced by the toilet neutralizes the *yang chi* that enters the door.

There are two adages that are not being disclosed by the Form School of *Feng Shui* and these are very crucial to having a complete understanding of the teachings of *Feng Shui.* These are:

(1) As in front, so behind.

(2) As above, so below.

These means that in the placement of any important element of the house we not only have to consider what is in front of it and what violation exists at the back of it but also what is being placed above it as well as what is beneath it. This is overlooked even by professional *geomancers.* Failing to consider these rules will result in not being able to rectify and improve the living conditions of their clients.

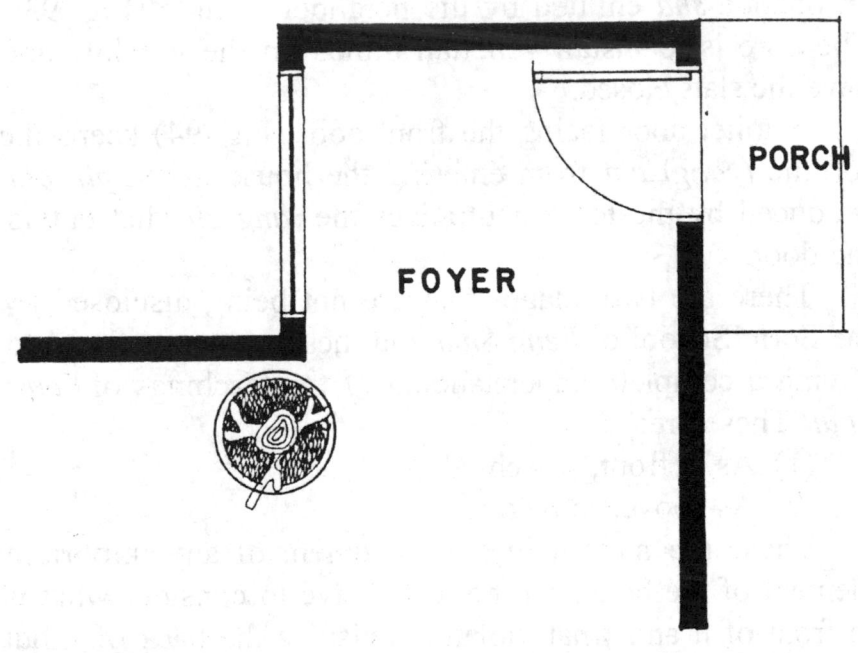

PORCH

FOYER

(Fig. 91) The plan of a door opening to a window.

*(Fig. 92) The perspective of a window
in line with the main door.*

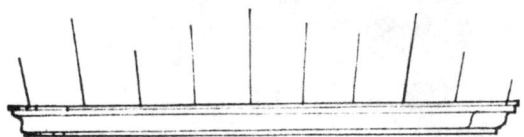

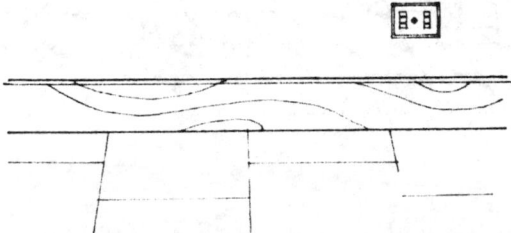

(Fig. 93) The neighbor's gable pointing to the main door through a window.

Fig. 95 shows why the family fortune is being 'flushed' away from the house. Having a toilet above the front door ensures unnecessary expenditure and is a drain to family fortune. Some people are perplexed why fortune continues to be evasive even though the door is correctly positioned by *geomancers* according to the higher techniques of *Feng Shui*.

Once form is violated as in the above case, it is very difficult to rectify the situation. Hence the importance of having the house designed according to *Feng Shui* principles before the construction begins. This will avoid incurring huge unnecessary expense to rectify it at a later stage.

Fig. 96 exemplifies the second adage "As above, so below." The violation is that the sewer pipe is installed running out the front door. The fortune *chi* is prevented from entering the house by the flushing effect of the water closet.

Another case that escapes the attention of most *geomancers* is that they do not work or analyze the *Feng Shui* of a house with an accurately scaled house plan in Fig. 97. This is the reason why the author painstakingly has in most cases illustrated both the perspective view and the plan of the house to familiarize everybody with the situation at hand.

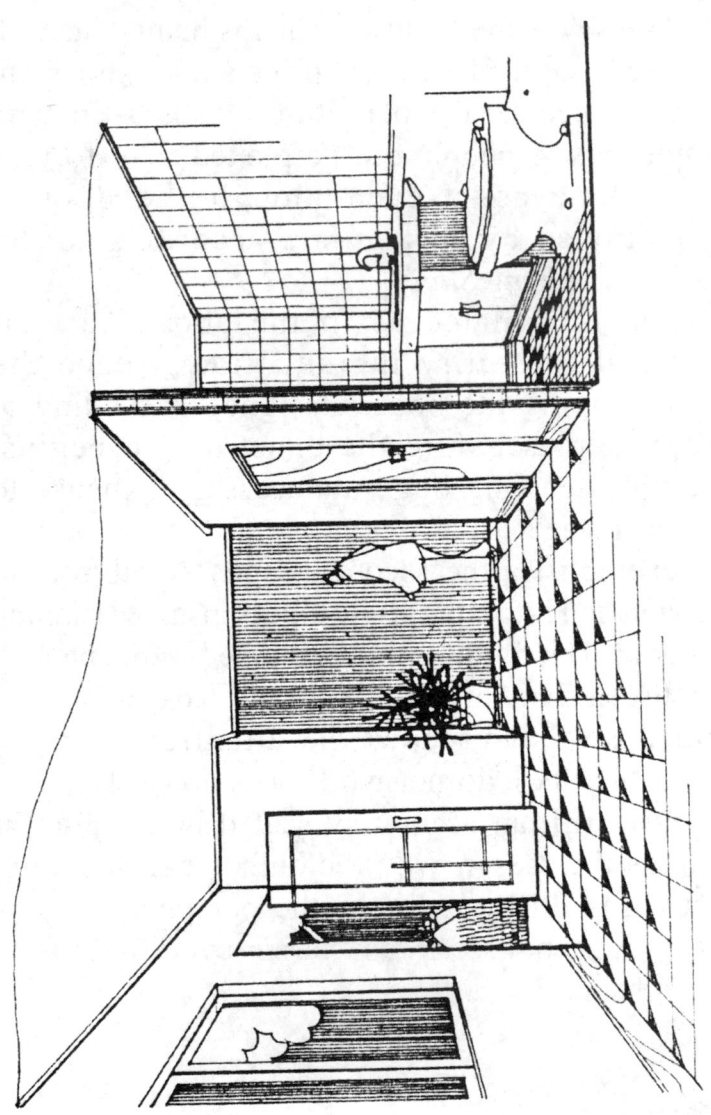

(Fig. 94) The main door opens to a toilet door.

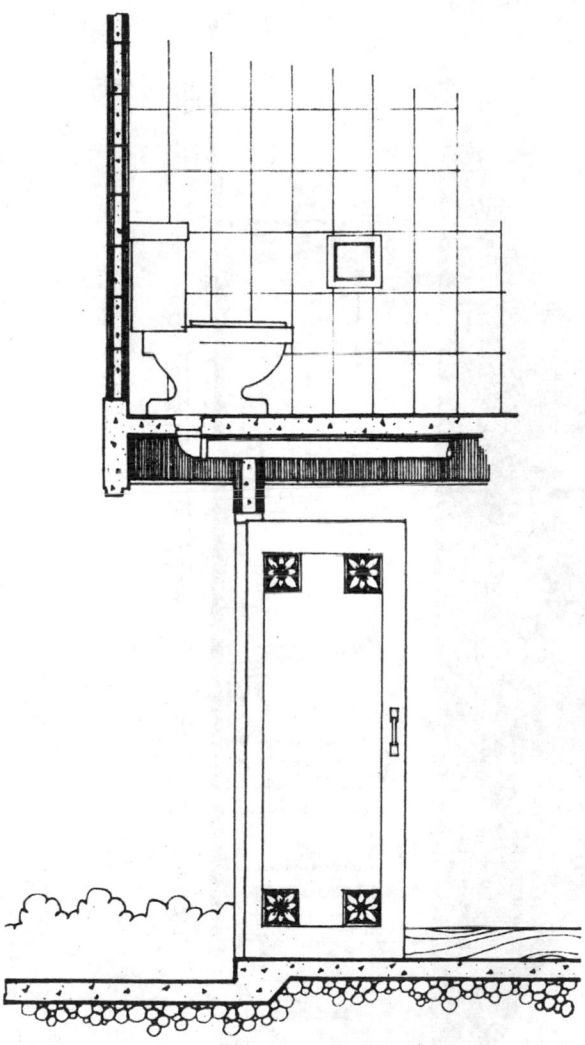

(Fig. 95) A water closet above the front door.

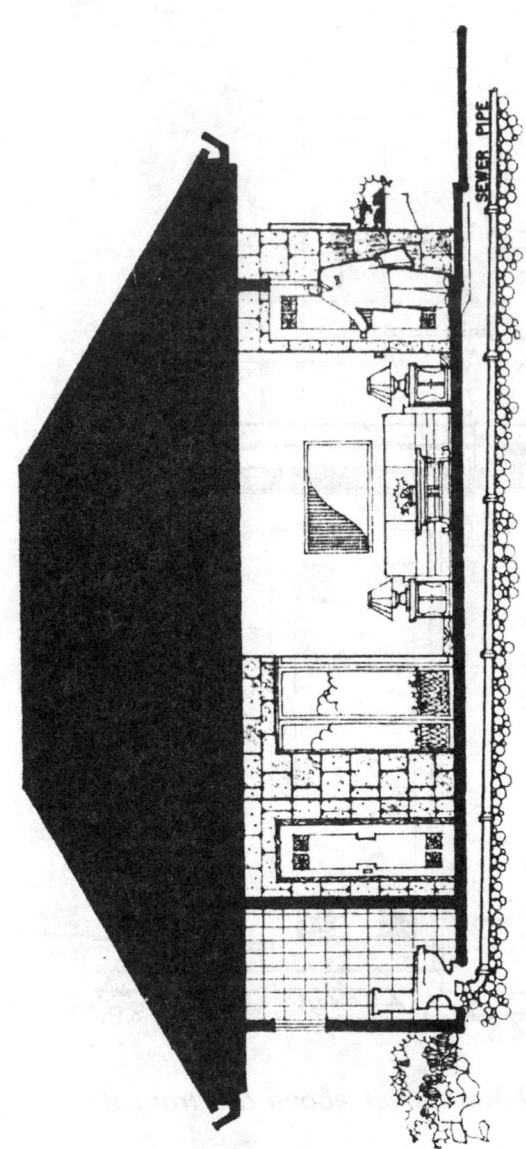

(Fig. 96) A sewer pipe running out the front door.

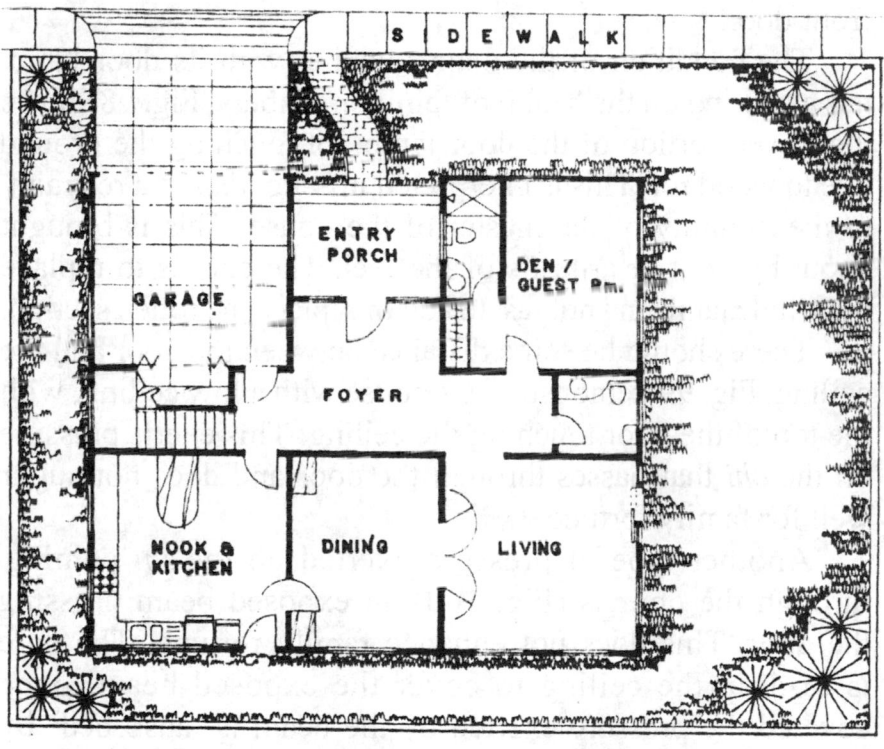

(Fig. 97) A toilet before the main door.

The placement of the front door (Fig. 97) does not encourage fortune *chi* to be coursed into the house because the adjacent water closet 'flushes' out whatever *yang chi* that enters the house.

The cure for the above two cases is to relocate the front door.

The condition of the door, together with its door jamb, has a bearing on the health of family members. Fig. 98 shows the lower portion of the door jamb not touching the ground due to wood rot. This is interpreted in *Feng Shui* as a restraint to the mobility of the master of the house. This is brought about by gout or arthritis of the feet. The cure is to replace the whole jamb and not just to add or replace the rotten section.

There should be some distance between the door and the ceiling. Fig. 99 demonstrates a house with a low ceiling, with the top of the door touching the ceiling. This exerts pressure on the *chi* that passes through the door and does not augur well for family fortune.

Another type of pressure exerted on the *chi* coming through the door is (Fig. 100) an exposed beam crossing the door. This does not enhance family fortune. The cure is to drop the ceiling to cover the exposed beam, once covered the pressure exerted by the beam is 'absorbed' by the ceiling panel.

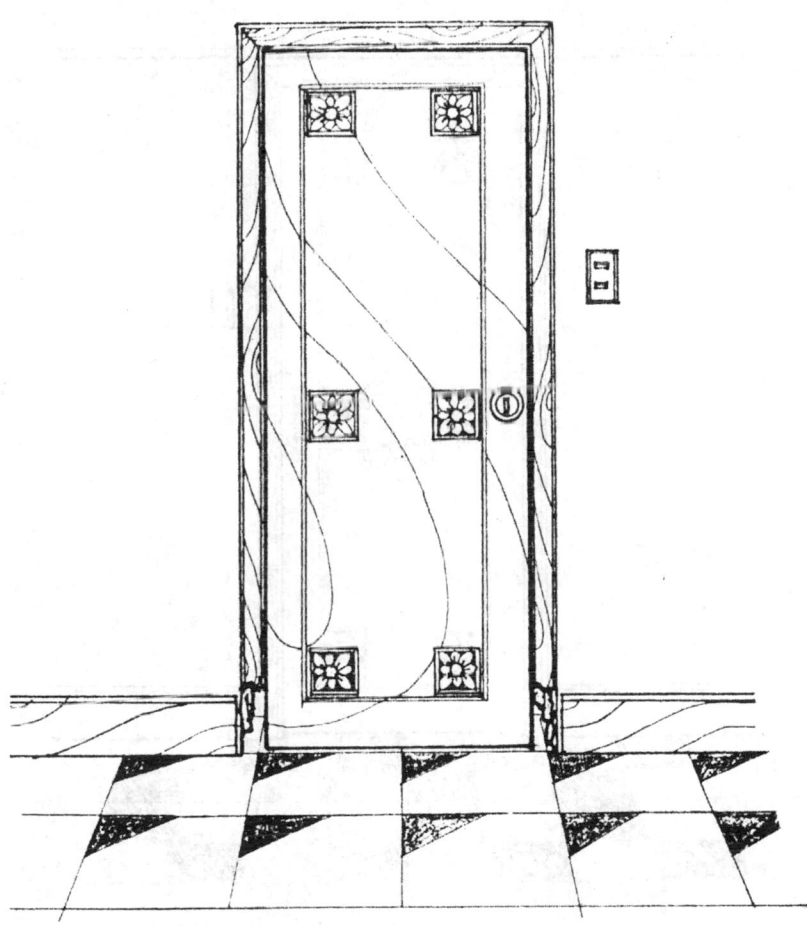

(Fig. 98) A door with rotten jamb.

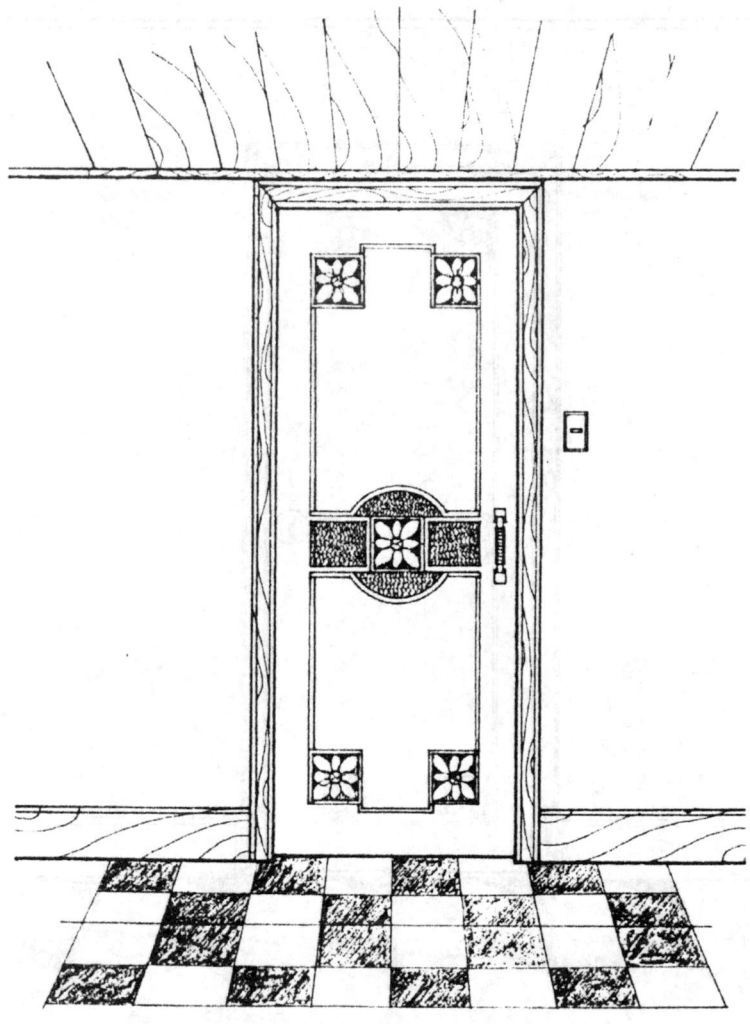

(Fig. 99) A door reaching the ceiling.

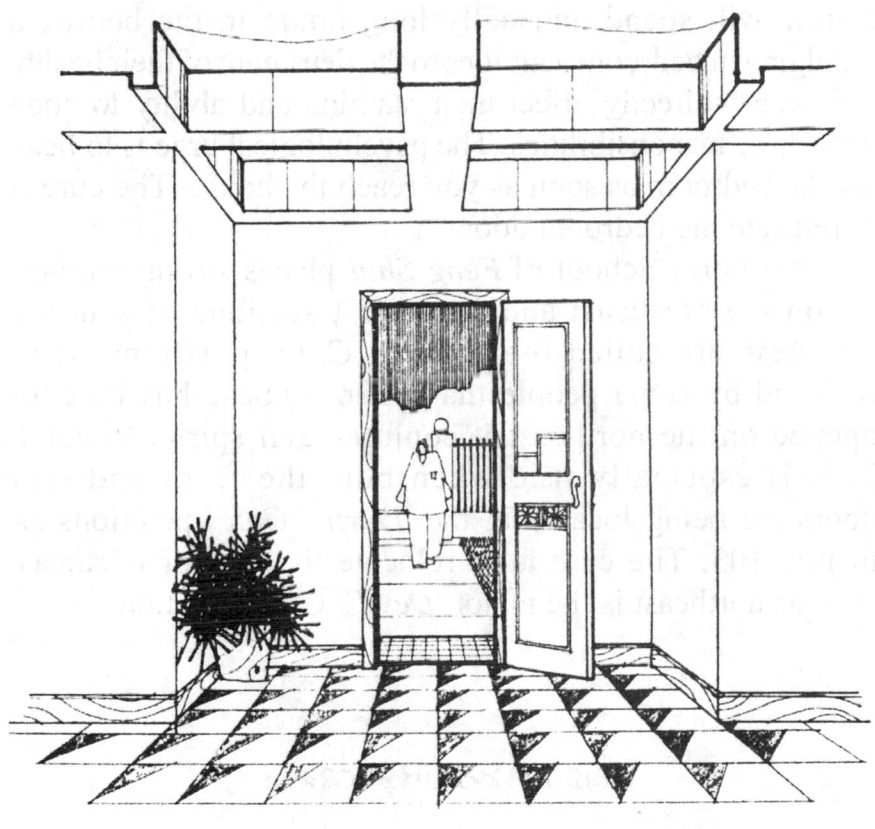

(Fig. 100) An exposed beam on top of the front door.

Figs. 101 and 102 illustrate the setup where the health of the couple occupying the bedroom is being amorously affected. A bedroom door that opens to the front door indicates the couple will spend unusually long hours in the bedroom indulging in bedroom activities to the detriment of their health. This can indirectly affect their stamina and ability to cope with other responsibilities. The psychological urge is to head for the bedroom as soon as you reach the house. The cure is to relocate the bedroom door.

The Form School of *Feng Shui* places strong emphasis on the northeast and southwest sections of a house for these are called the *'Devil's Gate'* positions. It is believed by some people that when a house has its door opened on the northeast it conjures evil spirits to enter. This is especially true when both the front and rear doors are being located in the *'Devil's Gate'* positions as in Fig. 103. The cure is to relocate the rear or northeast door as northeast is the major *'Devil's Gate'* position.

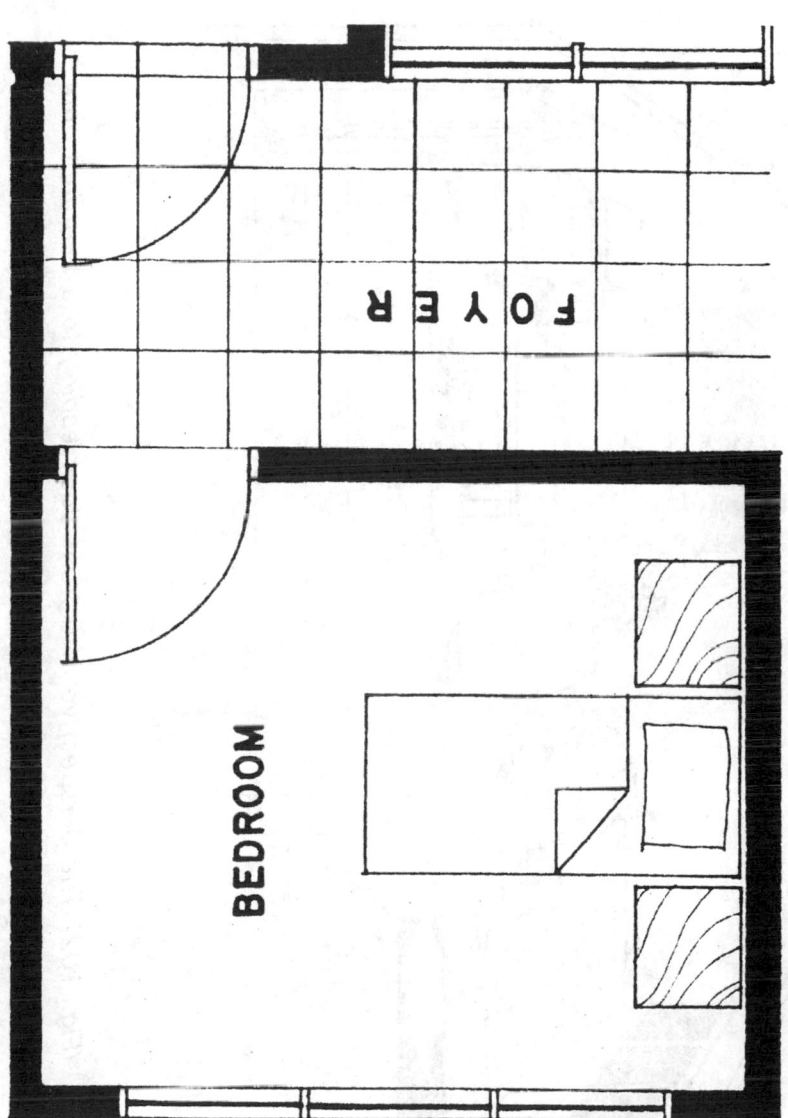

(Fig. 101) The plan of a bedroom door facing the front door.

(Fig. 102) The perspective of a front door leading to a bedroom door.

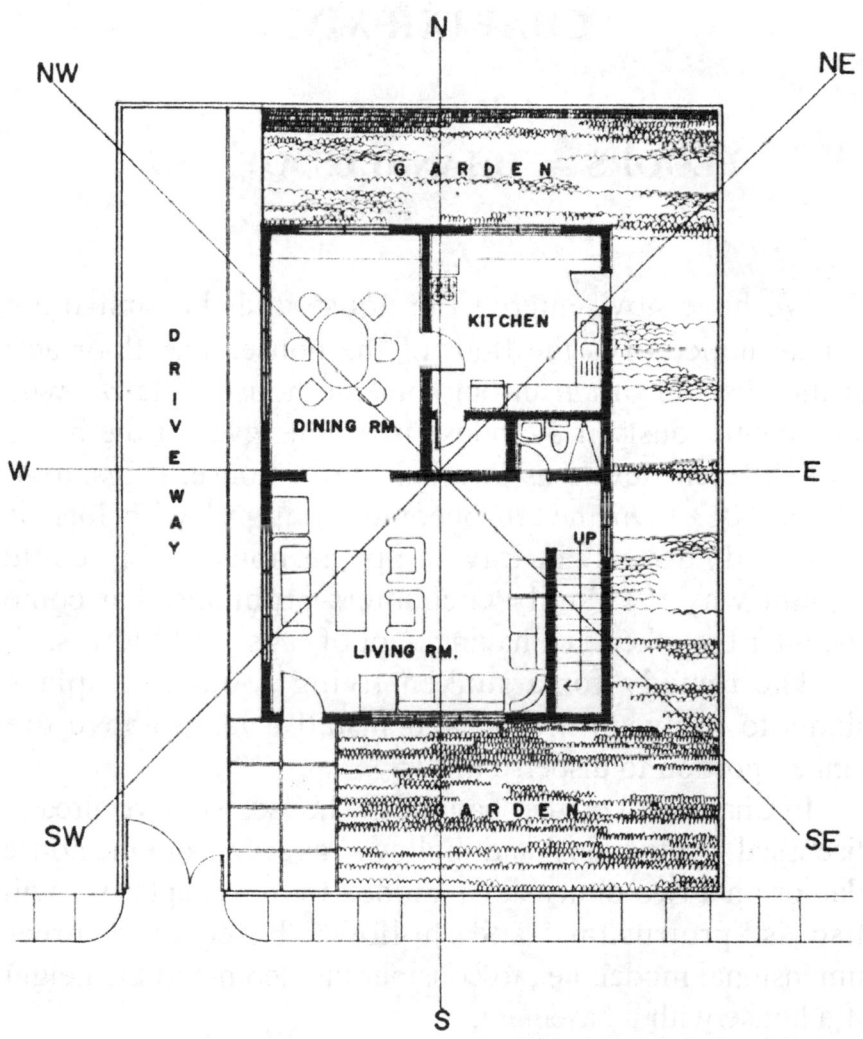

(Fig. 103) Doors on the devil's gate positions.

CHAPTER XIV

FLOORS = CHANNELS OF *CHI*

We have now entered the house and the first thing to take notice of is the floor of the house. The floor acts as the channel of *chi* throughout the house. The *chi* will flow continuously if the house is of one level. If the house is of different levels as in a split-level house, (Figs. 104, 105 & 106) then the *chi* becomes 'bumpy' with lots of 'ups' and 'downs' in traversing the house. This could explain why the family encounters problems that come one after the other, i.e., having a lot of 'ups' and 'downs.'

The remedy for a sunken living room is to place plants to bring up the *chi* and install a lamp above the sunken portion to disperse the *chi*.

In Chapter XI on the shape of the house, we have already discussed 'protrusions' and 'hollows' as seen from the house plan or on a two-dimensional model. In this chapter we will discuss 'protrusions' and 'hollows' based on a three-dimensional model, i.e., to consider the depth and the height of a house with a basement.

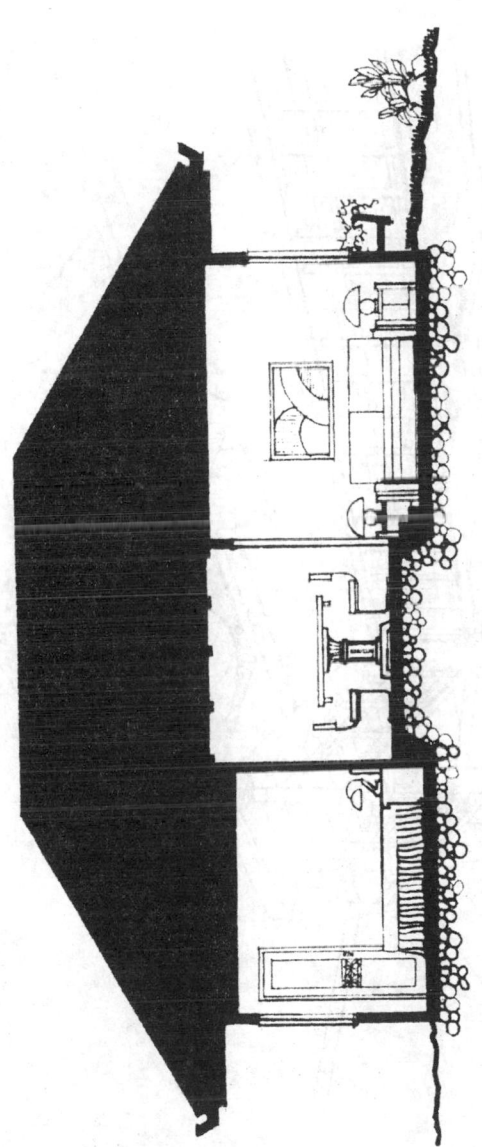

(Fig. 104) A house with different floor levels.

(Fig. 105) A split-level house.

In *Feng Shui*, the *chi* is the energy that moves on the earth's surface, a basement is considered as a 'hollow.' A basement or a cellar under the house will have an effect on certain members of the family depending on its position. If the basement is situated at the center of the house (Fig. 107), this will cause the disintegration of the family as this is a 'hollow' at the center of the house.

If there is a lower level having the same area as the house then this is not considered a 'hollow' and is permissible in *Feng Shui*.

ଚ୍ଚ୍ଚ

(Fig. 106) A sunken living room.

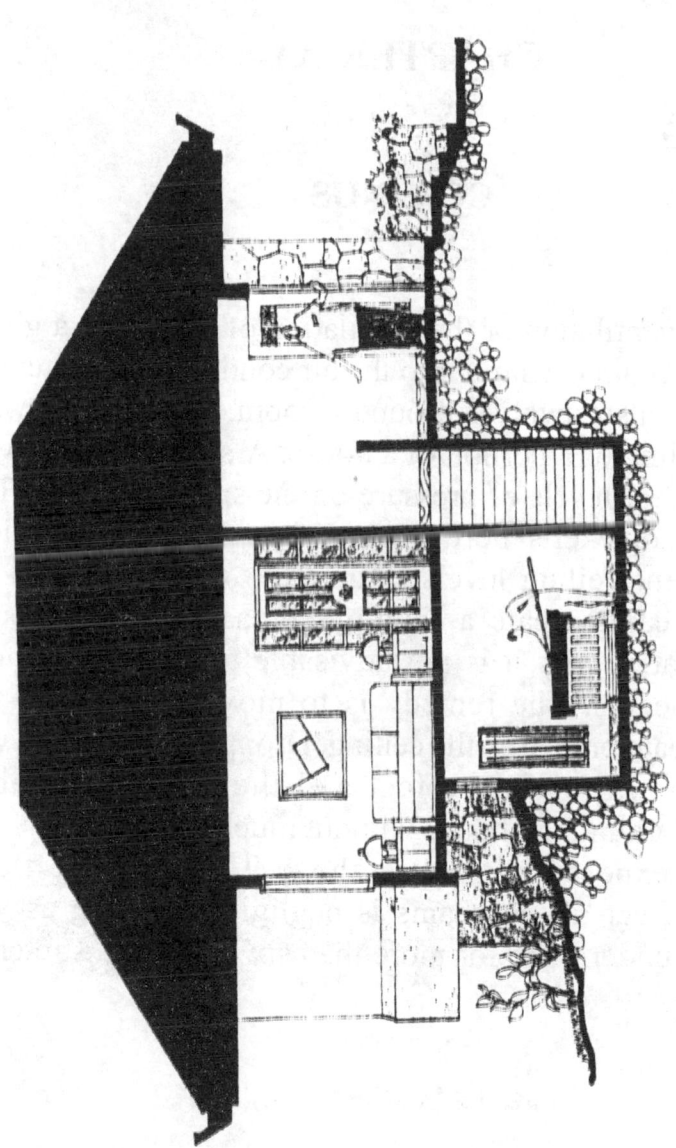

(Fig. 107) A basement at the center of a house.

CHAPTER XV

CEILINGS

Chi is ventilation or the circulation of energy in a given space. It acts almost similar to the air conditioning system in that the *chi* also revolves around a room. Fig. 108 shows a slanted ceiling of a portion of a house. A slanted ceiling will exert different levels of pressure on the space below it. The lowest portion exerts more pressure than the highest portion.

Different ceiling levels (Figs. 109 & 110) created by exposed beams create a 'bumpy' pressure on the space below. That is why it is not advisable to be seated under exposed beams. The remedy is to move away from the exposed beam or to drop the ceiling. Dropping the ceiling will give a smooth ceiling effect and the *chi* will be able to revolve around the house without much obstruction.

If the exposed beams are above 9 ft. from the floor, then the effect of the beams is negligible as long as you don't stay under them for more than six hours at a stretch.

(Fig. 108) A slanted ceiling of a house.

(Fig. 109) A house with different ceiling levels.

(Fig. 110) Exposed beams on the ceiling.

CHAPTER XVI

STAIRS = CONDUITS OF *CHI*

Stairs are used to convey motion from one level to another. It is a conduit for *chi* to be brought up or down and be distributed throughout the level. The placement of the stairs affects family fortune and unity.

Chi is like water, it flows easily from an upper level to a lower level. Unlike water, *chi* also moves upward. It is carried by the movement of activity that establishes the energy pattern of the next level.

Fig. 111 illustrates a staircase leading to the front door. This is one of the reasons the family finds it difficult to accumulate wealth. The fortune *chi* rushes down and out through the door. The remedy is to redirect the position of the stairs so that it comes at an angle 90 degrees (Fig. 112) to the door. This will prevent the loss of *chi* from the house.

Another situation worth checking when the household expenses seem to get out of hand is (Fig. 113) a staircase that leads to a toilet. This flushes the *chi* down the drain. The cure is to install an automatic door closer, have a curtain over the door and put plants inside the toilet to bring up the *chi*.

(Fig. 111) The front door opening to a staircase.

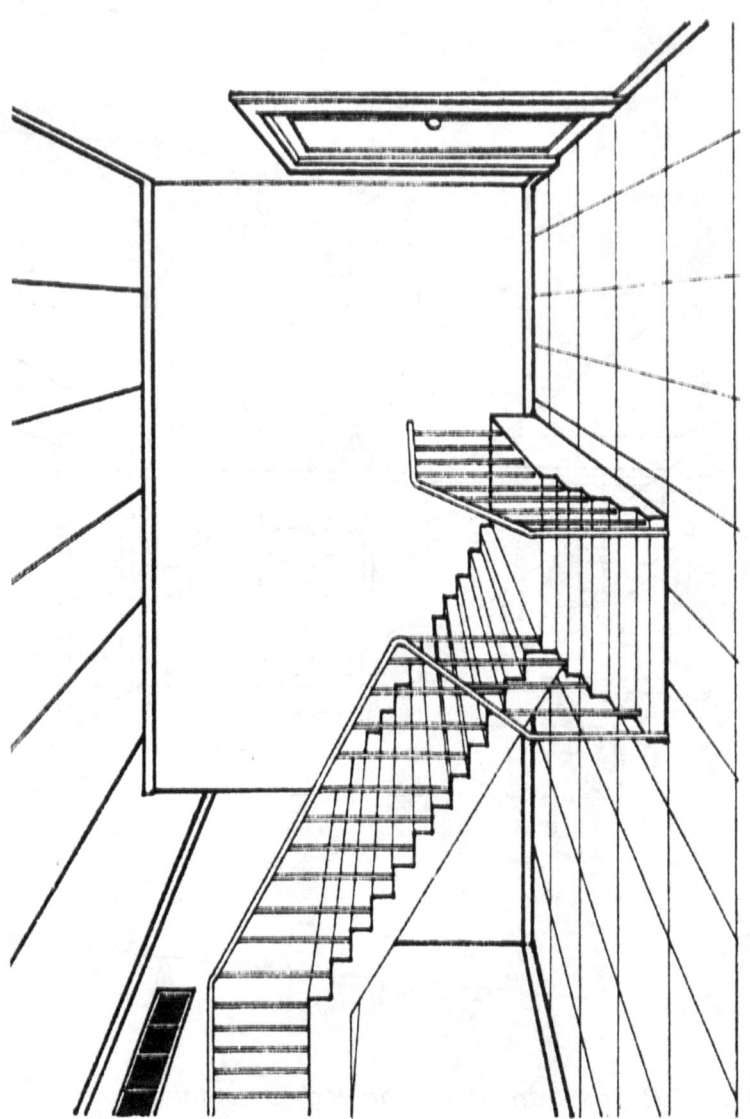

(Fig. 112) The cure for a staircase leading to the front door.

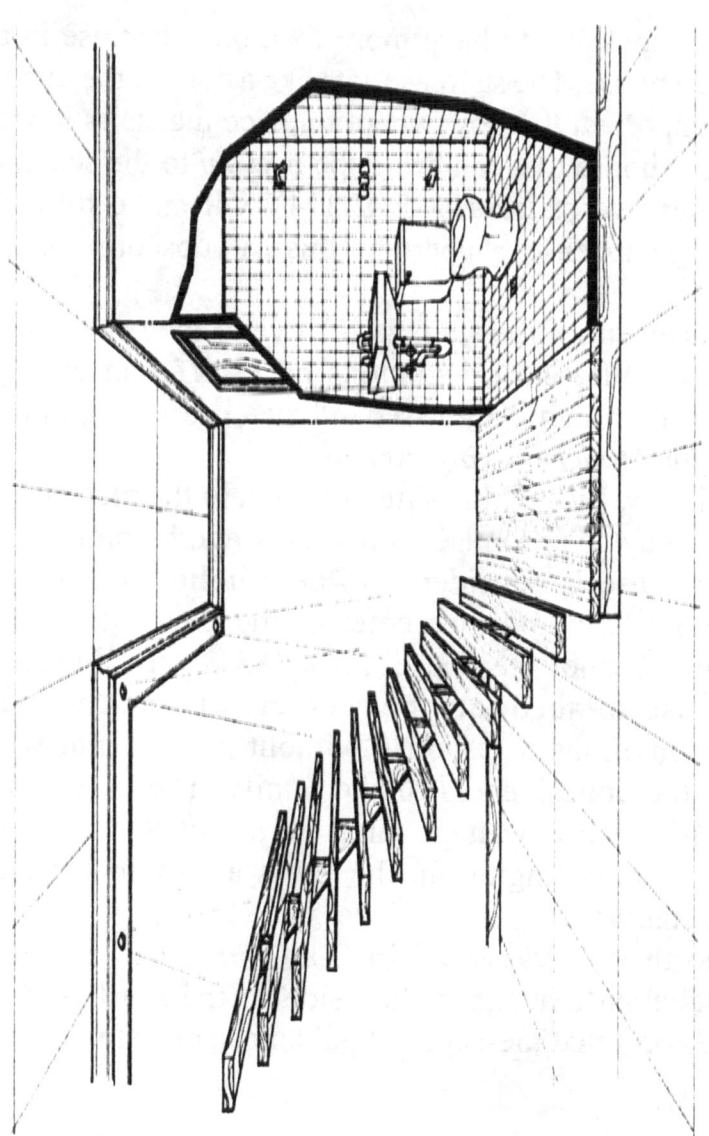

(Fig. 113) A staircase leading to a toilet.

It is not advisable to have more than one staircase in a modest-sized house. The staircase acts like a door to the upper level. It is important to know where to place the stairs in the section of the house that can bring the best *chi* to the second level. Having two staircases (Fig. 114) will make the *chi* flowing on the upper level aberrant; this will upset the *chi* of this level.

The placement of the stairs is relative to the orientation of the house. Different orientations have different energy grids. This is thoroughly discussed in Level III of the *Applied Feng Shui for Modern Living* course.

We will now discuss the situations where the placement of the stairs may compromise family unity and harmony.

The staircase is considered to be a hollow or empty space in *Feng Shui* and the center of the house is considered as the heart of the house. Figs. 115 & 116 illustrate the staircase placed at the center of the house. This is synonymous to a house without a heart and will jeopardize the cohesiveness of the family. The cure is to install a 24-hour low wattage lamp on top of the stairs to bring up the *chi.* Bringing up the *chi* is a way to fill the void of the stairwell.

The north is held sacred in *Feng Shui.* The ancient Chinese believed that the gods reside in the north and it is from the north that messages of guidance emanate.

(Fig. 114) A house with two staircases.

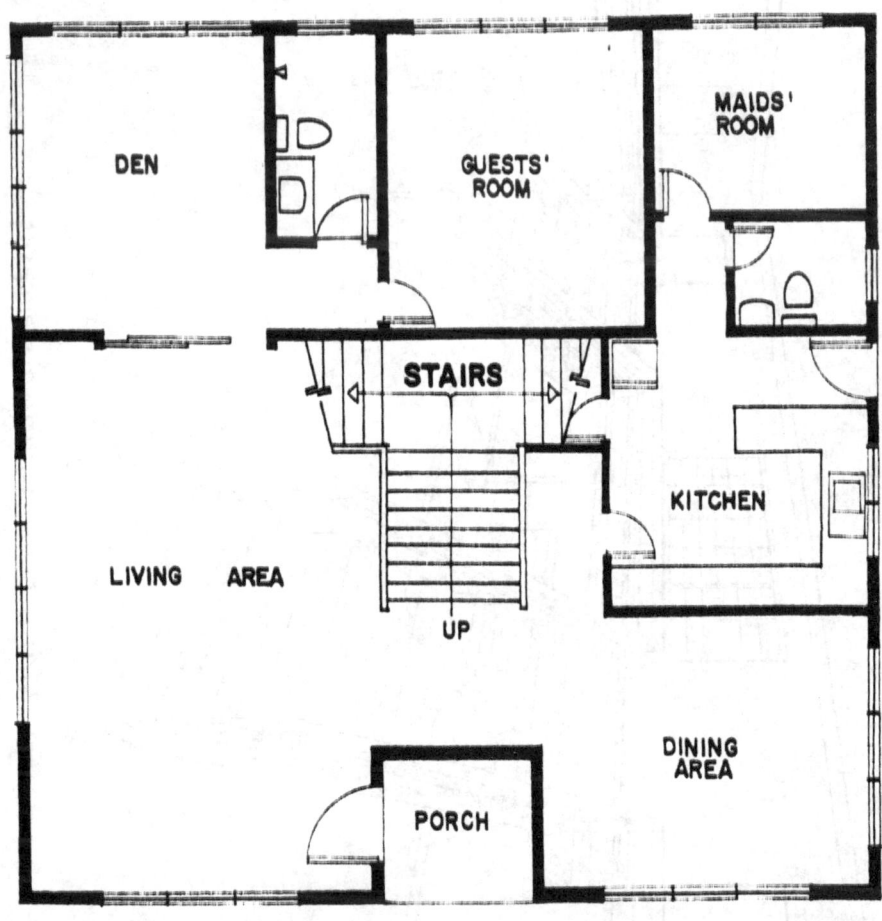

(Fig. 115) The plan of a stairwell at the center of a house.

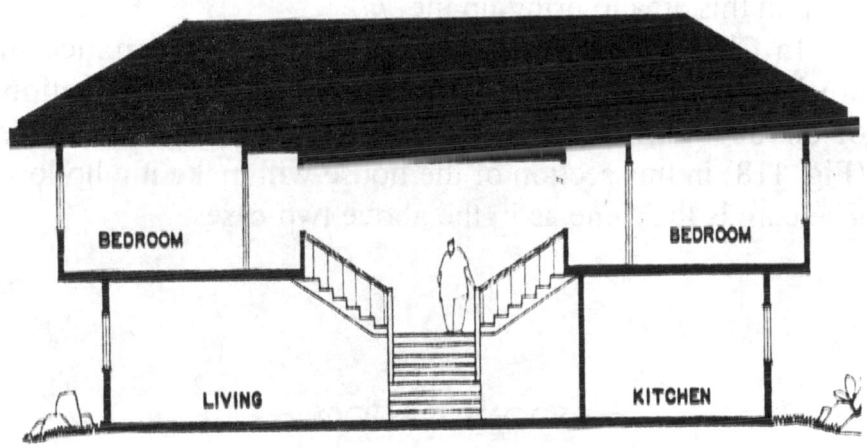

(Fig. 116) The perspective of a stairwell at the center of a house.

This is especially true for travelers as they look to the North Star to guide them in their journey. Even modern science validates the path of magnetism to be traversing from the north to the south.

A staircase in the north (Fig. 117) is equivalent to having a hollow in the north. This does not augur well for family solidarity for it connotes insubordination and loss of fortune. The cure is to install a 24-hour low wattage lamp in this area to bring up the *chi*.

In Chapter III we have discussed the importance of northwest in *Feng Shui*. This being the *'Gua'* or section of the house where authority emanates, placing a staircase (Fig. 118) in this section of the house will make it a hollow. The cure is the same as in the above two cases.

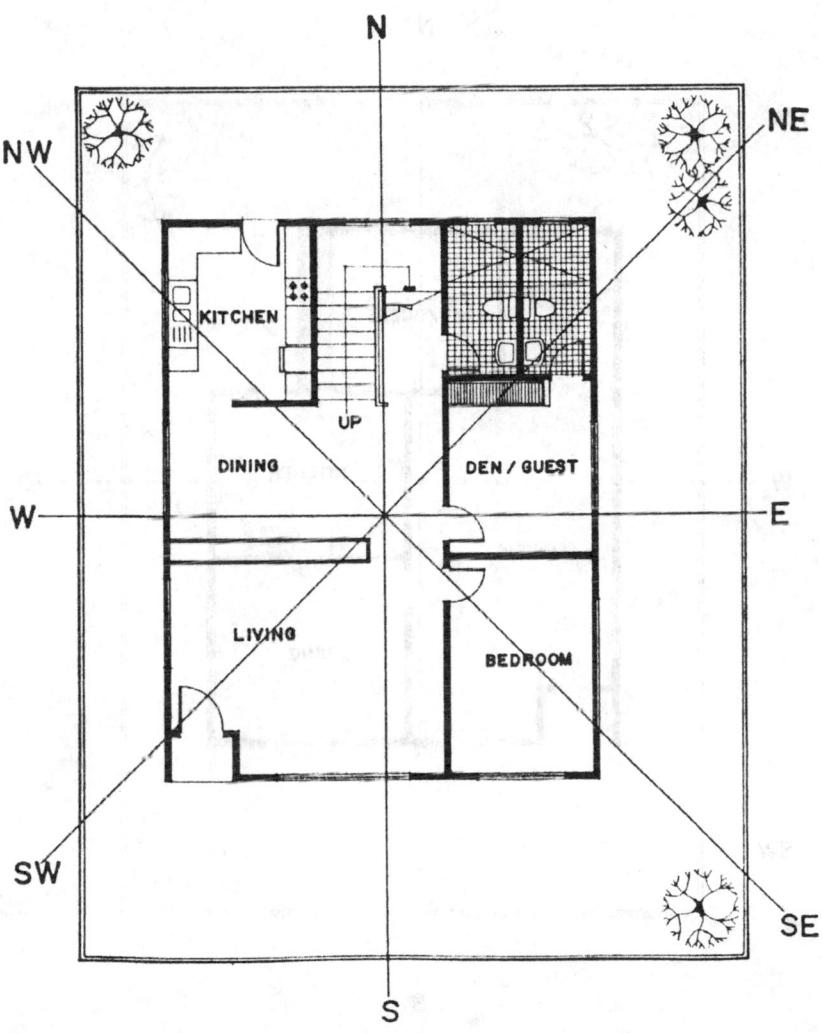

(Fig. 117) A staircase in the north section of a house.

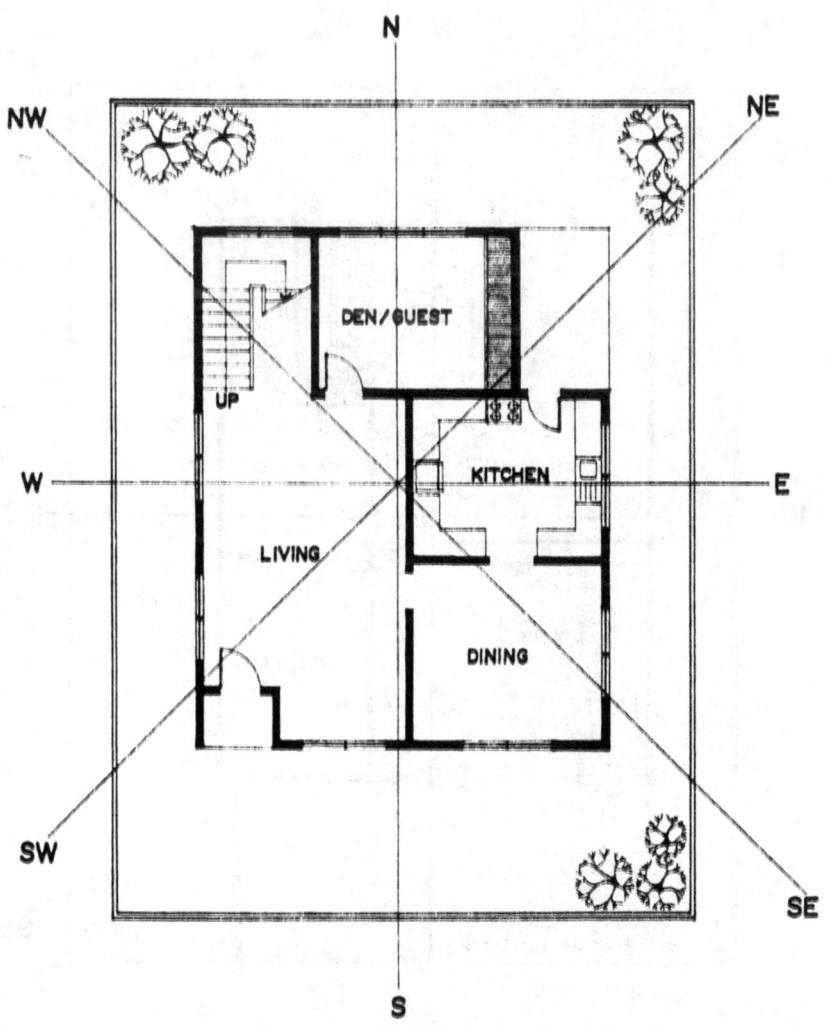

(Fig. 118) A staircase in the northwest of a house.

CHAPTER XVII

CENTER (HEART) OF A HOUSE

In this chapter we will deal with what element of the house is best placed at the center of the house and what should not be placed here.

In *Feng Shui* the universe is believed to be made up of five elements, namely: water, wood, fire, earth and metal. The center of any given space is considered to be the element of earth. It is from the earth that all living things come. Even in religion it is believed that God created man from a patch of clay which represents the element earth. It is the earth that nurtures almost all the nutrients required to sustain life, so when the earth element is violated then the lifeline of the area is adversely compromised.

We will cite some instances to show that the center of the house is 'hollow.' Due to the irregular shape of the house (Fig. 119) its center is found to be outside. A regular shaped house with an atrium at its center (Fig. 120) is considered as a house without a heart. Fig. 121 shows a skywell located at the center of the house, this does not enhance family unity.

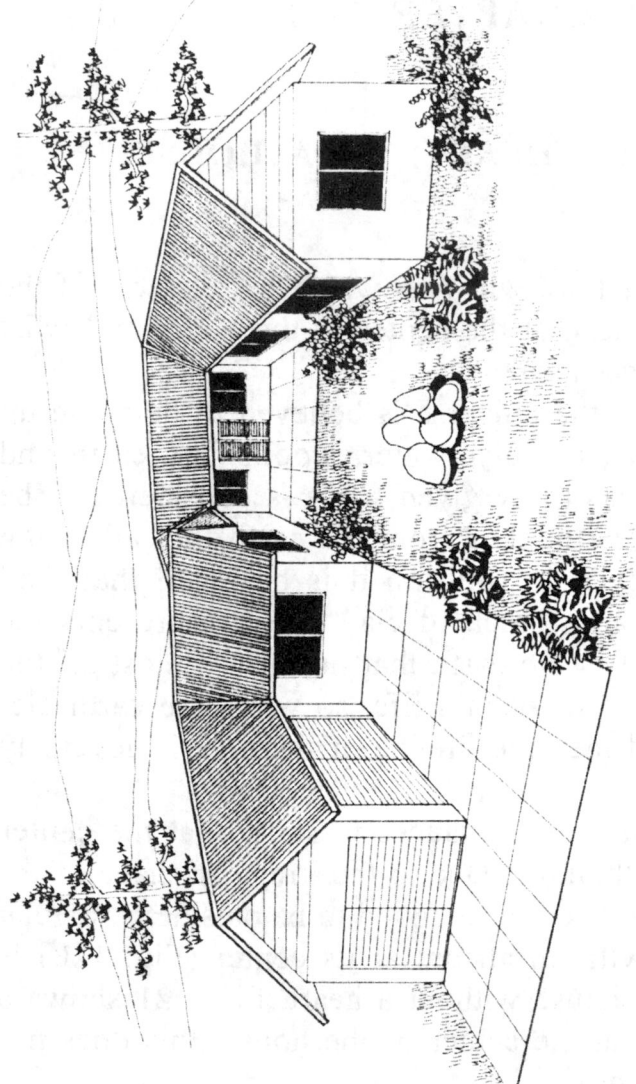

(Fig. 119) An irregular-shaped house.

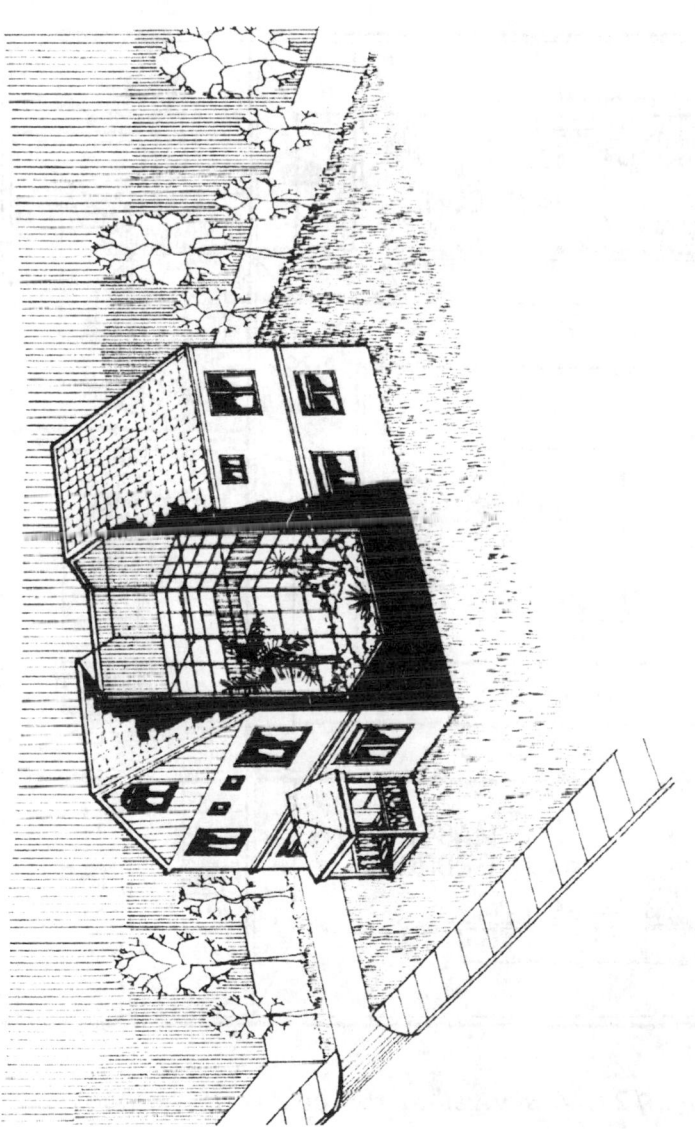

(Fig. 120) A house with a central atrium.

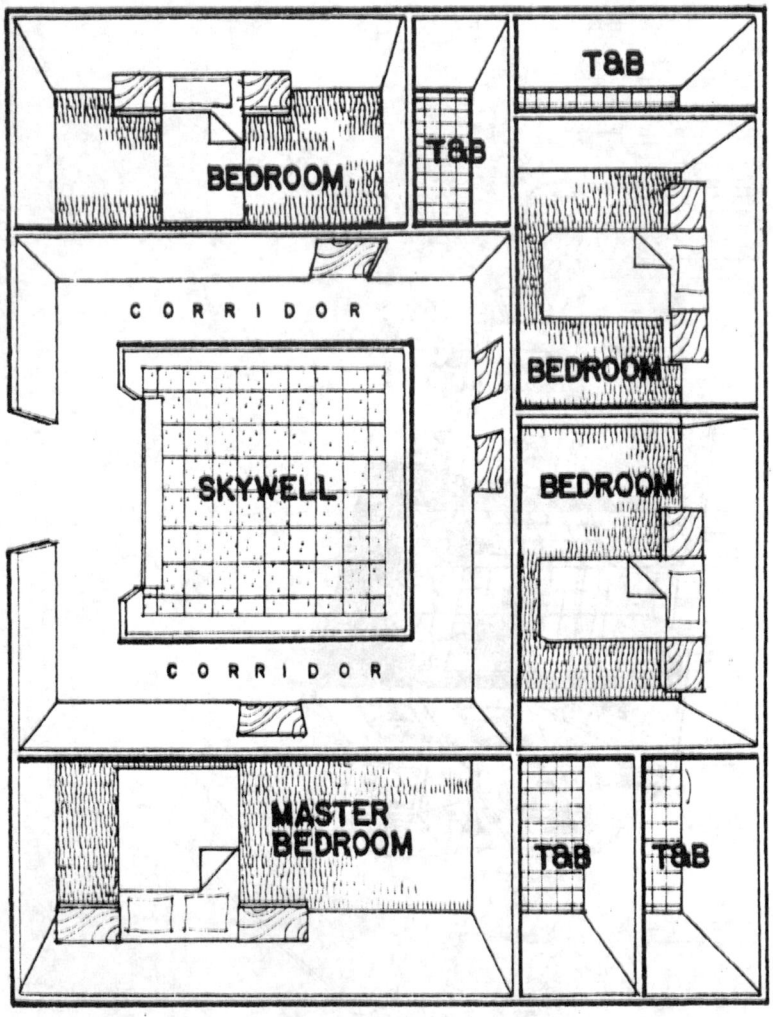

(Fig. 121) A skywell at the center of the house.

Knowing the important role played by the heart of the house, it is but logical to capitalize on this section by placing in this area the element of the house the activity of which can enhance family unity. In Fig. 122 the family room is located at the center of the house; this will assist in nurturing a warm and closely knit family. The family area should be placed at the heart of the house as it is here where all members of the family get together to enjoy sharing activities and experiences with each other.

The master of the house, being the central figure at home, is the nucleus of the family. It is auspicious to place the master bedroom at the center of the house (Fig. 123) as it will act as the cohesive force that brings the family together.

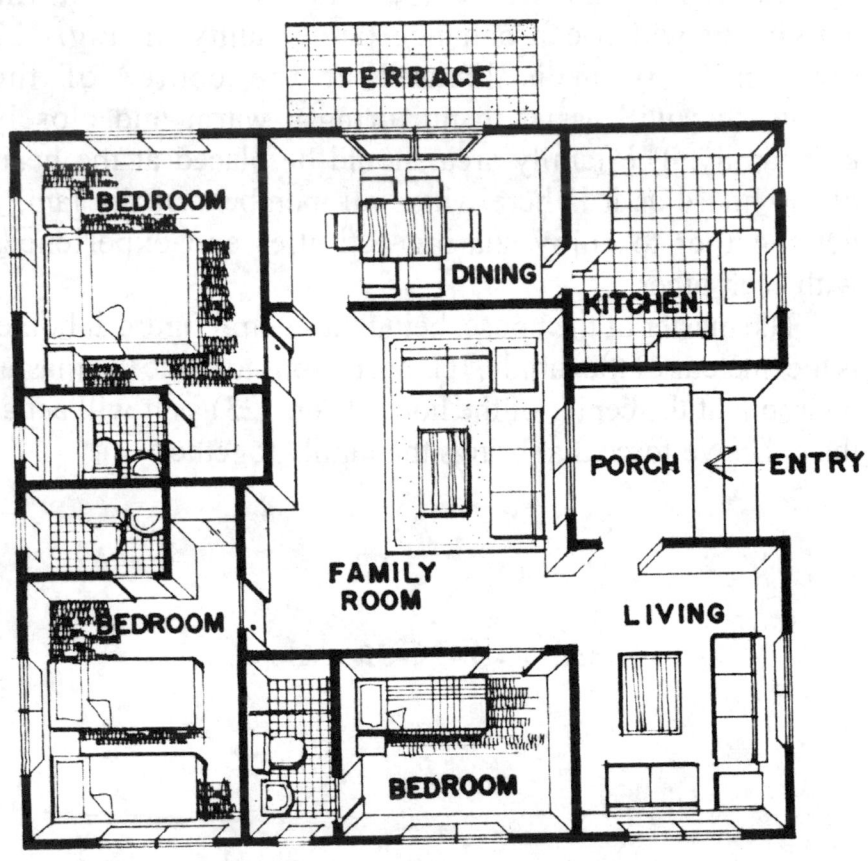

(Fig. 122) A family room at the center of the house.

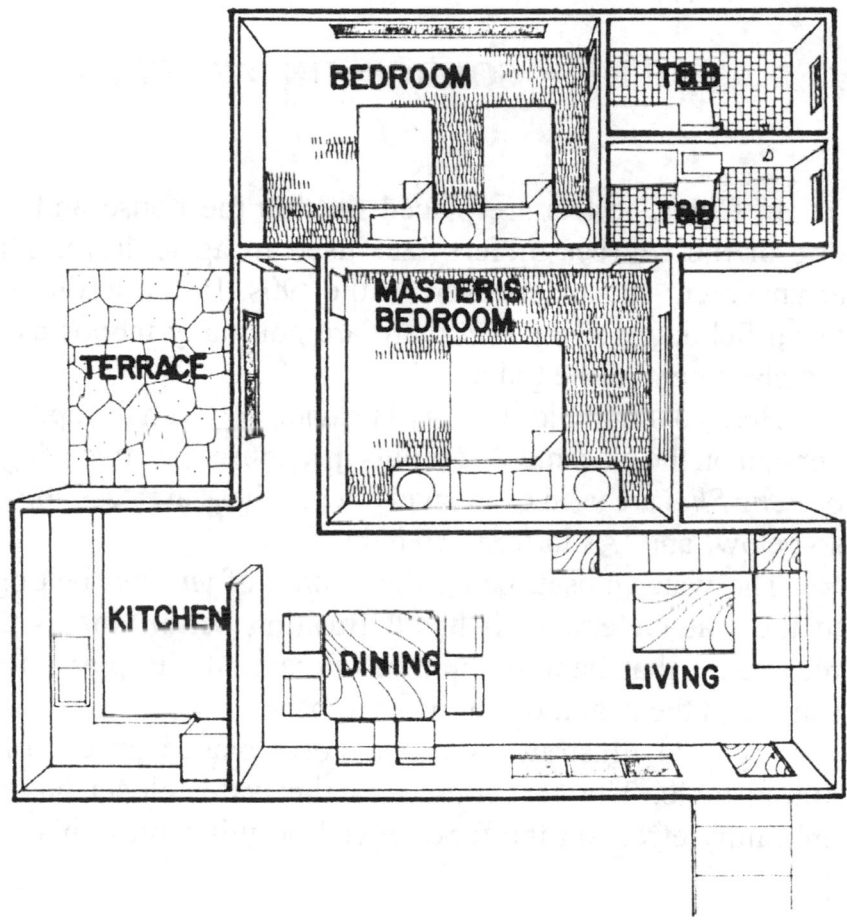

(Fig. 123) The master bedroom at the center of the house.

CHAPTER XVIII

TOILET = SOURCE OF *YIN CHI*

In China, toilets are placed outside the house and are one of the sources of fertilizer used in agriculture. This arrangement still exists even in the '90s. In the traditional Form School of *Feng Shui* there are not many taboos as to the placement of the toilet.

Here your humble guide will provide you with the updated version on the placement of toilets in a house. The two adages of *Feng Shui* are used extensively here. These are: 'As above, so below' and 'As in front, so behind.'

The water closet, being the source of *yin chi,* belongs to the water element. It has a flushing action and is the receptacle that handles human excrement. Its placement can affect the health of family members.

Fig. 124 illustrates a water closet placed on top of a dining table. The *chi* emitted by the water closet has an unhealthy effect on the food served on this table. This will

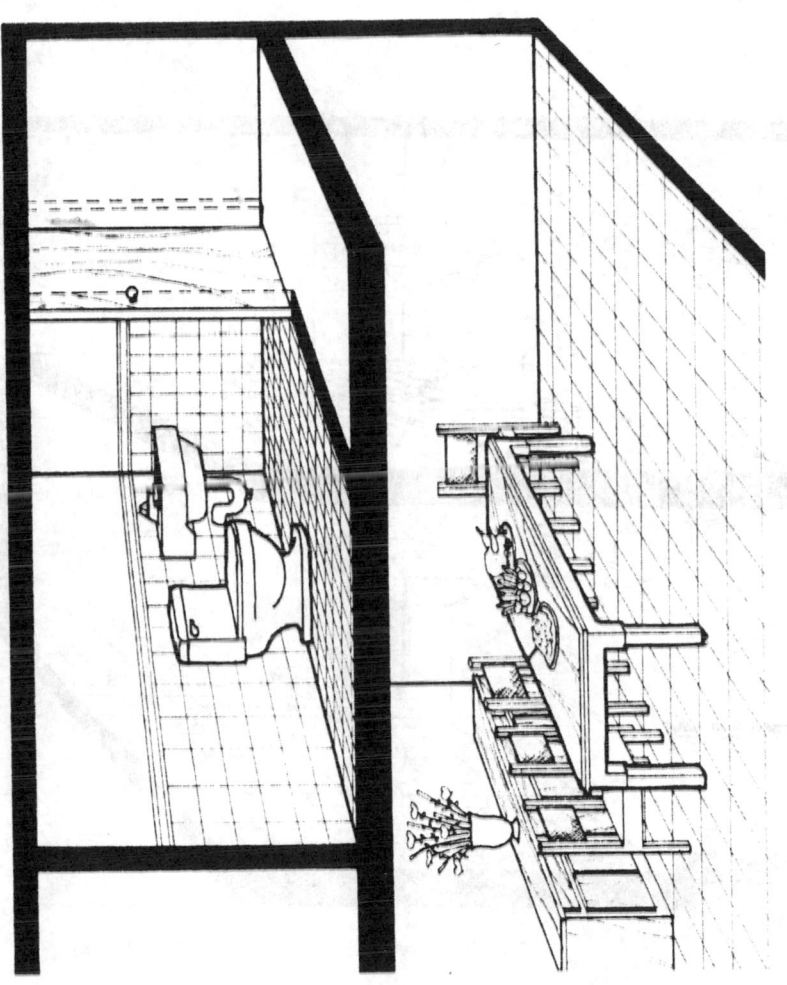

(Fig. 124) A water closet above the dining table.

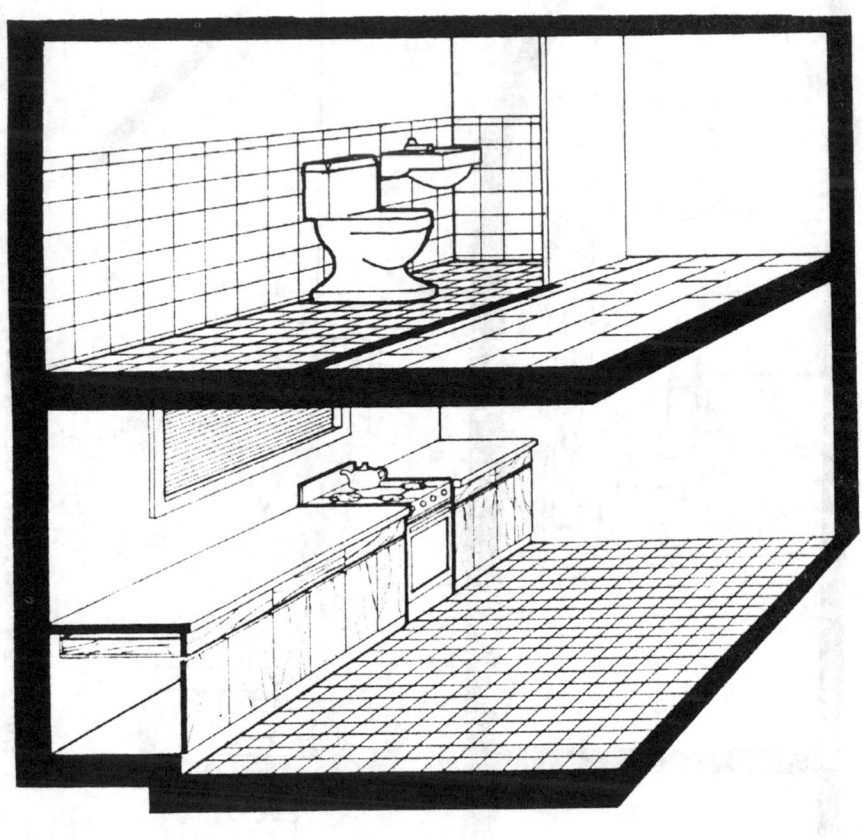

(Fig. 125) A water closet above a stove.

affect the fortune of anyone who is seated directly under it. The cure is to relocate the dining table out of range of the water closet.

Fig. 125 shows the arrangement of a household that is always sickly and in financial distress. In *Feng Shui,* the stove symbolizes family wealth and its element is fire. The primary responsibility for all of us is to feed our families. This is in turn translated into the food cooked and served on the dining table. A water closet placed on top of a stove is not only unhealthy but also endangers the family fortune because the water *chi* emitted by the toilet puts out the fire *chi* of the stove.

Fig. 126 illustrates why the sleeper on the bed below the water closet is always sickly and unlucky. The remedy is to relocate the bed.

Fig. 127 depicts that one of the reasons for a sleeper suffering from insomnia is having a water closet placed behind the bed. The flushing energy pattern is formed, hence the auric field of the sleeper is disturbed. The cure is to relocate the bed.

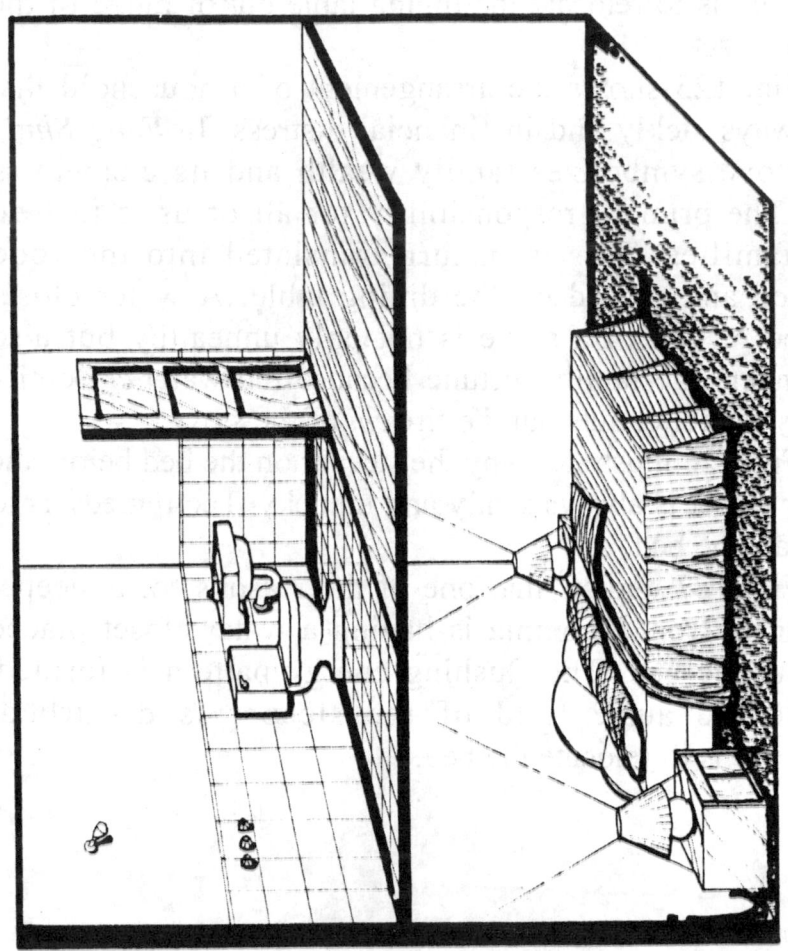

(Fig. 126) A water closet above a bed.

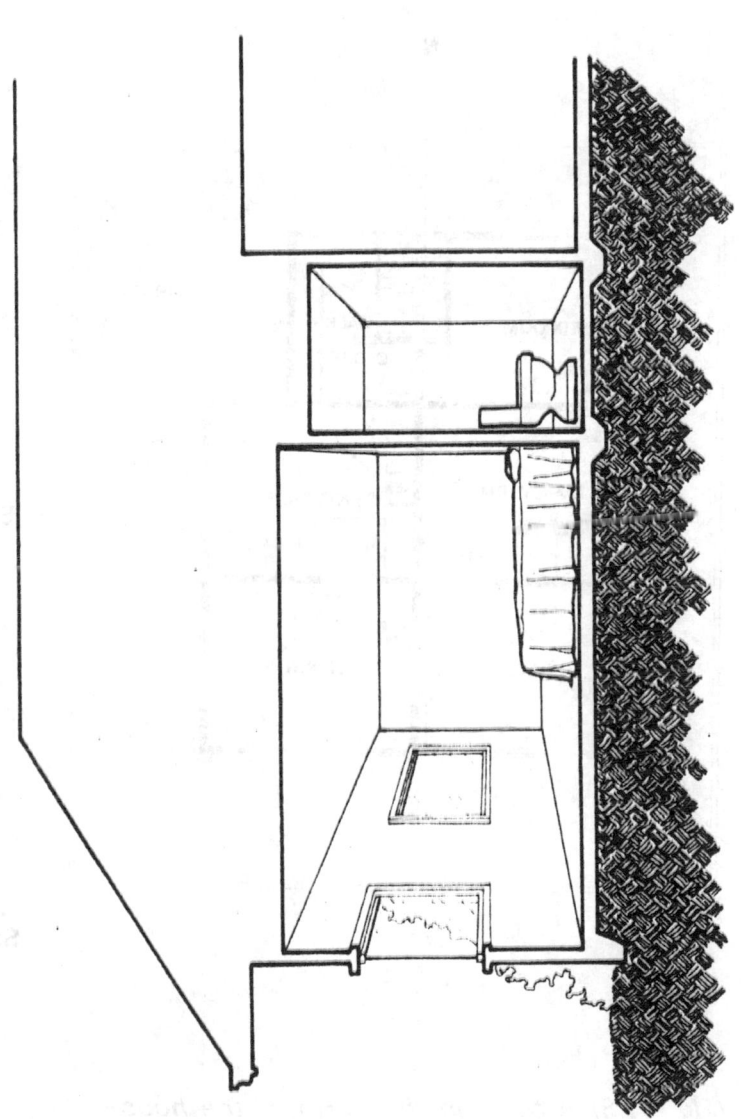

(Fig. 127) A water closet behind the bed.

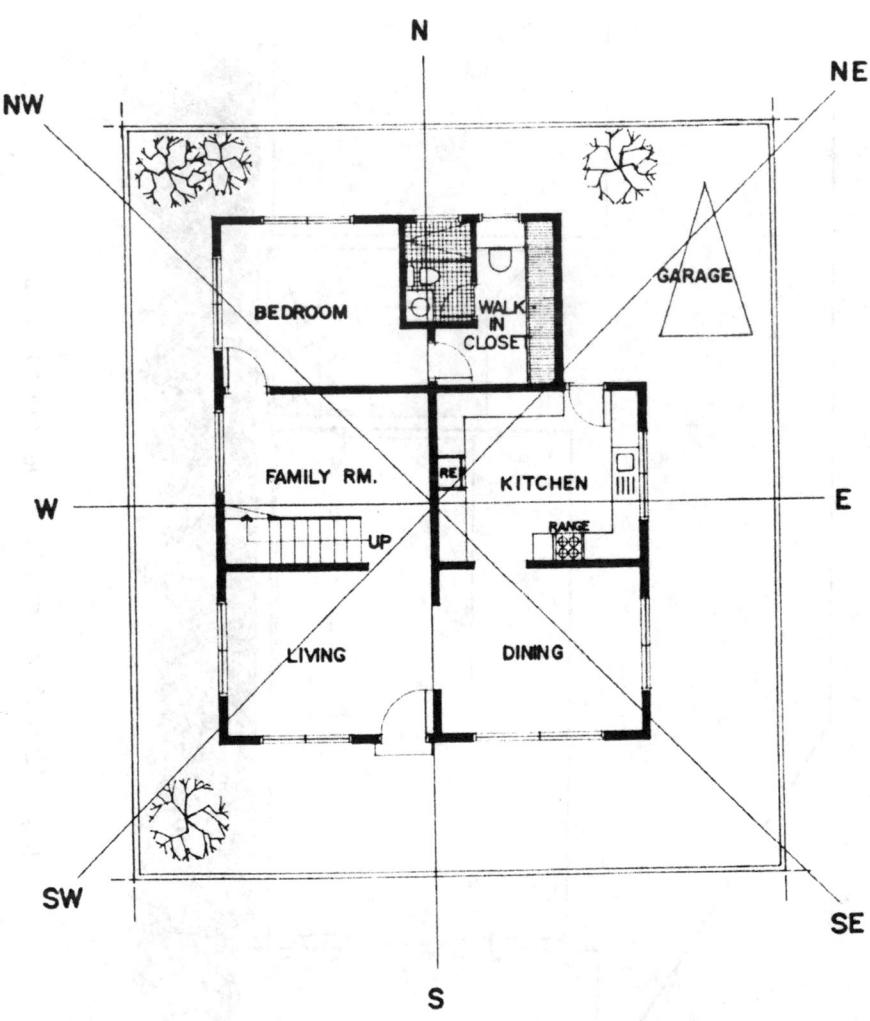

(Fig. 128) A toilet in the north of the house.

For the same reason as in the placement of the staircase (Chapter XVI), toilets or water closets, to be more precise, should not be placed in the (Fig. 128) northern section of a house as this will unfavorably affect the fortune and health of the family.

Water closet in the northwest (Fig. 129) will diminish the status of the master of the house making him ineffective. This will affect the harmony within the family.

In the preceding chapter we learned that the center of the house belongs to the element earth, a toilet placed here (Fig. 130) will be the source of conflicting energies in the family; as earth is the nemesis of water.

ഇ൮ഇ൮ഇ൮ഇ൮ഇ൮

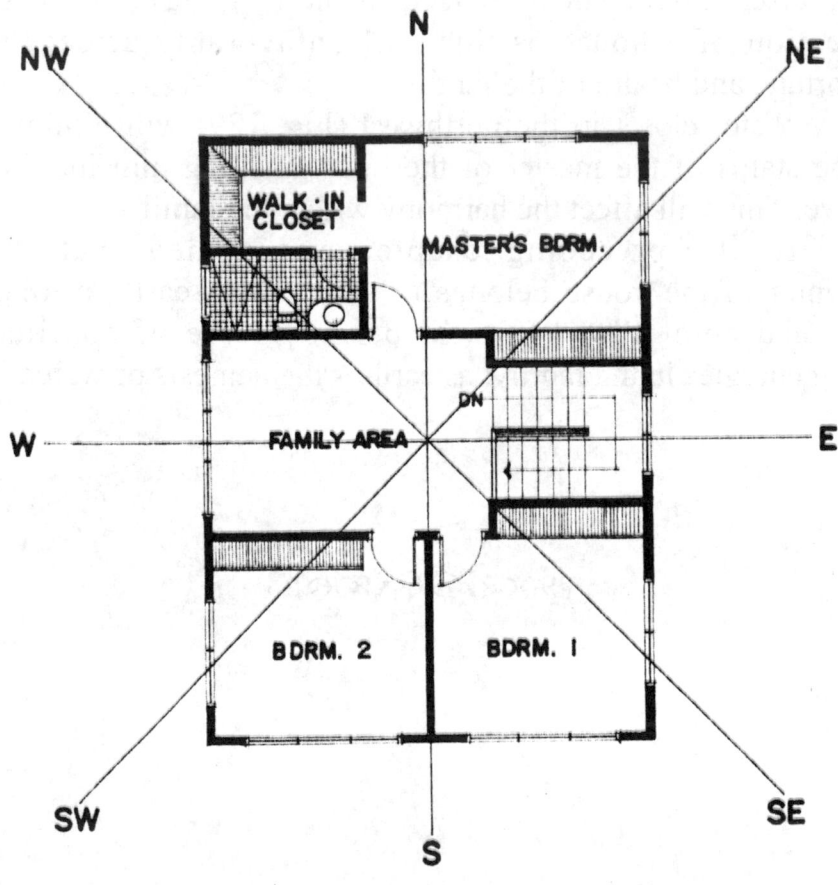

(Fig. 129) A toilet in the northwest of the house.

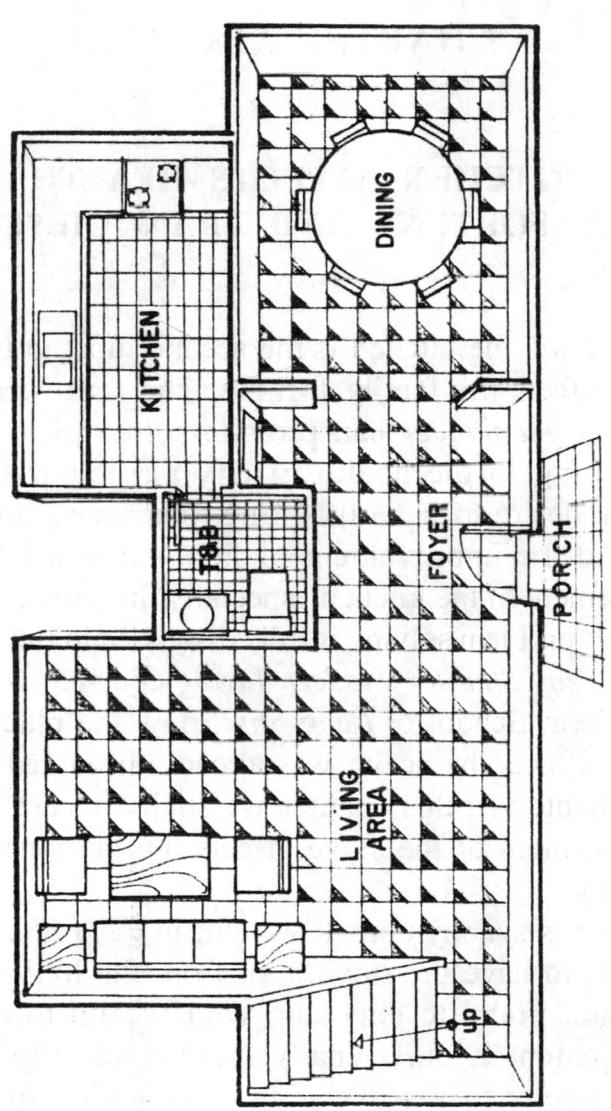

(Fig. 130) A toilet at the center of the house.

CHAPTER XIX

THE KITCHEN AFFECTS HEALTH, FAMILY FORTUNE AND TRANQUILITY

In *Feng Shui,* the kitchen is the second most important factor that affects the family fortune. The first being the main door. A *geomancer* can provide solutions to problems pertaining to the health of any particular family member, the desire to have offspring, marriage problems, litigation and the improvement of family fortune by the correct placement of the kitchen especially the stove.

All of this problem solving is fully discussed in Level II of the *Applied Feng Shui for Modern Living* course.

In the Form School of *Feng Shui*, how the placement of the stove affects the health was already discussed in the preceding chapter. In this chapter we shall concentrate on how the placement of the stove affects the family fortune and tranquility.

The stove is synonymous to wealth in *Feng Shui*. It is not advisable to have the stove seen from the living room as this is tantamount to exposing your wealth to others. This arrangement is most unadvisable especially if the front door opens to a stove (Fig. 131.) The *chi* from the outside is sucked into the house through the door, hitting the stove, which threatens the stability of

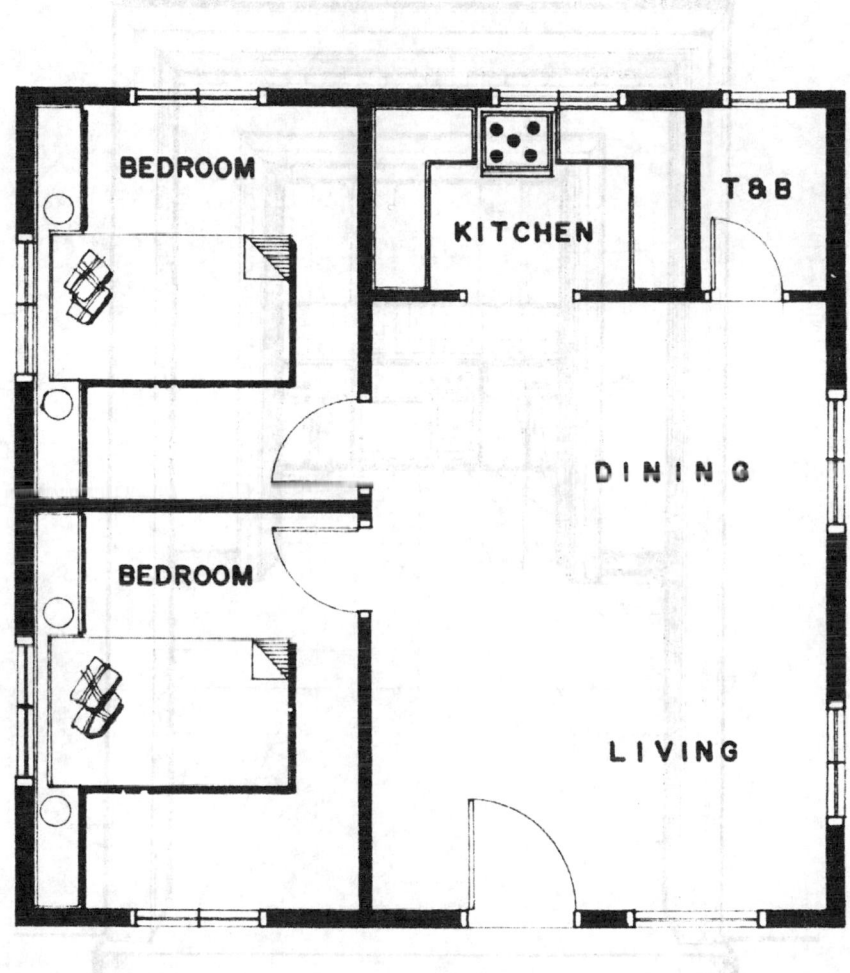

(Fig. 131) The front door opens to a stove.

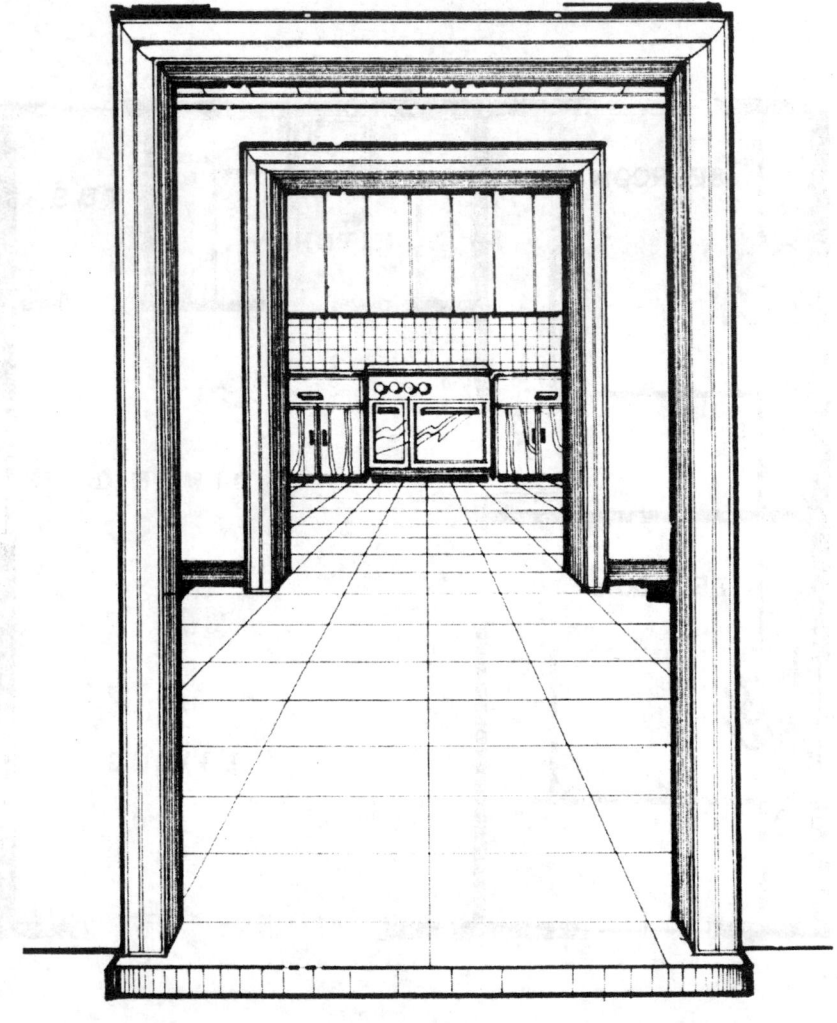

(Fig. 132) Two doors in line with a stove.

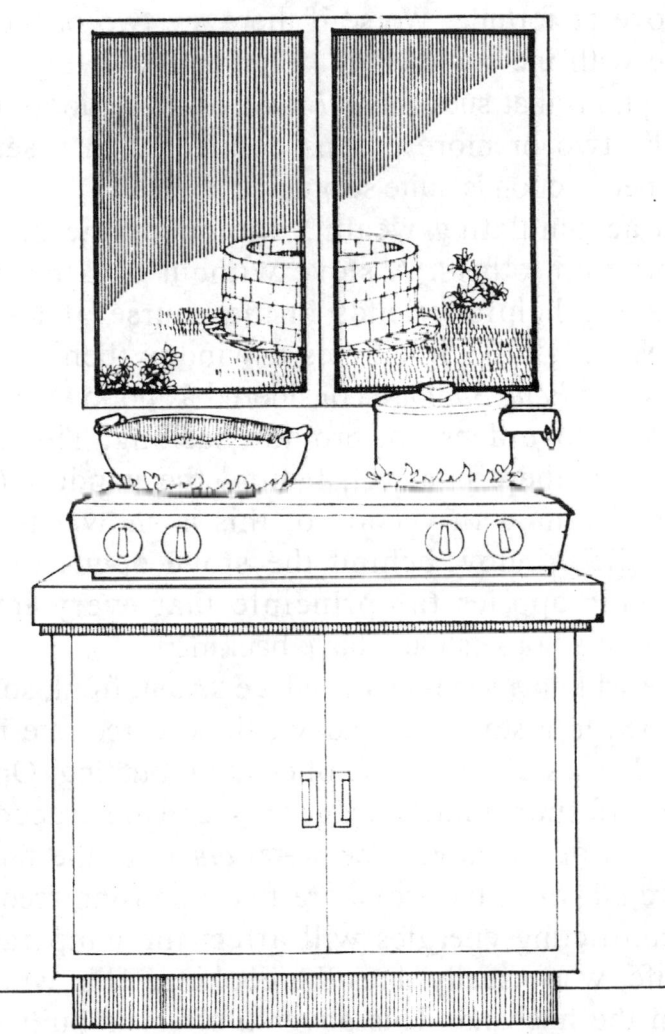

(Fig. 133) A window behind a stove.

the stove or fortune. Worse if there are two or more doors in line with the stove (Fig. 132) because every door acts like a pump that sucks in *chi,* two or more doors in a row are like two or more pumps connected in a series, the combined suction is quite strong.

In accumulating wealth, one needs the backing or support from others. A stove without backing connotes not having helpful friends in the course of transacting business. Fig. 133 illustrates a window behind a stove, windows in *Feng Shui* are considered as hollows; a window behind a stove does not provide backing. This situation is worse if there is a well behind the window (in rural areas). The modern version of this is shown in Fig. 134 where the window behind the stove opens to a water tank. This applies the principle that every important element of a house should have backing.

We will now see how the adage "As in front, so behind" is applied to a stove. Nowadays, the divorce rate is on the rise and cases of broken families are mounting. One of the causes of such family tragedies can be traced to the placement of the stove. The water *chi* from the faucet and the fire *chi* from the stove are two opposing frequencies. The conflicting energies will affect the temperament of the wife, who usually does the cooking. This will take its toll on the husband. This adverse effect is built up daily

(Fig. 134) A water tank behind a stove.

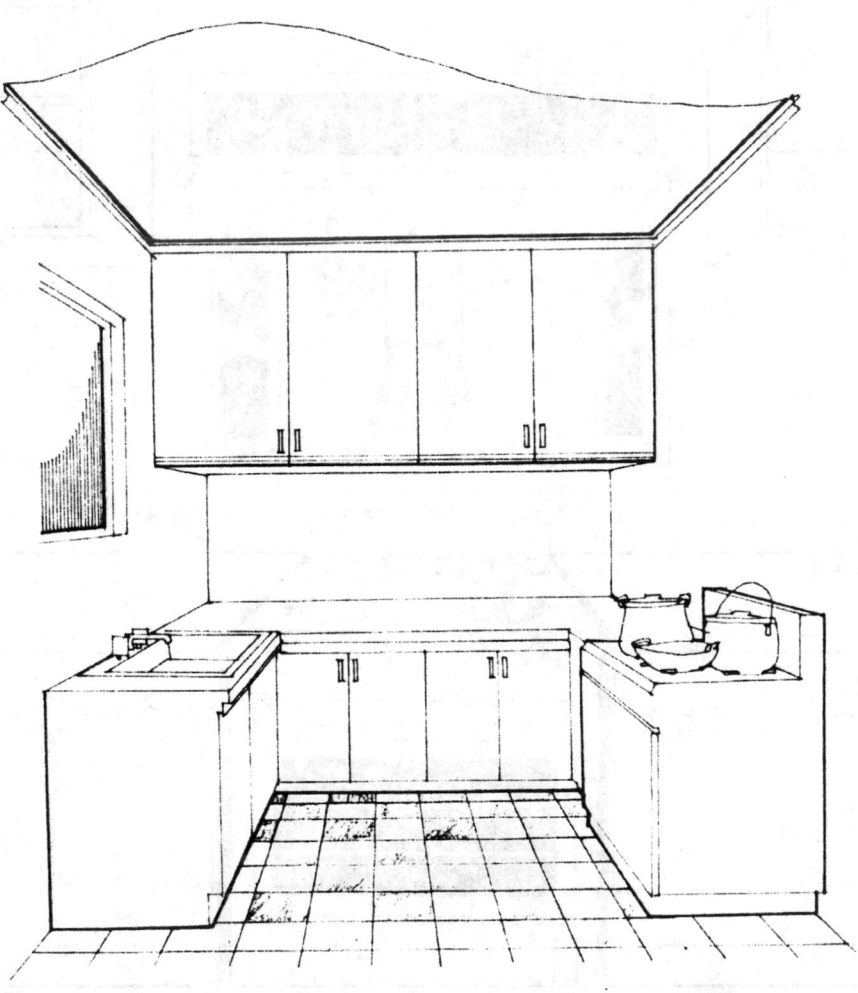

(Fig. 135) A sink opposite a stove.

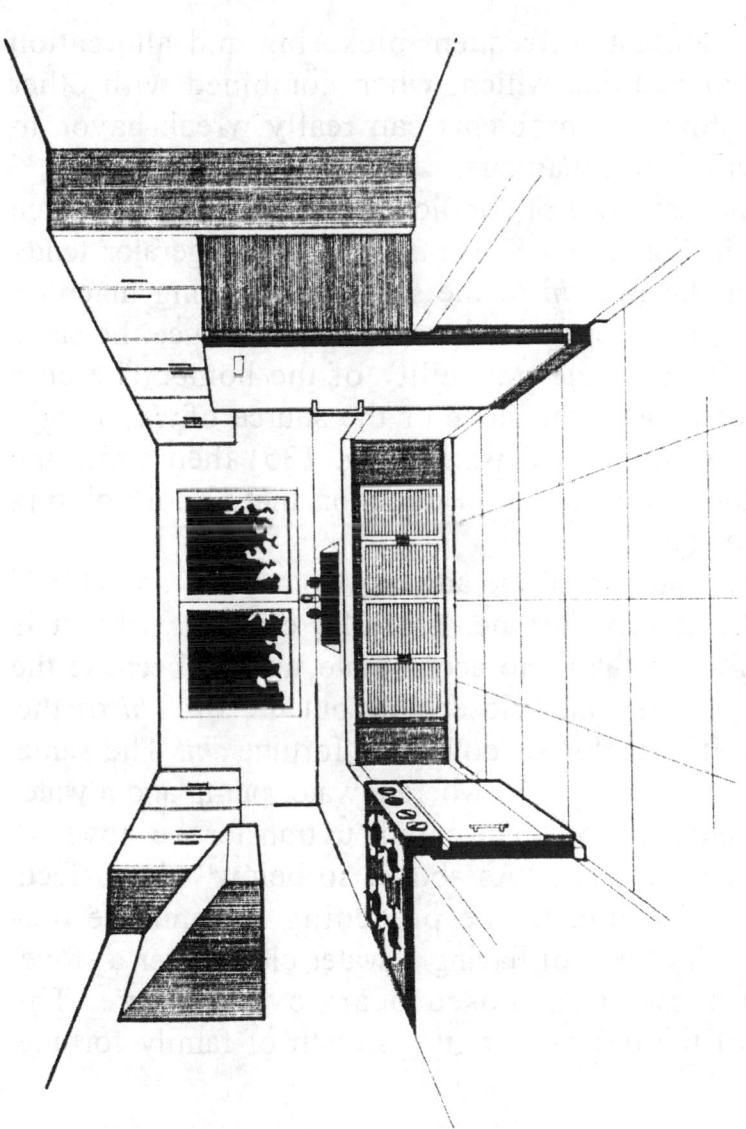

(Fig. 136) A refrigerator opposite a stove.

and can manifest in frequent bickering and altercation over trivial matters, which, when combined with other social or domestic problems can really wreak havoc to an otherwise happy marriage.

Another example of conflicting energies in the kitchen is shown in Fig. 136. The *yin chi* of the refrigerator tends to counter the fire *chi* of the stove. A washing machine (Fig. 137) placed opposite the stove will produce the same adverse effect on the tranquility of the home. The cure is to either transfer the stove or the source of *yin* energy. If neither solution is feasible (Fig. 135) then angle the swivel faucet and fix it to a direction that is not pointing toward the stove.

The second part of the adage "As in front, so behind" affects the family fortune. Fig. 138 explains why it is difficult for the family to accumulate wealth, because the water *chi* of the water closet puts out the fire *chi* of the stove and it also flushes down the fortune *chi*. The same effect is shown in Fig. 139 where a water pump and a water tank are behind a stove. The cure is to transfer the stove.

The second adage "As above, so below" also affects the family fortune. In the preceding chapter we discussed the ill effects of having a water closet over a stove. Fig. 140 shows an exposed beam over a stove. The pressure of the beam deters the growth of family fortune.

(Fig. 137) A washing machine opposite a stove.

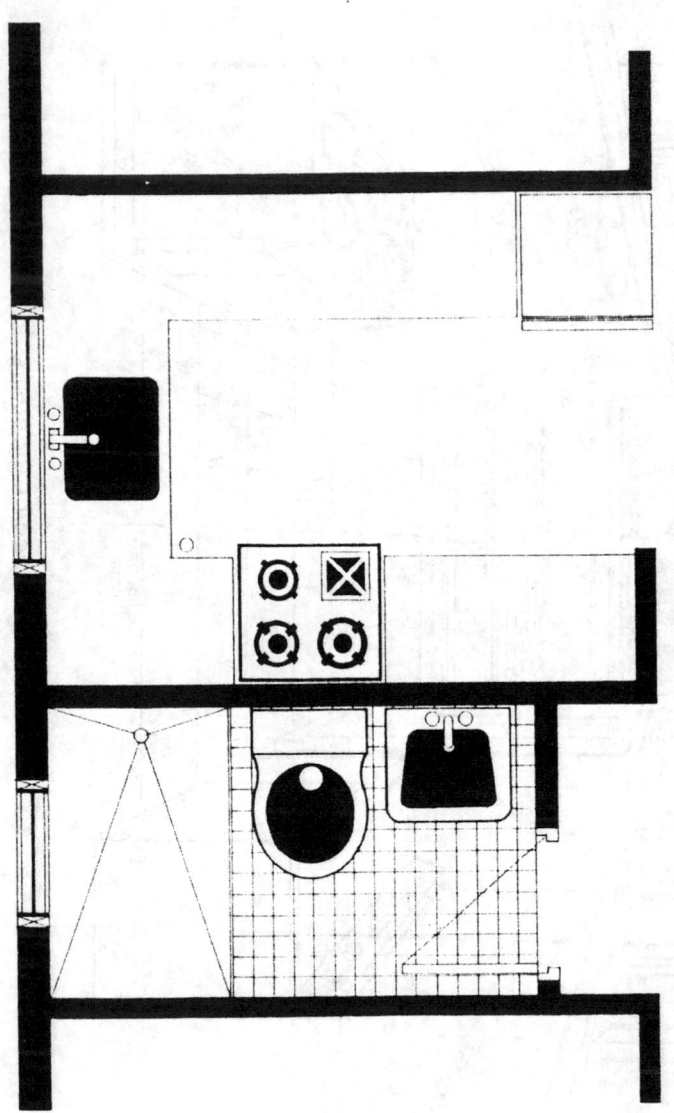

(Fig. 138) A water closet behind a stove.

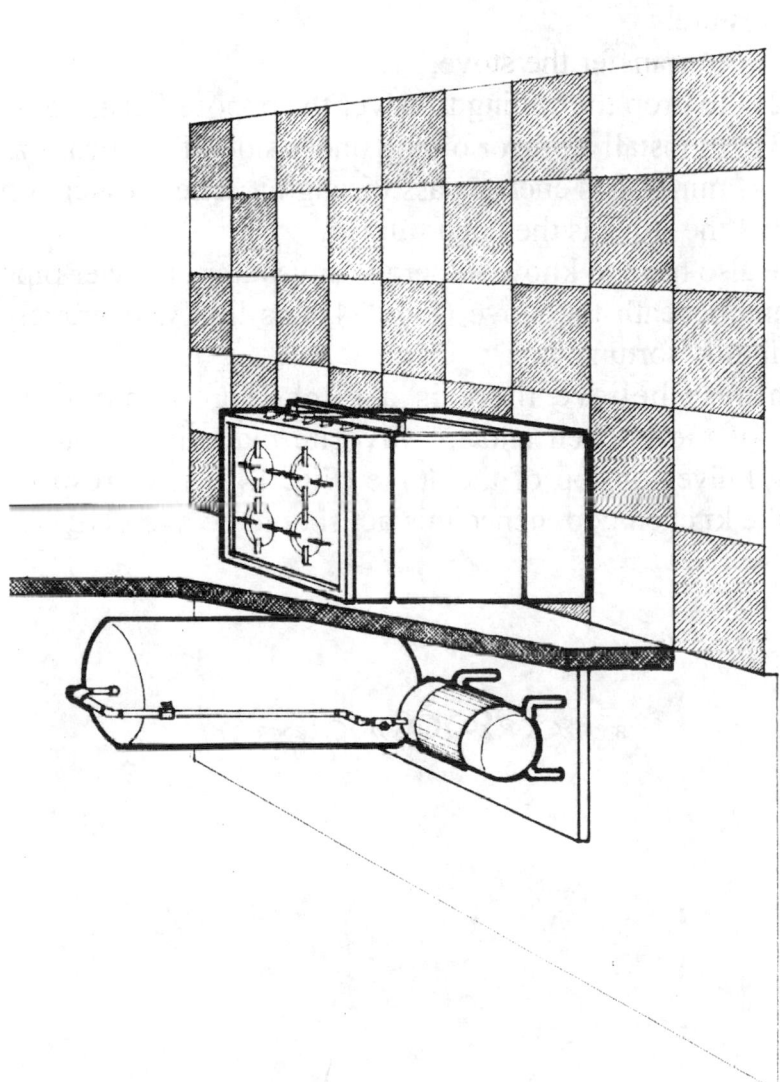

(Fig. 139) A water pump behind a stove.

The cures are:
- (1) to transfer the stove,
- (2) to drop the ceiling to cover the exposed beam or
- (3) to install a mirror on the under side of the beam as mirror lets energy pass through it. The pressure on the stove is then neutralized.

We also have to know if there is any water or sewer pipe that runs beneath the stove (Fig. 141) as this will gravely affect family fortune.

Chinese believe there is a kitchen god that is in charge of the kitchen and his favorite place is the stove. Putting knives on top of the stove (Fig. 142) is disrespectful to the kitchen god, hence this act should be avoided.

ಬೌಆ಄ಠಖಎಠಿಛಿಬೌಆ

(Fig. 140) An exposed beam over a stove.

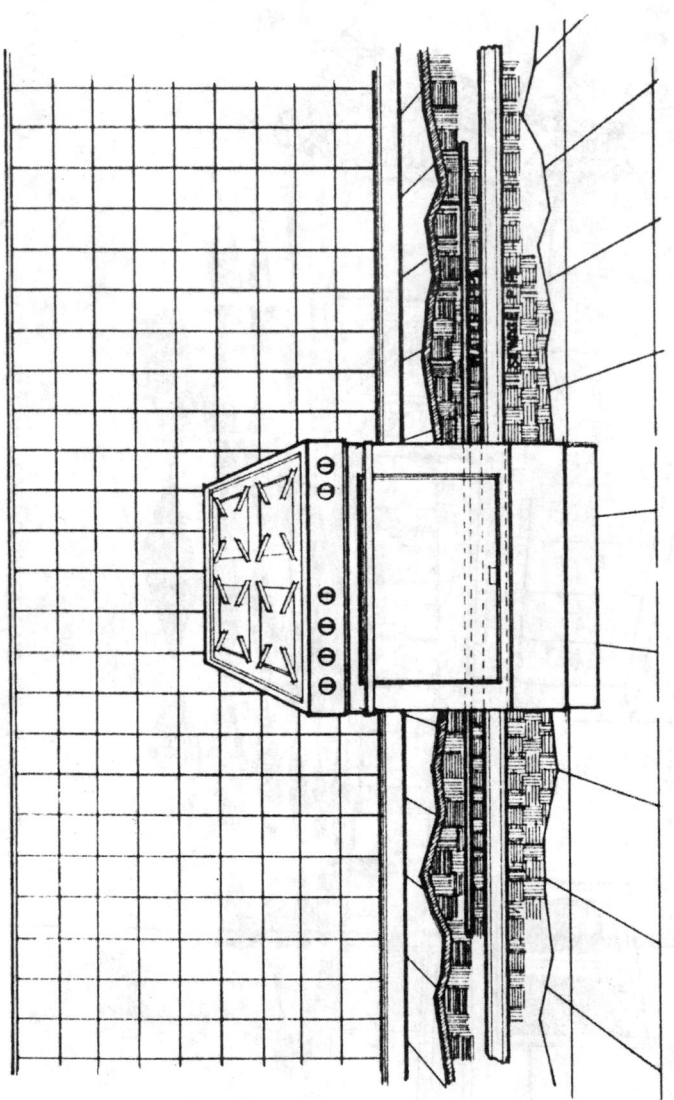

(Fig. 141) Water pipes beneath a stove.

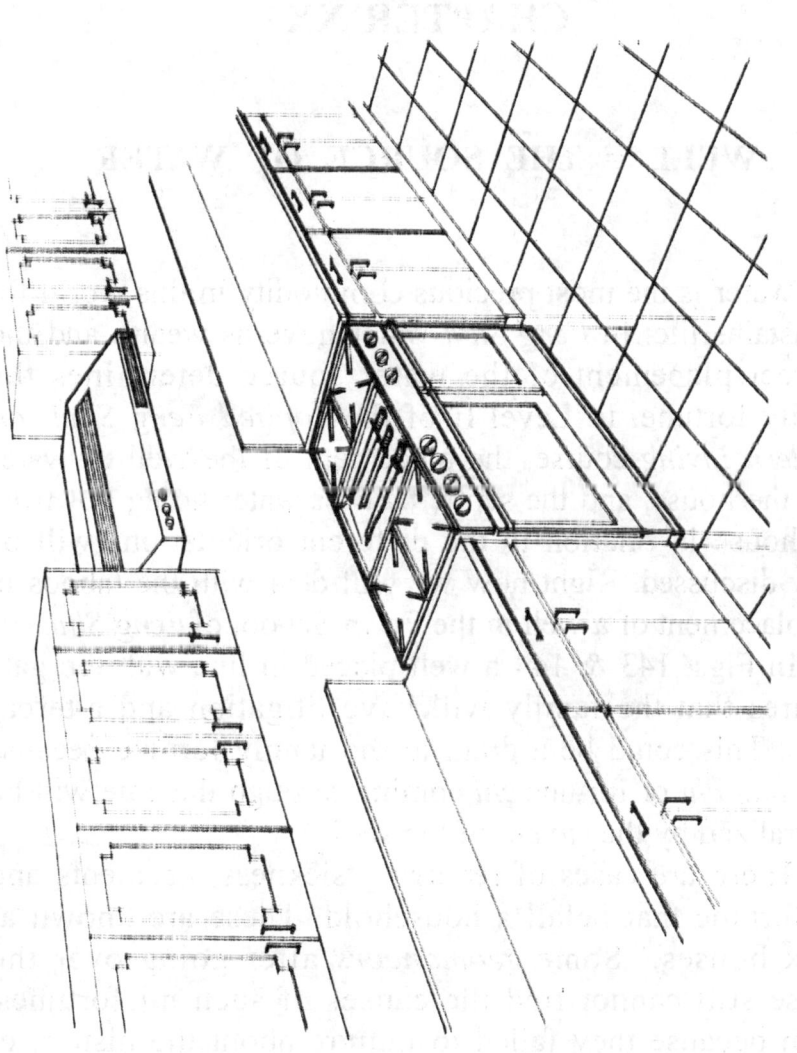

(Fig. 142) Knives on a stove.

CHAPTER XX

WELL = THE SOURCE OF WATER

Water is the most precious commodity in this world for it sustains life. In *Feng Shui* water governs wealth and the correct placement of the water source determines the family fortune. In Level II of the *Applied Feng Shui for Modern Living* course, the placement of the well or water into the house, and the septic tank or water going out from the house in relation to the different orientations will be fully discussed. Right now we will deal with the taboos in the placement of a well in the Form School of *Feng Shui.*

In Figs. 143 & 144 a well placed in line with the gate assures that the family will have litigation and altercations. This could be a drain to the family fortune because the *yang chi* or fortune *chi* coming through the gate will be neutralized by the *yin chi* of the well.

There are cases of recurring sickness, accidents and misfortune that befall a household. These are known as 'jinx houses.' Some *geomancers* after going over the house still cannot find the causes of such misfortunes, often because they failed to inquire about the history of the place such as "could the house been built over an old abandoned well?" (Fig. 145) Worse if the well had been

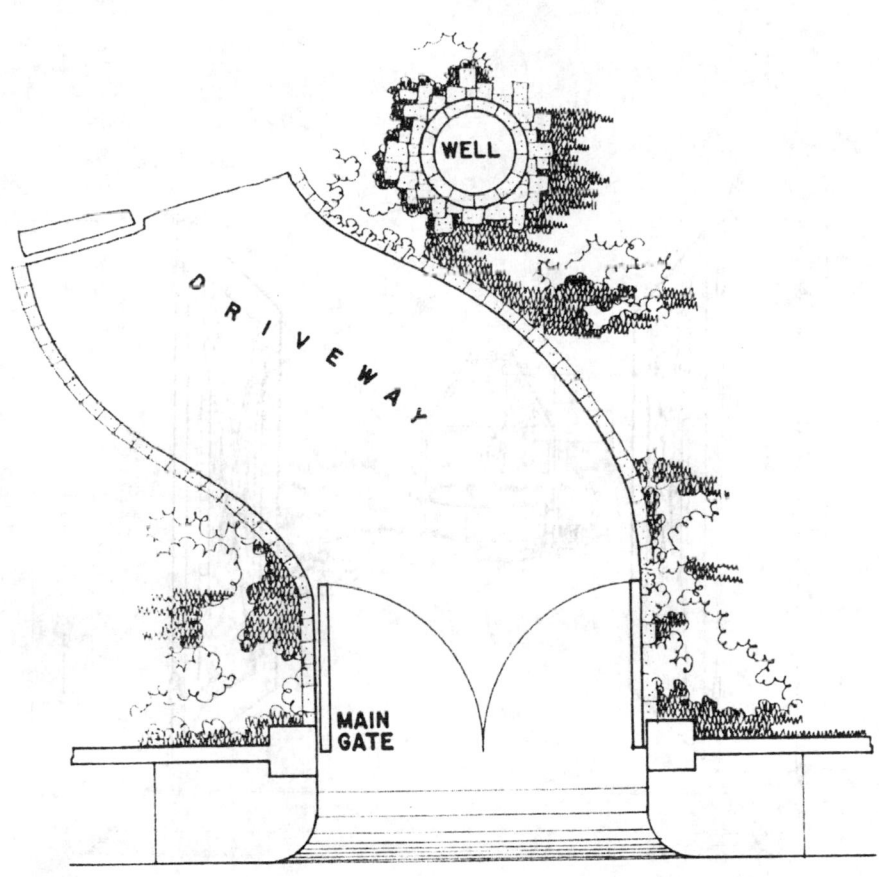

(Fig. 143) The plan of a well in line with the main gate.

(Fig. 144) The perspective of a gate that opens to a well.

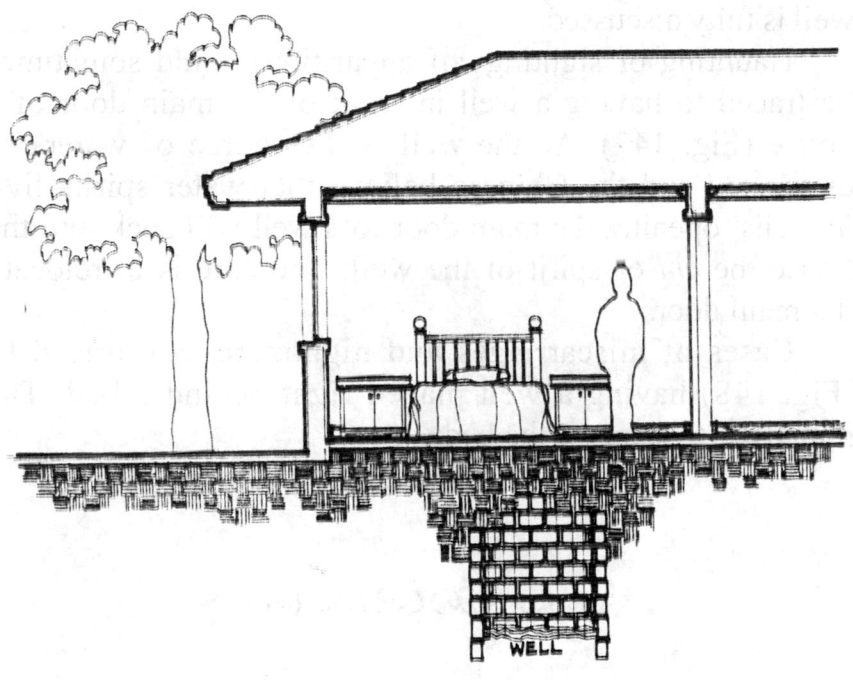

(Fig. 145) A house built over an abandoned well.

summarily filled up with garbage and filling materials from questionable sources (Fig. 146). This being the case the water *chi* will be violated or trapped, and this will cause sickness to recur especially if a bedroom is built on top of the well. In Level I of *Applied Feng Shui for Modern Living,* the correct procedures for filling up a well is fully discussed.

Haunting or sightings of apparitions could sometimes be traced to having a well in front of the main door of a house (Fig. 147). As the well is the source of water *chi* or *yin chi* and the Chinese believe that water spirits live in wells, opening the main door to a well will suck into the house the *chi* or spirit of the well. The cure is to relocate the main door.

Cases of miscarriages and nightmares are traced to (Fig. 148) having a well placed right behind a bed. The remedy is to relocate the bed.

ઝ૦ભ૪૦ભ૪૦ભ૪૦ભ૪૦ભ

(Fig. 146) A well improperly filled.

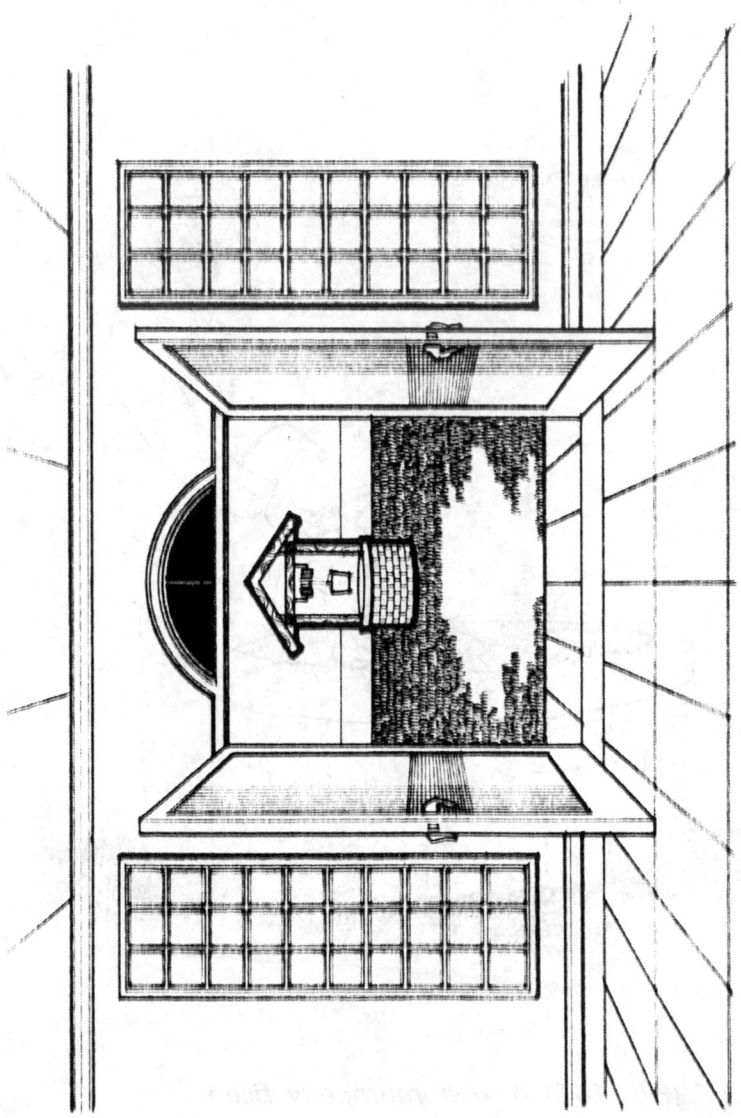

(Fig. 147) A well in front of the main door.

(Fig. 148) A well behind a bed.

CHAPTER XXI

BEDROOMS

As the saying goes: "The best wine is reserved for the last part." We have reached the penultimate topic of the Form School of *Feng Shui* which is the third most important factor of *Yang Feng Shui* — the bedroom.

The bedroom is where we spend one third of our lives. It should be treated as a sanctuary from the daily hassles and pressures of modern living. It is here where we can regain our lost energies. It is also here that the foundation of a happy marriage is built. The loving and harmonious energy built up by the beautiful marital interactions between the husband and wife is created in the bed and this energy permeates the bedroom. This is why it is so important that this energy be preserved.

Fig. 149 illustrates an irregular-shaped bedroom. The pressure exerted by the shape of this room on the bed is jagged and aberrant which disperses whatever loving energy is created. A room with cracked walls (Fig. 150) also can not hold the *chi* of the bedroom and it gives the impression of a cracked relationship.

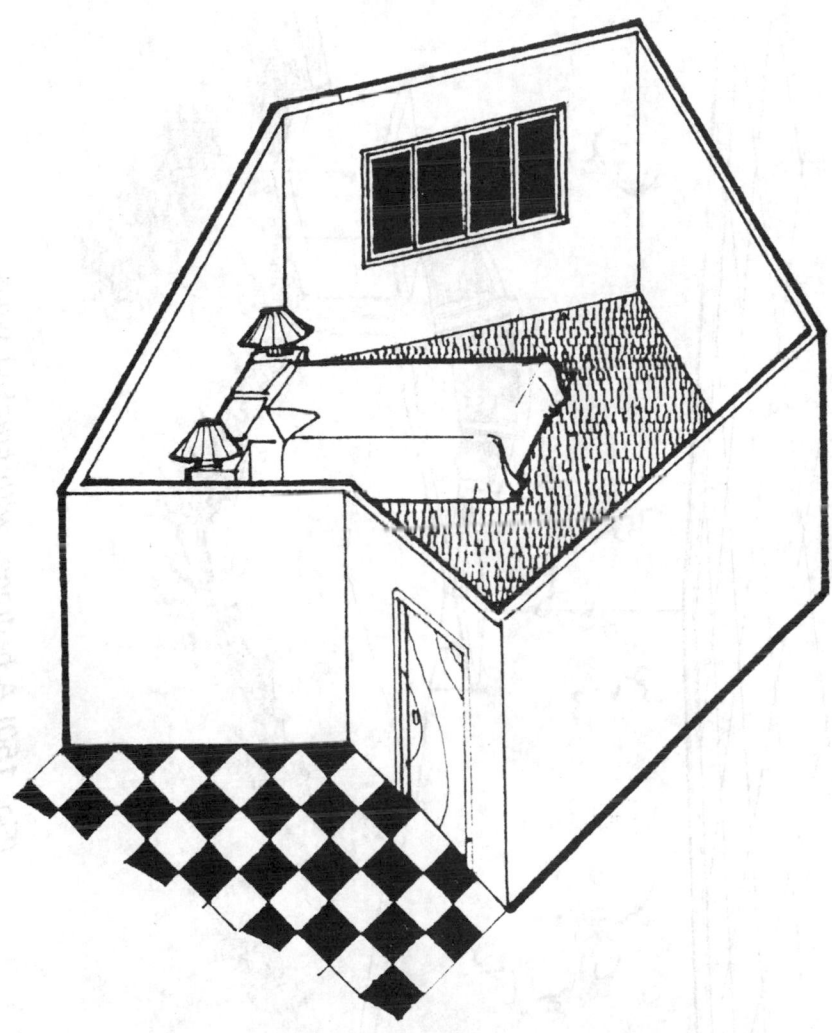

(Fig. 149) An irregular-shaped bedroom.

(Fig. 150) A bedroom with cracked walls.

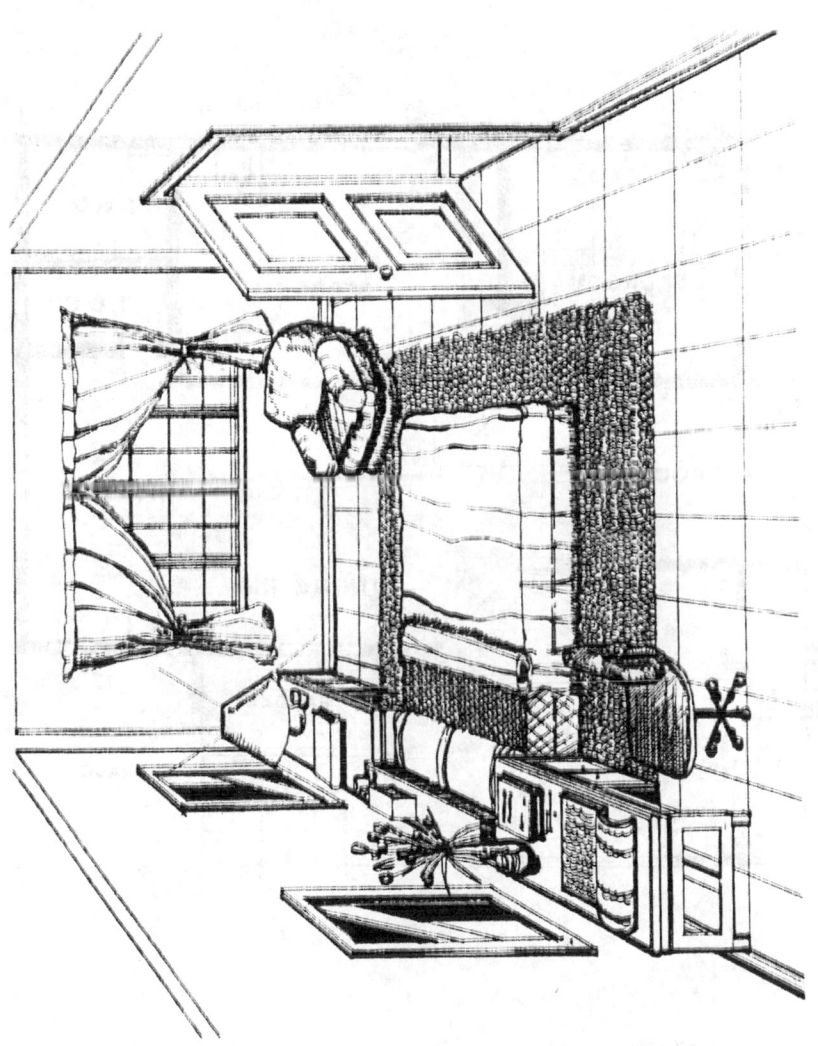

(Fig. 151) Bedroom door that opens to a bed.

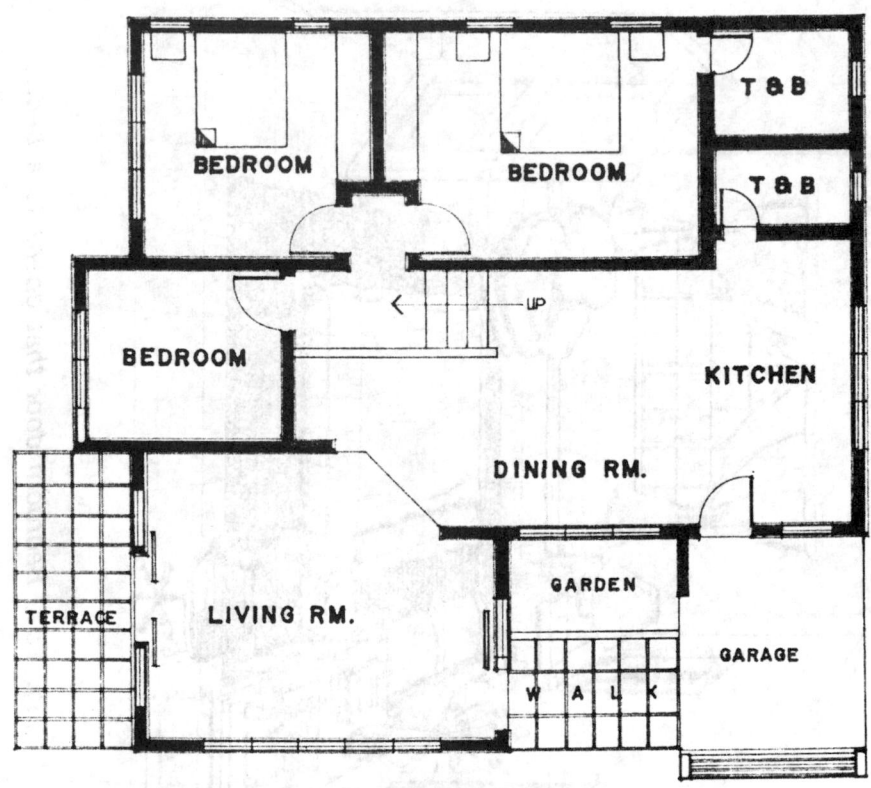

(Fig. 152) A staircase in line with a bedroom door.

A bedroom door that opens to a bed (Fig. 151) disperses the *chi* of the bed especially if a staircase is in line with the bedroom door (Fig. 152). Should the stairs run down towards the bedroom door then the *'chiong'* of the door to the bed is reinforced. The cure is to hang a convex mirror over the door facing the staircase. If the bedroom door opens to a staircase that runs down to a lower level, then the *chi* of the bedroom is dragged down every time the bedroom door is opened. The cure is to hang a concave mirror over the door facing the staircase.

Figs. 153 & 154 illustrate two bedroom doors facing each other. This is one of the causes of family bickering between the occupants of these two rooms as both doors competes for the *chi*. Worse if the door opens to a bed as in Fig. 155. When the door opens to a portion of the bed, it will manifest in arthritis in the part of the sleeper's body that is being hit. If a bathroom door opens to a bed (Fig. 156) and hits the sleeper's body this will often result in a urinary tract infection of the sleeper. The cure is to move the bed out of range of the door or to place a divider in between the bed and the door to act as a shield.

A bedroom door in line with a kitchen door (Fig. 157) will suck into the room unhealthy *chi* from the kitchen and could adversely affect the health of the sleeper. The cure is to install an automatic door closer on the kitchen door.

The bed being an important element in *Feng Shui*

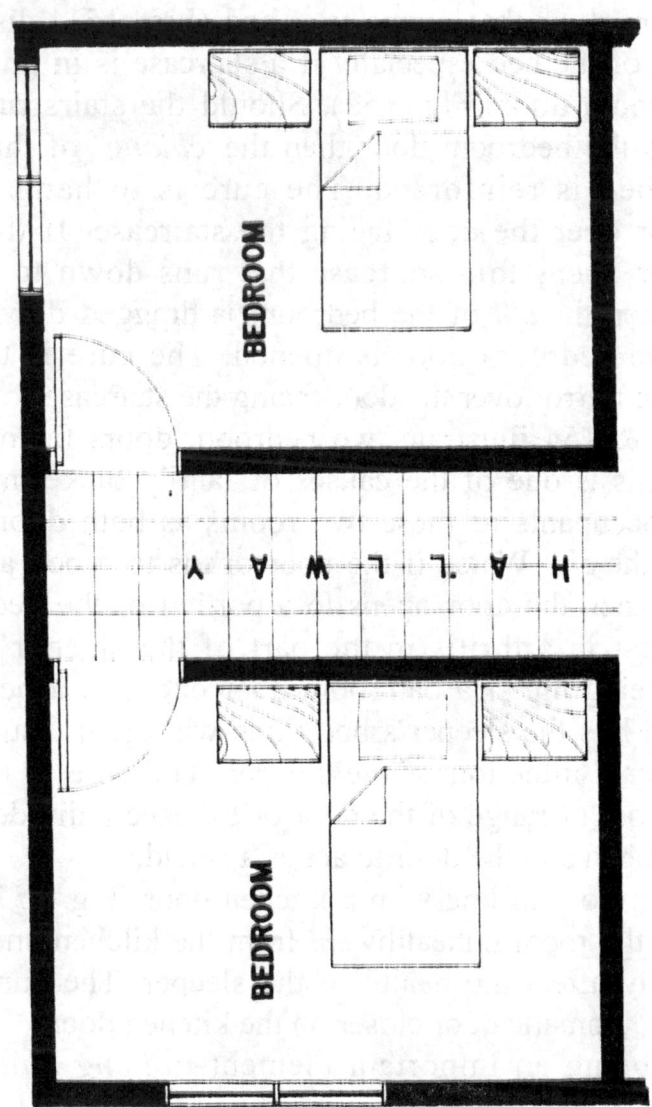

(Fig. 153) The plan of two bedroom doors facing each other.

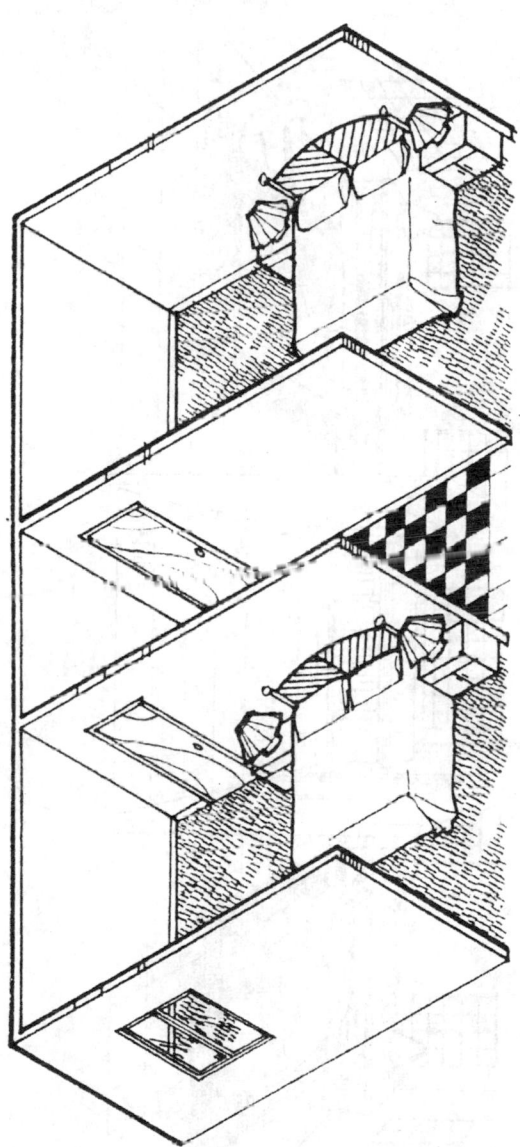

(Fig. 154) The perspective of two bedroom doors in line with each other.

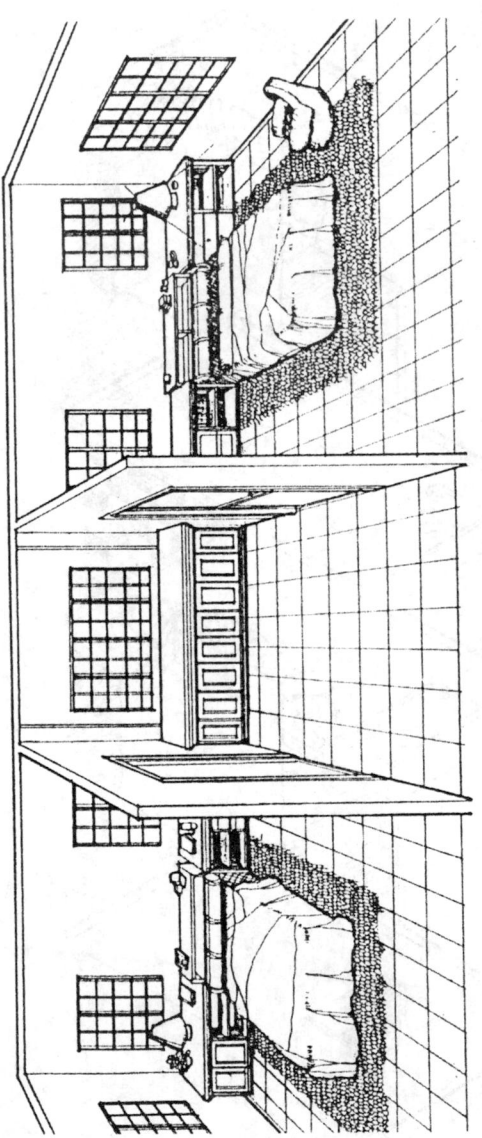

(Fig. 155) Bedroom doors open to the beds.

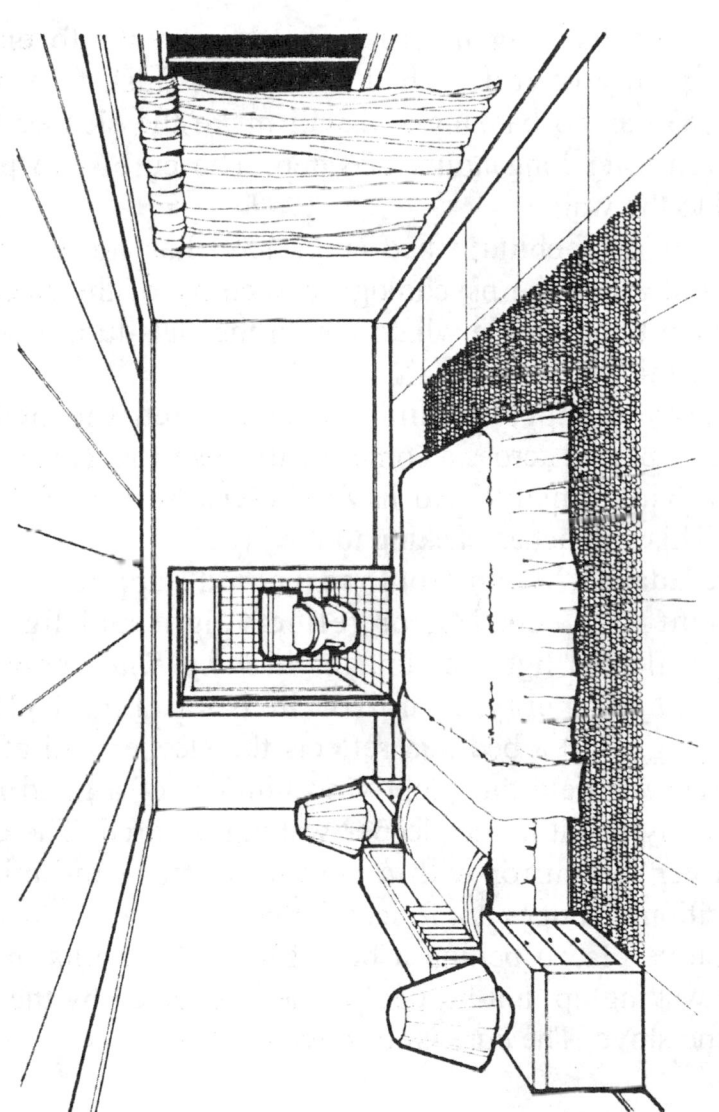

(Fig. 156) A bathroom door in line with a bed.

should have backing in order for the sleeper to enjoy a good quality of rest. A bed that is not flush to a wall (Fig. 158) has no backing and will make the sleeper feel tired even after long hours of sleep. The cure is to push the bed to the wall.

A window behind a bed (Fig. 159) has no backing. This could affect the psychological security of the sleeper. A venetian blind on the window with the slats turn upward can solve this problem.

Energy escapes behind the bed when the bed is diagonally placed across a corner of the bedroom (Figs: 160 & 161). The remedy is to have shelves built to fill the corner. This will act as backing to the bed.

The adage: "As in front, so behind" applies to the placement of a bed. Mirror reflects light and light is energy, reflected lights or images in *Feng Shui* connotes movement of energy. A mirror in front (Fig. 162) or behind (Fig. 163) a bed that reflects the sleeper will affect his/her energy field thus depriving him/her of a good rest. This usually result in the sleeper waking up tired. The cure is to cover the mirror with a curtain or move the mirror to a position that does not reflect the bed.

A stove placed behind a bed (Fig. 164) results in the sleeper waking up 'hot-headed' as he is affected by the fire *chi* of the stove. The cure is to move the bed.

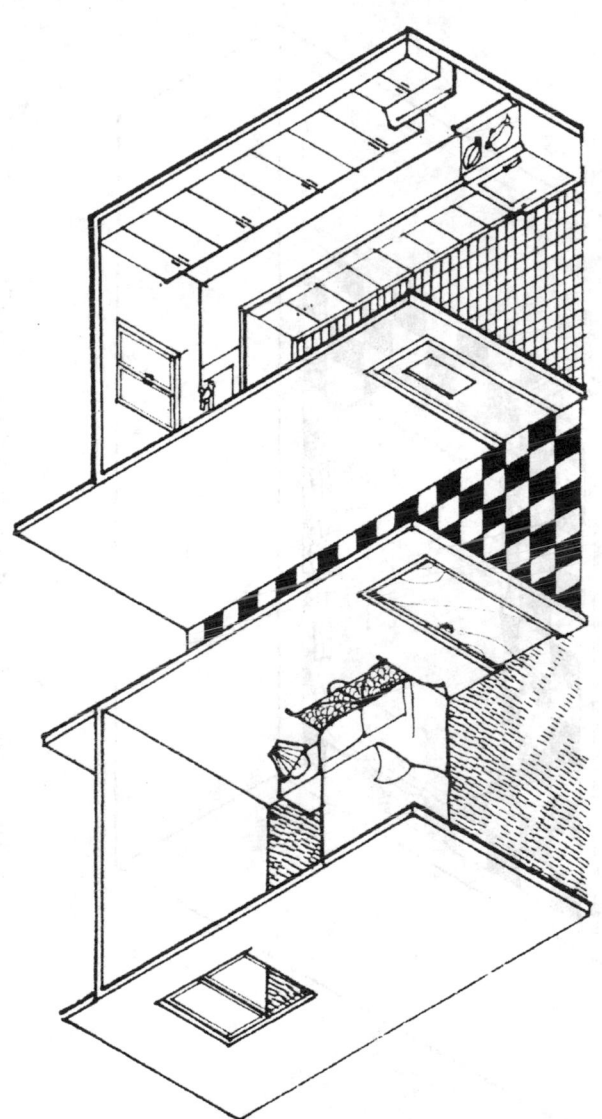

(Fig. 157) A bedroom door in line with the kitchen door.

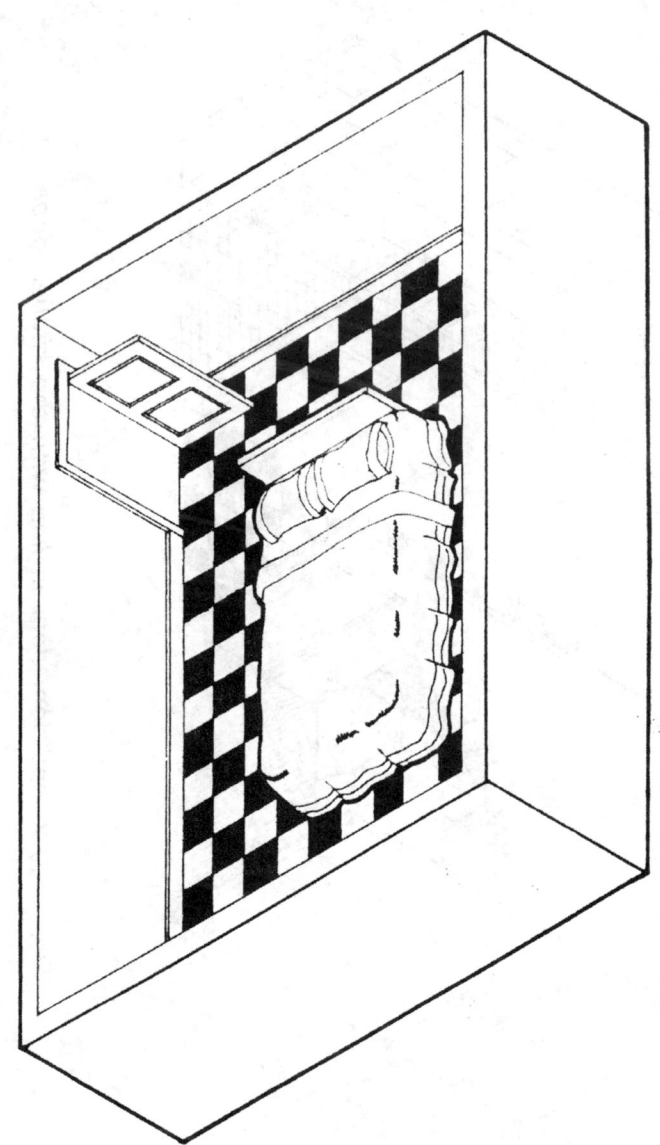

(Fig. 158) A bed not flushed to the wall.

(Fig. 159) A window behind a bed.

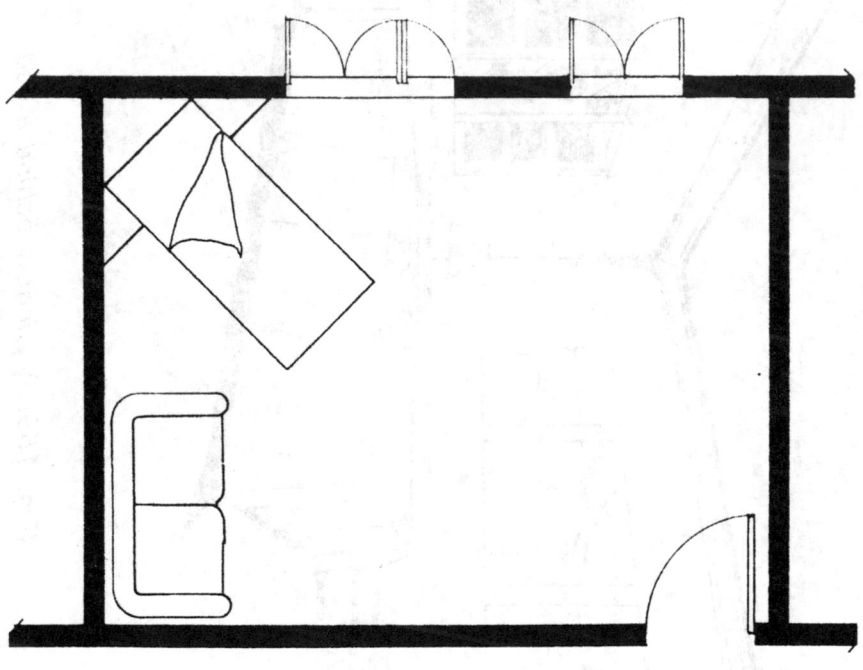

(Fig. 160) A bed placed diagonally across a corner.

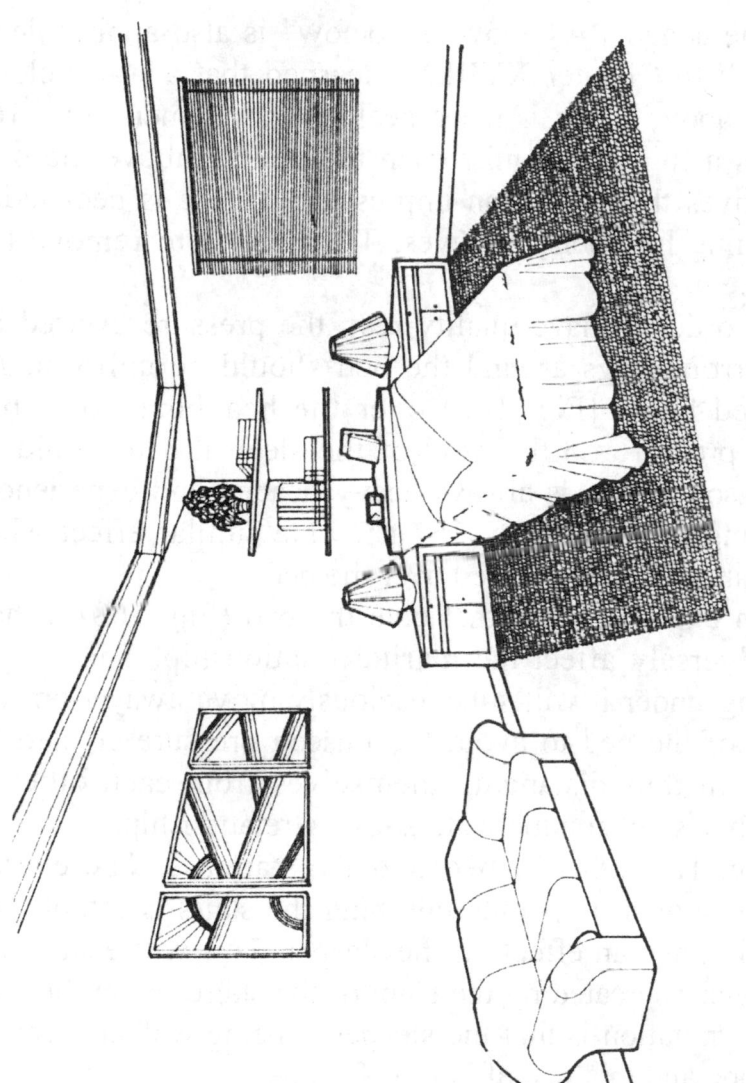

(Fig. 161) The cure for a bed diagonally placed at the corner.

The adage: "As above, so below" is also applicable to the bed. In Chapter XVIII we learned that a water closet placed above a bed is not a healthy arrangement. Fig. 165 depicts a full length mirror on the ceiling above the bed. This gives the sleeper an impression that he is bed-ridden everytime he opens his eyes. The cure is to remove the mirror.

In order to have quality rest, the pressure exerted by the surroundings around the bed should be uniform. An exposed beam (Fig. 166) over the headboard of a bed exerts pressure on the head of the sleeper. This could be the reason he/she is always heavy headed and experiences recurring migraine. Fig. 167 shows a similar effect when a hanging cabinet is placed over the bed.

An exposed beam that cuts the bed (Fig. 168) in half can adversely affect the marital relationship. The couple sleeping under it will subconsciously move away from the center of the bed to avoid the unseen pressure created by the beam thus distancing themselves from each other in bed. This is not conducive to a loving relationship.

Fig. 169 shows a bed under a staircase. The energy pattern created by people climbing the stairs is established and will have an effect on the sleeper. This will exacerbate the pressure created by the slant of the staircase on the bed. The connotation is that the sleeper is being walked over by everyone and this will affect his fortune.

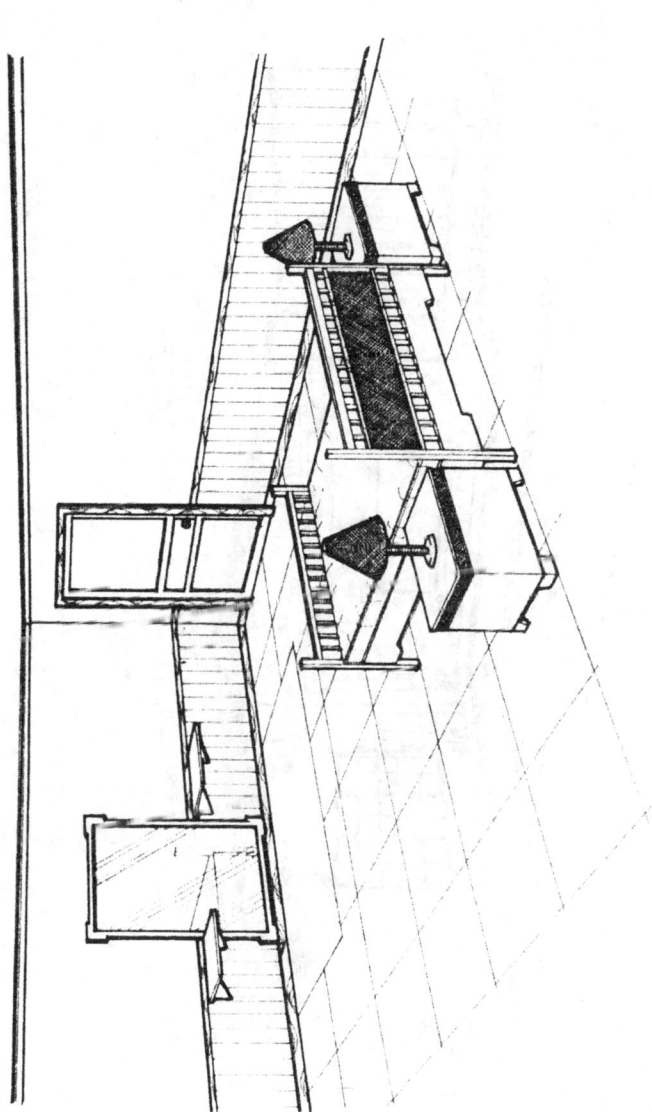

(Fig. 162) A mirror in front of a bed.

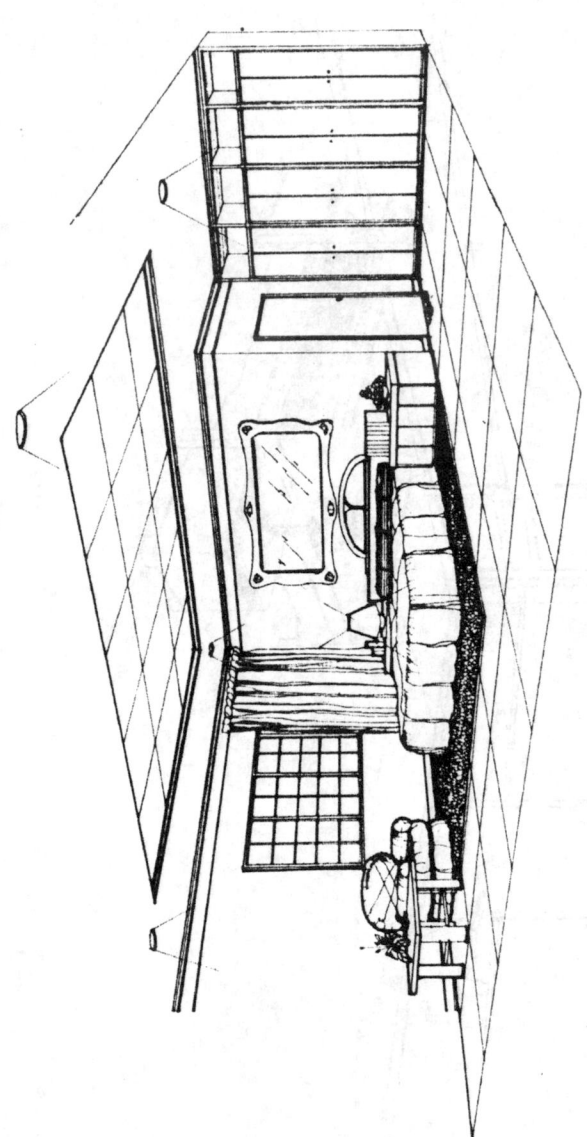

(Fig. 163) A mirror behind a bed.

(Fig. 164) A stove behind a bed.

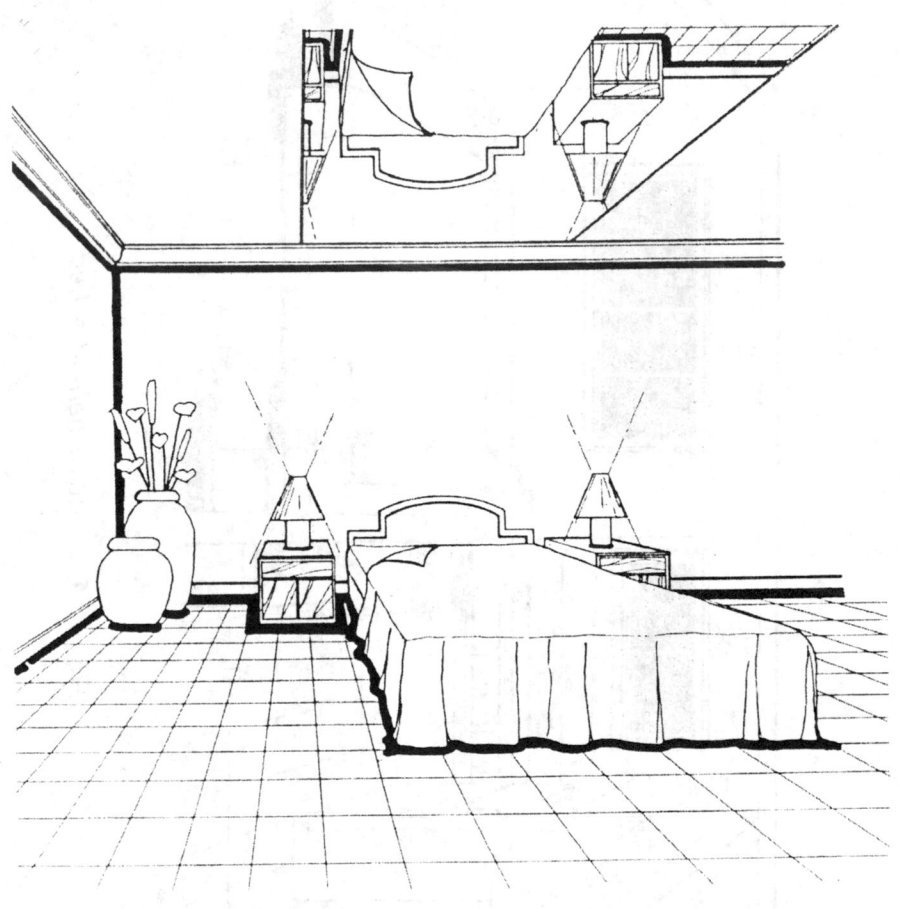

(Fig. 165) A mirror above a bed.

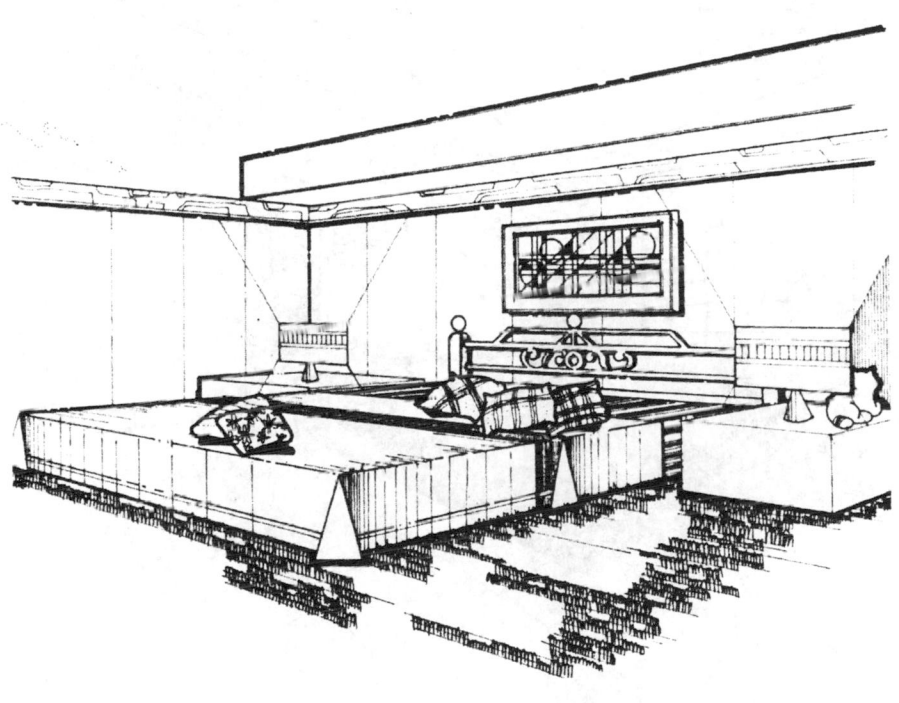

(Fig. 166) An exposed beam over a bed.

(Fig. 167) A hanging cabinet over a bed.

If a person feels he is agitated for no reason at all and flares up easily, then it is not a bad idea to check if his bed is on top of a stove (Fig. 170.) This is synonymous to sleeping on a hot place as the fire *chi* from the stove accumulates beneath the bed. The cure for the above cases is to move the bed to a position that is clear of the aforementioned violations.

The bed should have no moving lines of energy beneath it as this will affect its stability and consequently the quality of sleep. It is very obvious why the sleeper in Fig. 171 does not feel rested even after a long sleep. Water beds are not approved in *Feng Shui*, aside from having continuous motion and not being stable, the water *chi* which is *yin* will hamper the circulation of the *yang chi* within one's body that is needed to recharge and restore oneself.

A marriage that shows signs of instability could also be traced to having a bed placed on the cantilevered portion of the house (Fig. 172). As there is no support or solid foundation beneath the bed, the relationship will be shaky.

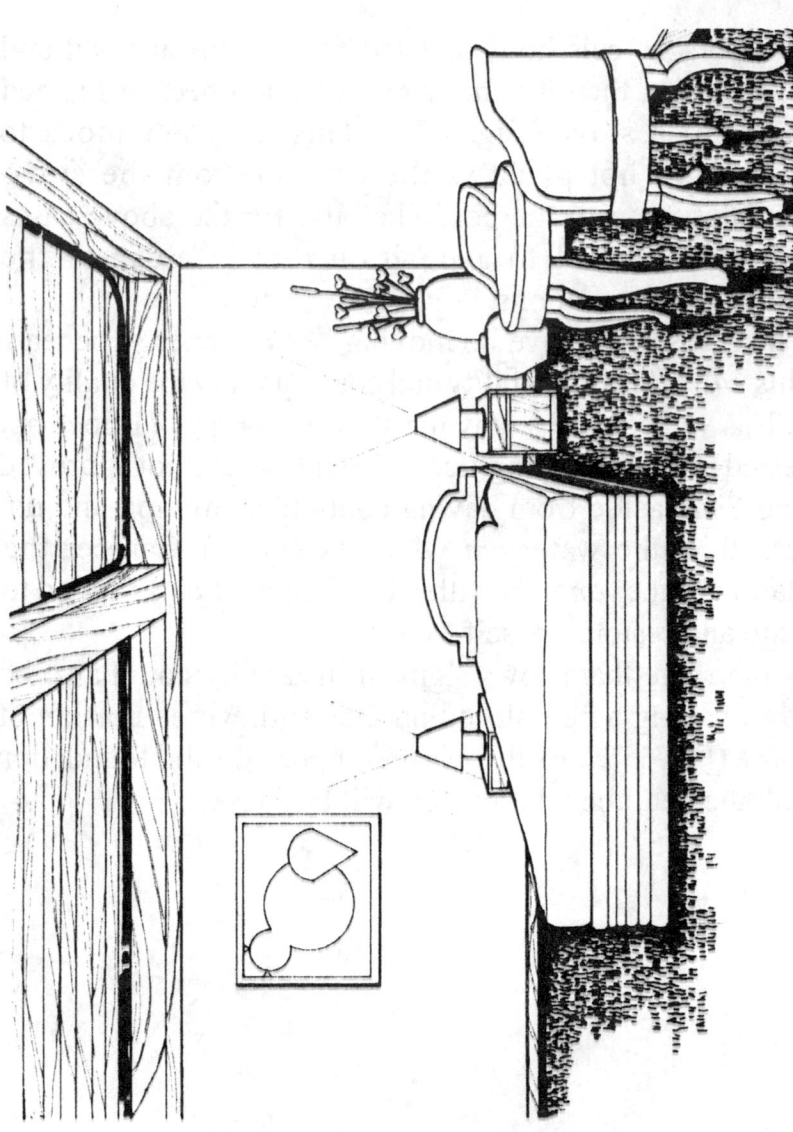

(Fig. 168) An exposed beam deviding a bed.

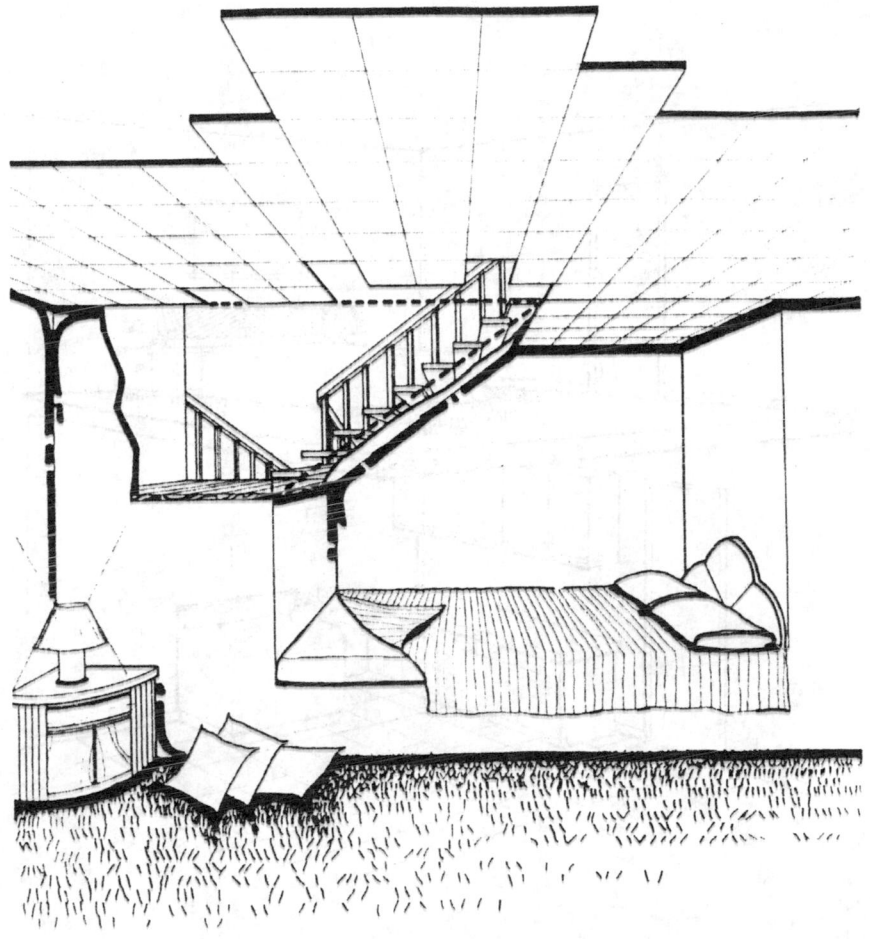

(Fig. 169) A bed beneath a stairwell.

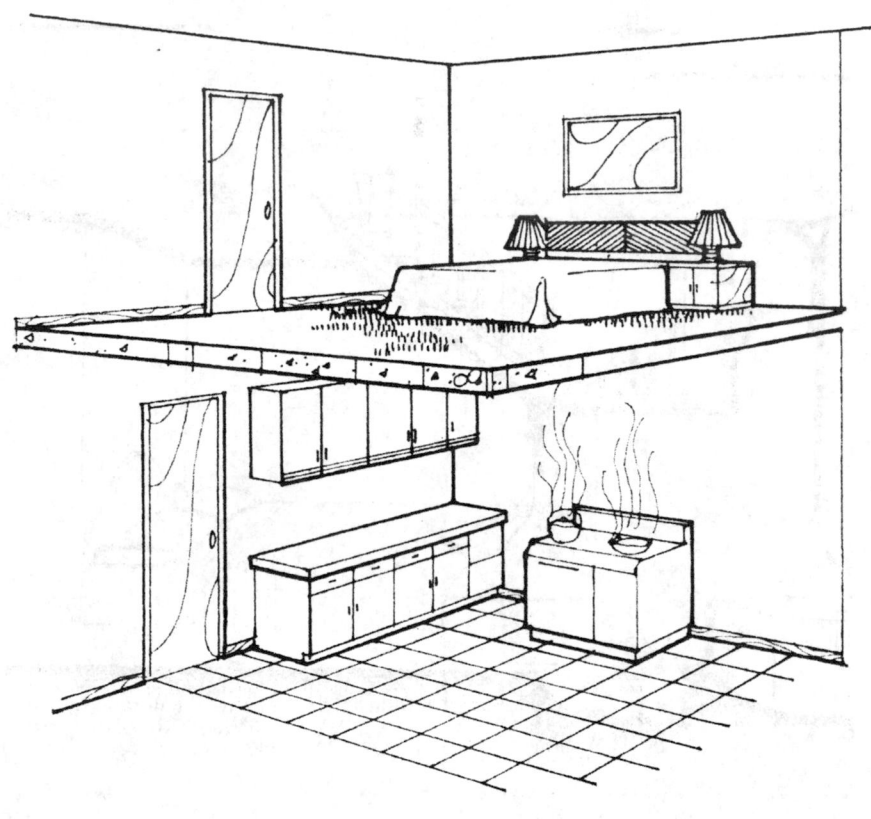

(Fig. 170) A bed above a stove.

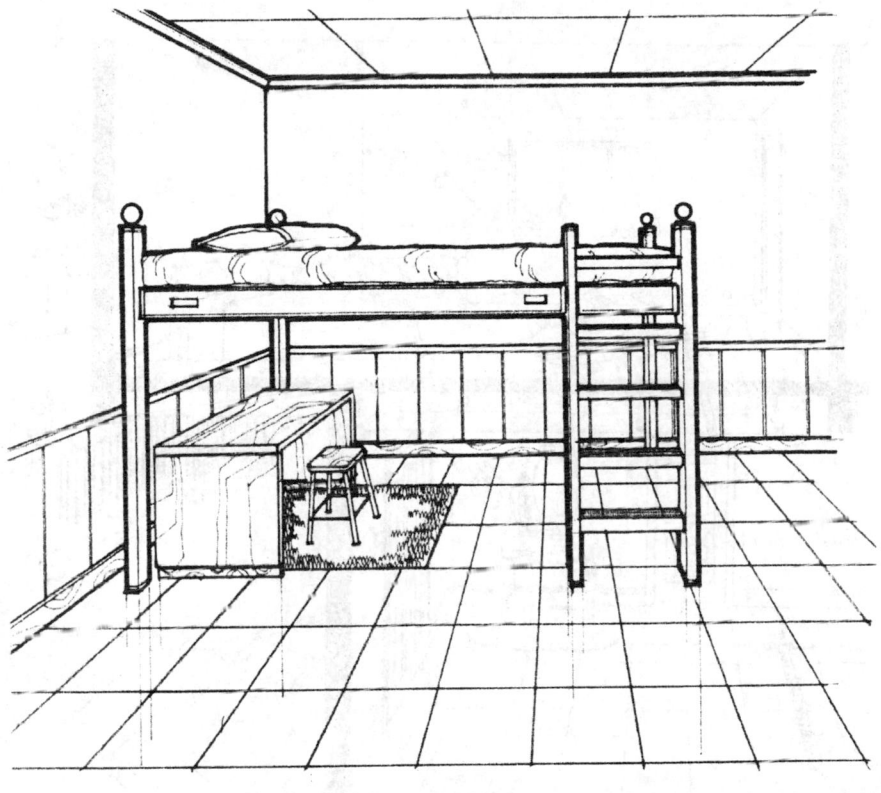

(Fig. 171) Moving lines under a bed.

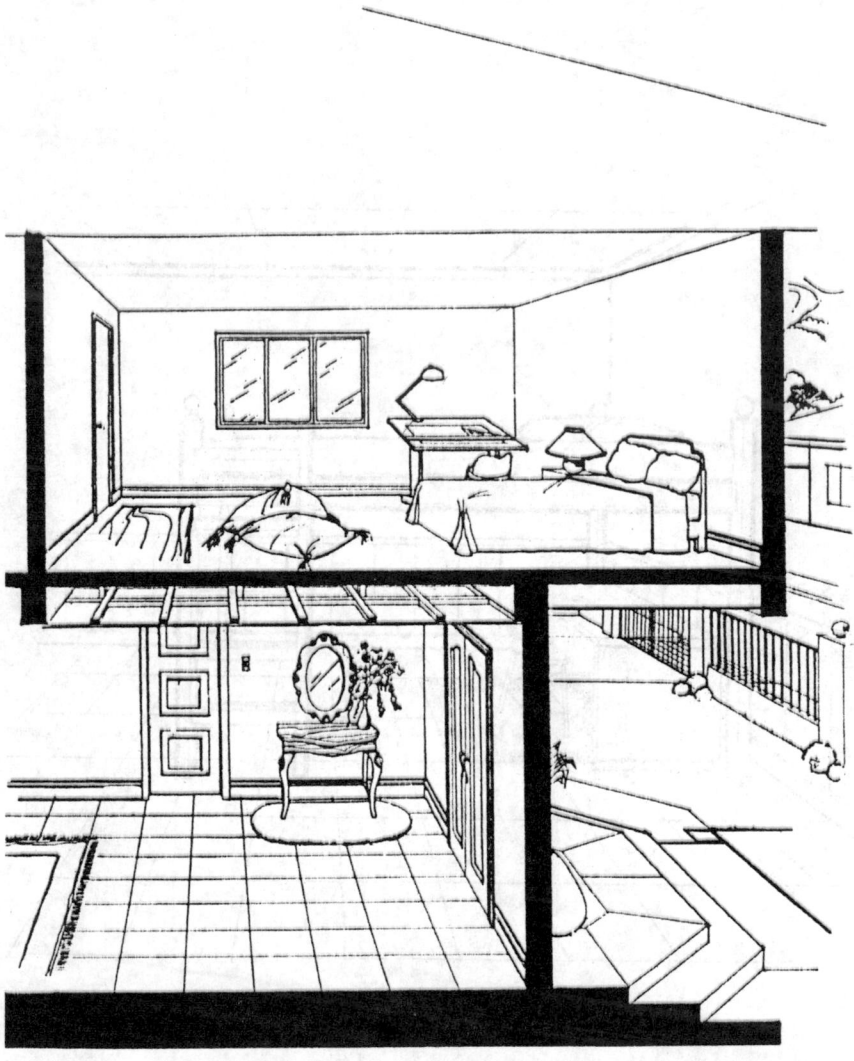

(Fig. 172) A bed on the cantilever portion of the house.

The pillar on the ground floor supports (Fig. 173) the bed and this is not considered to be cantilevered.

A garage beneath a bedroom (Fig. 174) is not recommended for the reason that the daily revving up of the automobile will produce unhealthy gases that will be trapped inside the bedroom.

Elder's room is recommended to be placed on the ground floor to avoid the aged from climbing (Fig. 175) the stairs several times a day which is not good for their heart and blood pressure.

A bedroom in the basement (Fig. 176) is unhealthy because it is *yin*. The *chi* above the ground is *yang*, it is considered to be *yin* when it is below the ground. That is why the *Feng Shui* for the dead is called *yin feng shui* and the *Feng Shui* for the living is known as *yang feng shui*. Aside from being damp in the basement it is not savory to be reminded that one is sleeping six feet under.

In Level II of the *Applied Feng Shui for Modern Living* course the correct placement of individual bedroom and bed positions that can solve problems of wanting to get married, to have a child or to recuperate from illness will be taught.

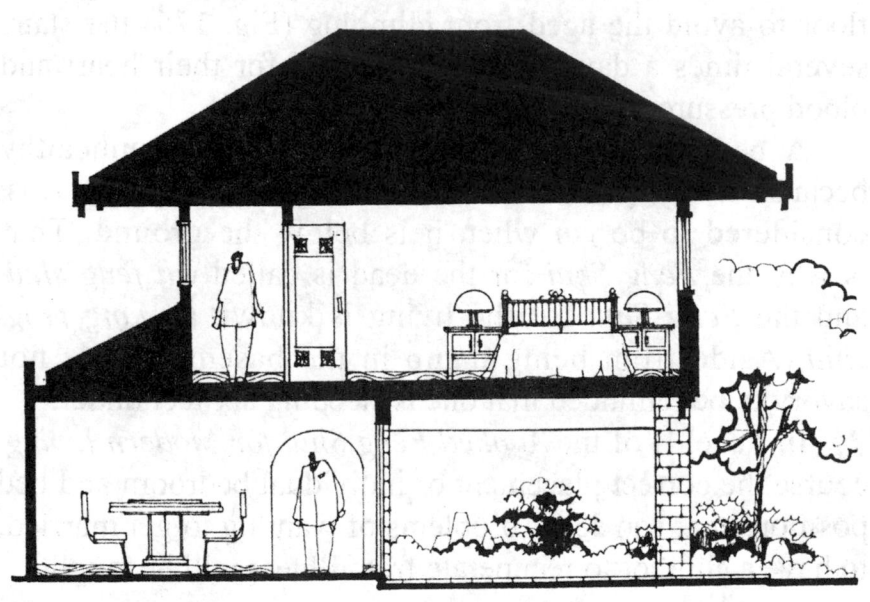

(Fig. 173) A bedroom supported by pillars.

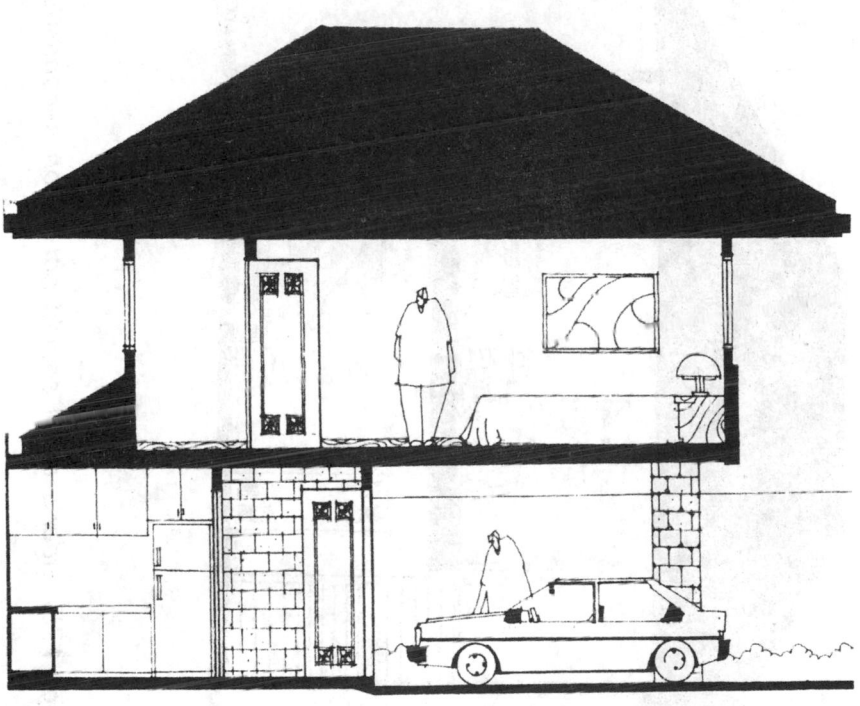

(Fig. 174) A garage beneath a bedroom.

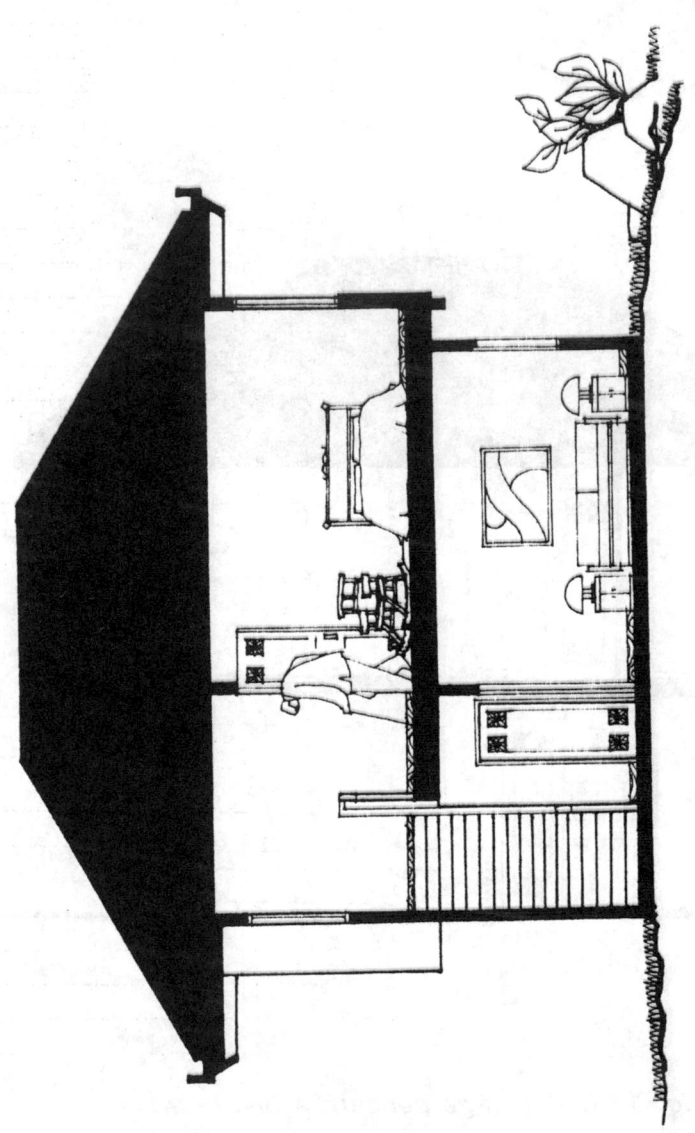

(Fig. 175) Elder's room should not be on second floor.

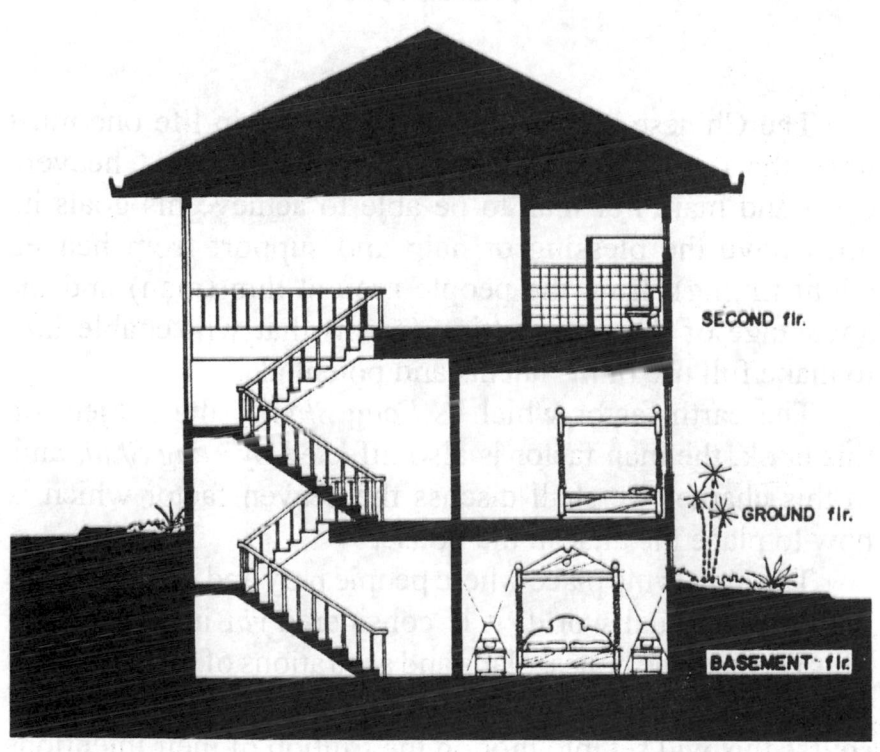

(Fig. 176) A bedroom in the basement.

CHAPTER XXII

ALTARS

The Chinese believe that to be fruitful in life one must have the right combination of three factors, i.e., heaven, earth and man. For man to be able to achieve his goals he must have the blessing or help and support from heaven (right timing), from the people around him (man) and the advantage of the right setting (earth) that will enable him to make full use of his talents and potential.

The earth factor which is *Feng Shui* is the subject of this book, the man factor is also affected by *Feng Shui,* and in this chapter we shall discuss the heaven factor which is how to place the altar in the house.

The altar is the place where people pray and communicate with the spiritual world, it is considered *yin* in *Feng Shui.* This is where the hopes, plans and aspirations of the occupants are repeated daily in the *yin* sphere of existence and in due course this will set into motion the fruition of their intentions in the *yang* or actual world of existence. This is comparable to the modern trend of affirmations and positive thinking to achieve one's goal.

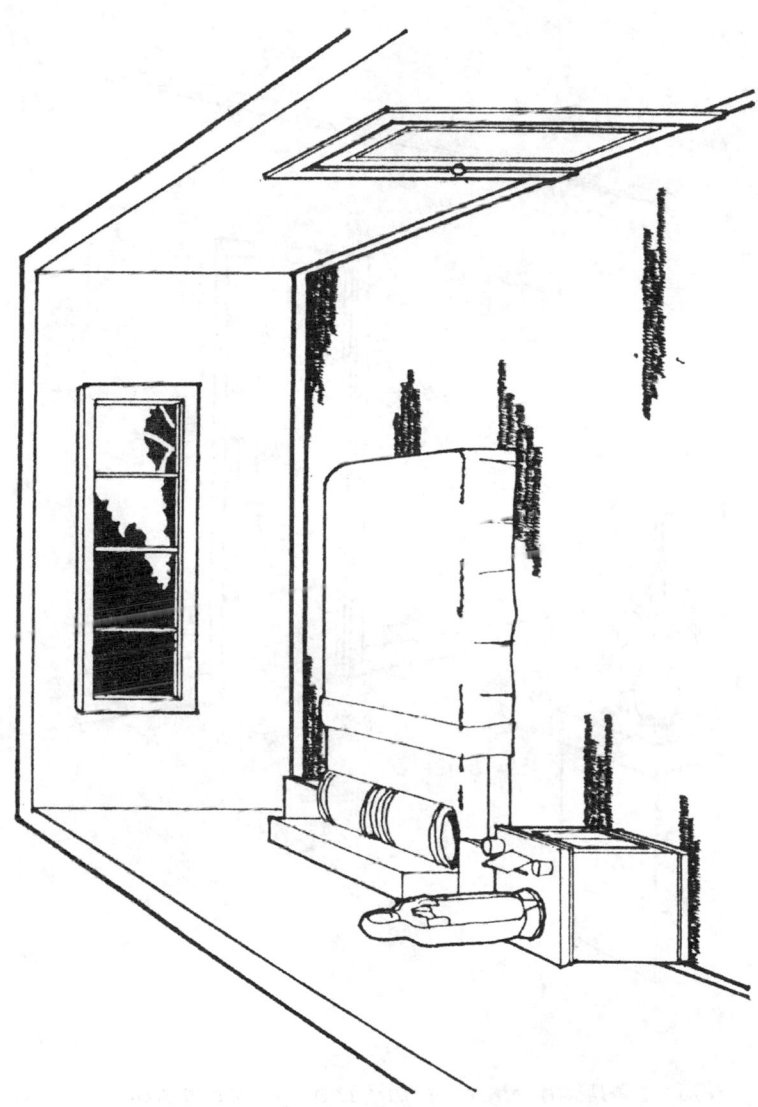

(Fig. 177) An altar inside the bedroom.

(Fig. 178) An altar facing the bedroom door.

(Fig. 179) An altar at the landing of a staircase.

As the altar is *yin,* it should be rightly placed in the house to assure that there will be no adverse effect on the health, fortune and efficiency of the occupants. This will be fully expounded in Level II and III of the *Applied Feng Shui for Modern Living* course.

Often the altar is placed inside the master's bedroom as in Fig. 177. This is not favorable for a place of rest because when one sleeps there is no activity or *yang chi* generated. The atmosphere already being *yin* is exacerbated by having the altar inside the bedroom. This is not to mention acts committed inside the bedroom that are disrespectful to the gods.

An altar placed outside the bedroom in line with the bedroom door (Fig. 178) is not advisable. *Yin chi* is sucked into the bedroom everytime the door is opened, this is not conducive to good health. The door being in line with the altar generates a *'chiong'* to the altar that disperses the energy built up by the prayers said there. Another case of having a *'chiong'* to the altar is (Fig. 179) placing it on the landing of a staircase. The cure for the above cases is to transfer the altar.

The altar being an important element in *Feng Shui* should have solid backing, hence, it is imperative to have a wall behind it. We should also consider the adage: "As in front, so behind." Care should be taken that no water closet be placed directly behind the altar (Fig. 180) as the flushing action undermines the stability of the altar.

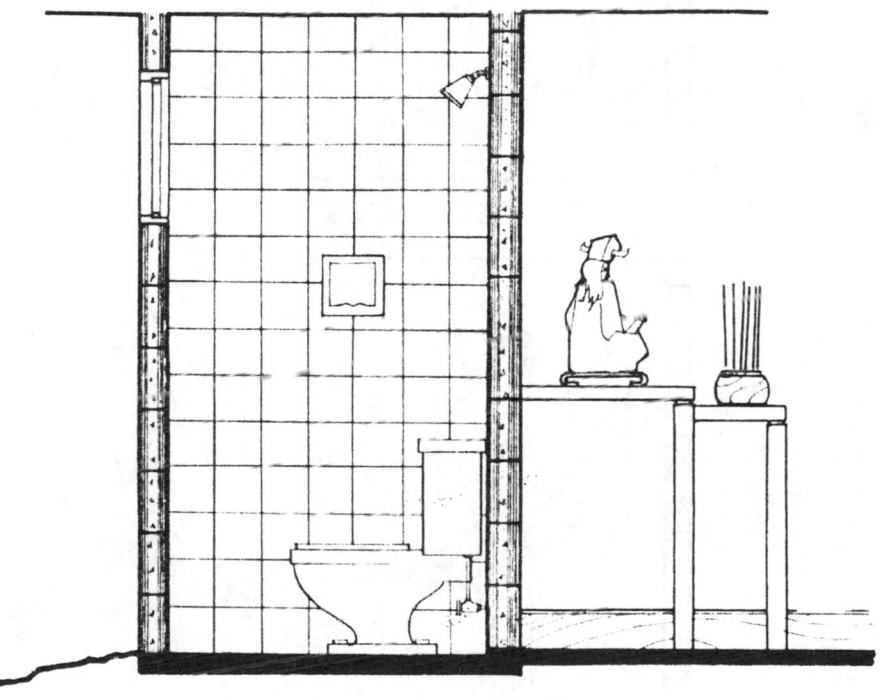

(Fig. 180) A water closet behind an altar.

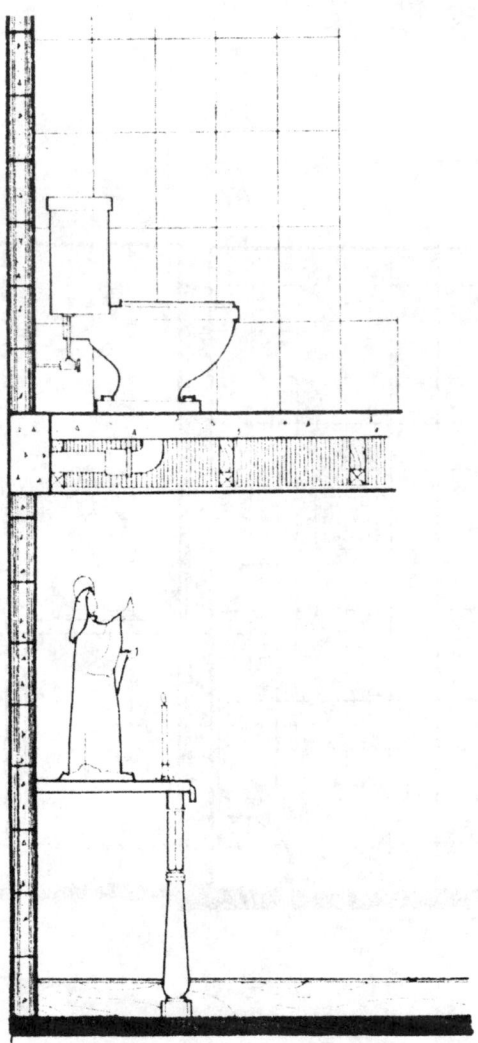

(Fig. 181) A water closet above an altar.

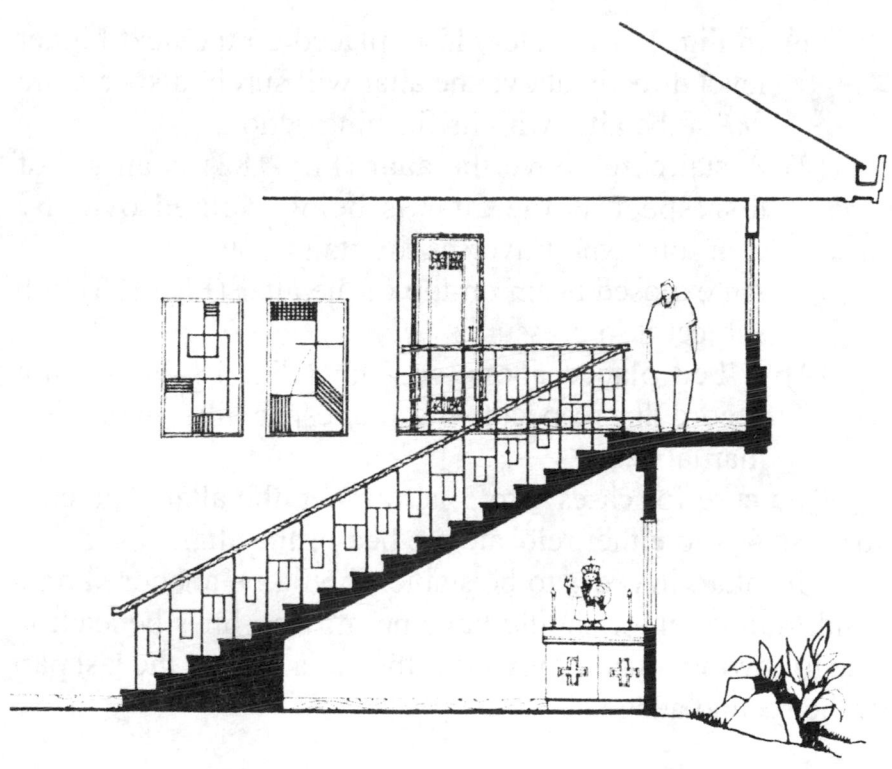

(Fig. 182) An altar under a staircase.

The second adage: "As above, so below" is also applicable to the placement of the altar.

The following illustrations depict violations on the first part of the adage:

(1) In Fig. 181 a water closet placed on the next higher level directly above the altar will surely disperse the *chi* of the altar with its flushing action.
(2) A staircase above the altar (Fig. 182) is an act of disrespect as the altar is being walked over by everyone who traverses the stairs.
(3) An exposed beam on top of the altar (Fig. 183) will subject it to pressure.
(4) A bed placed above an altar (Fig. 184) does not accord due respect to the altar especially when it is a marital bed.

The cure for cases 1 to 3 is to move the altar. The cure for case 4 is to either relocate the bed or the altar.

The altar, in order to be stable, should be anchored on a solid foundation or should have no moving lines beneath it. The following illustrations show the violations of the last part of the second adage:

(1) An altar on top of an aquarium (Fig. 185) does not provide stability for the altar. The cure is to transfer the aquarium.

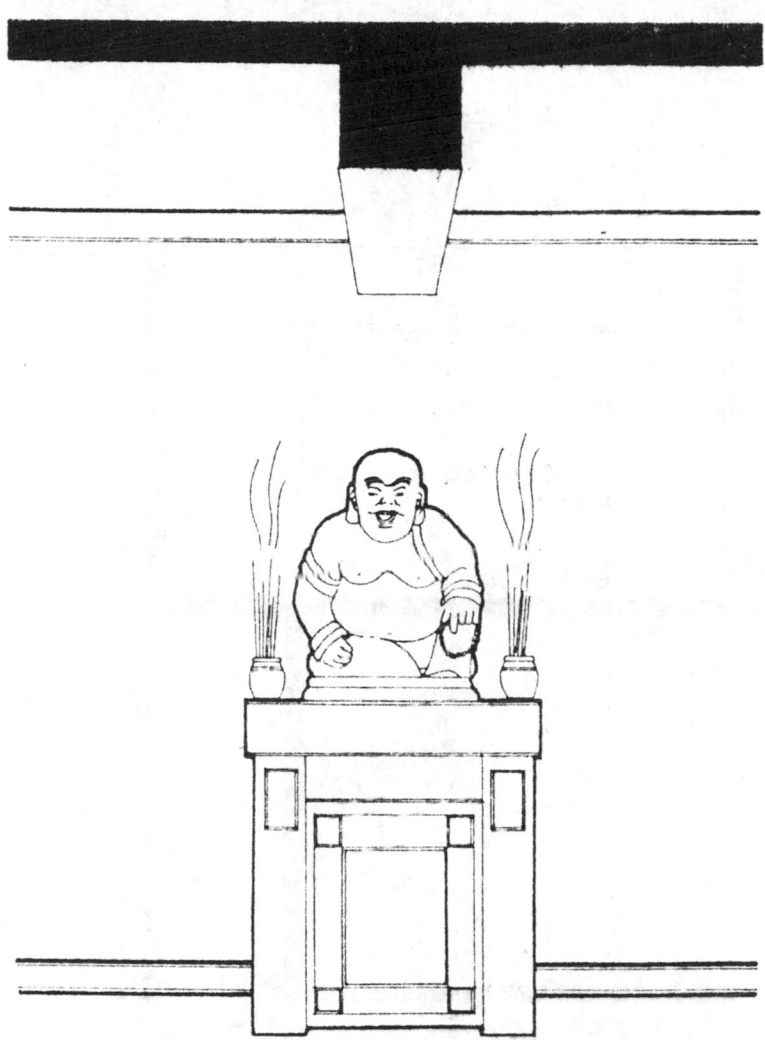

(Fig. 183) An exposed beam over an altar.

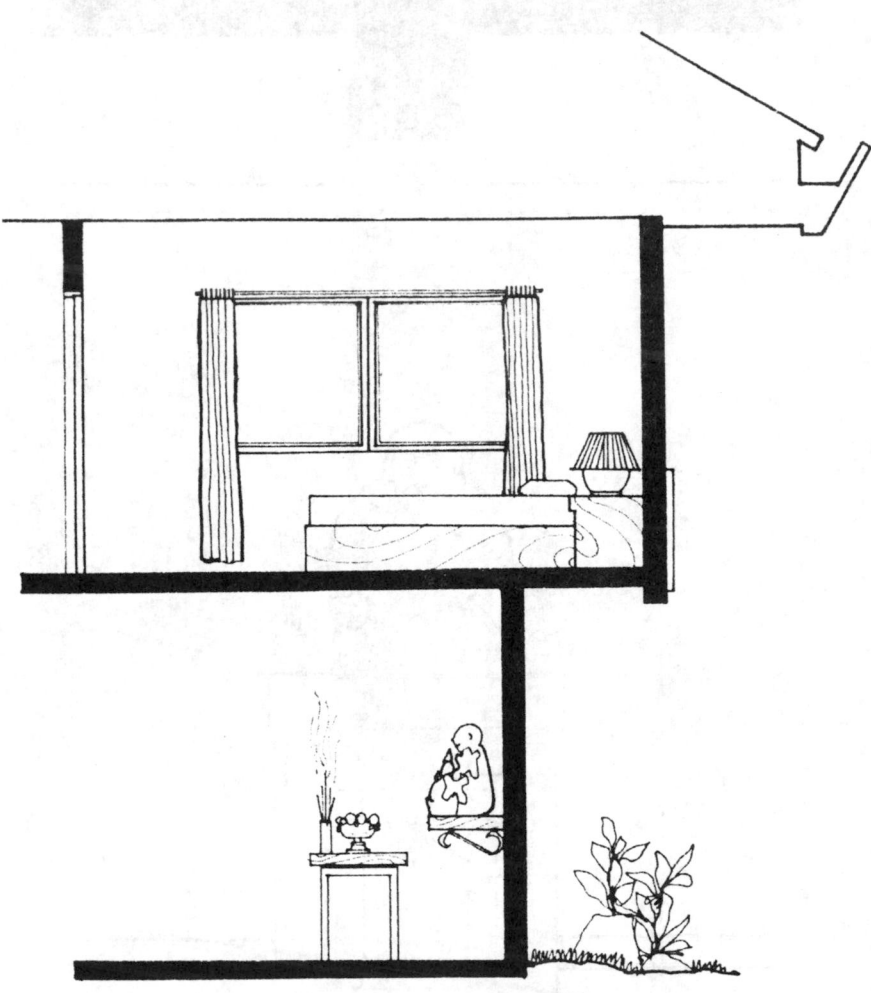

(Fig. 184) A bed above an altar.

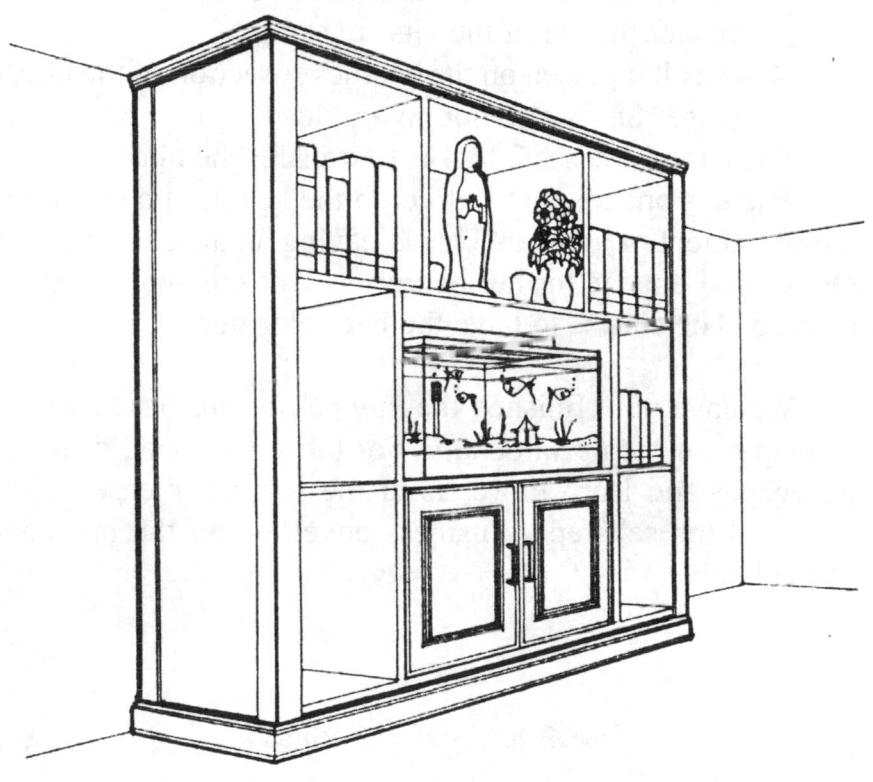

(Fig. 185) An aquarium beneath an altar.

(2) A water closet placed directly beneath an altar (Fig. 186) on a lower level does not provide 'solid' foundation to the altar due to its flushing action.

(3) A stove placed directly under an altar on a lower level (Fig. 187) is not desirable as this will agitate and render the *chi* of the altar unstable.

(4) An altar placed on the cantilever section of the house (Fig. 188) is also not favorable.

The cure for cases 2 to 4 is to transfer the altar.

There is one insidious effect to the health of a sleeper in the placement of an altar. This is having an altar in line with his/her bed outside his/her bedroom. This connotes sickness or dead. The cure is to have the bed relocated.

We have now finished the *Feng Shui* tour based on the Principles of the *Form School.* For those who would like to go deeper and learn more about the subject, please fill up and mail the self-reply business envelope on the last page of the book.

ಐಲ್ಲ ಐಲ್ಲ ಐಲ ಲ್ಲ ಐಲ ಲ್ಲ ಐಲ್ಲ

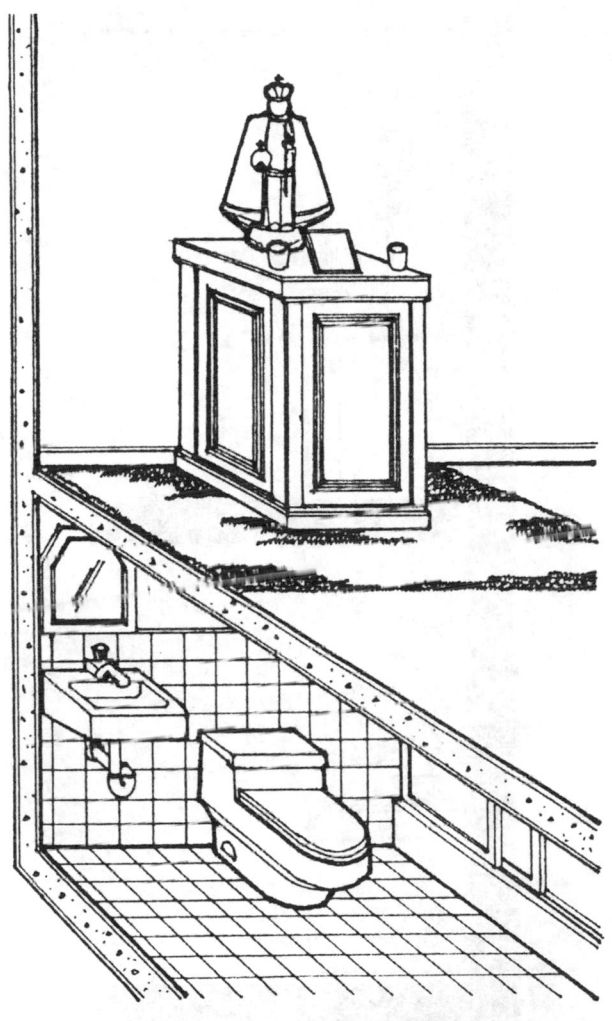

(Fig. 186) A water closet beneath an altar.

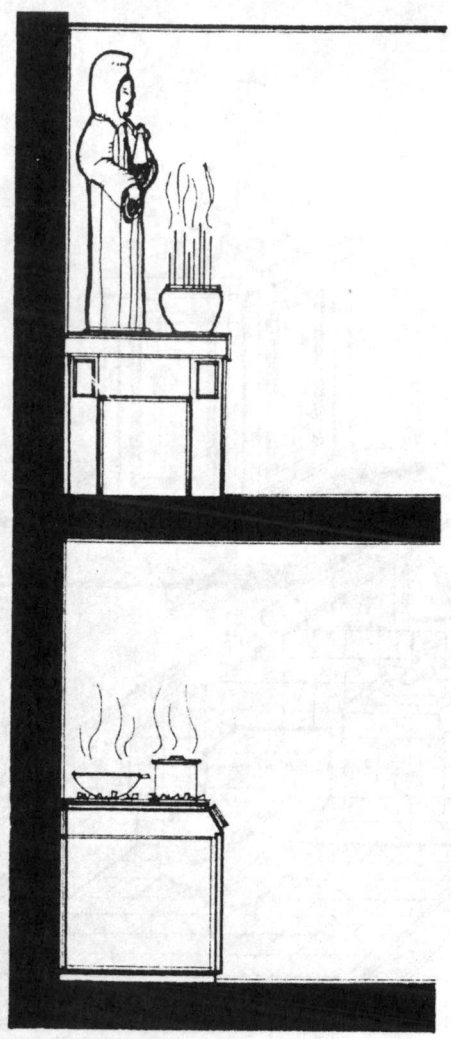

(Fig. 187) A stove under an altar.

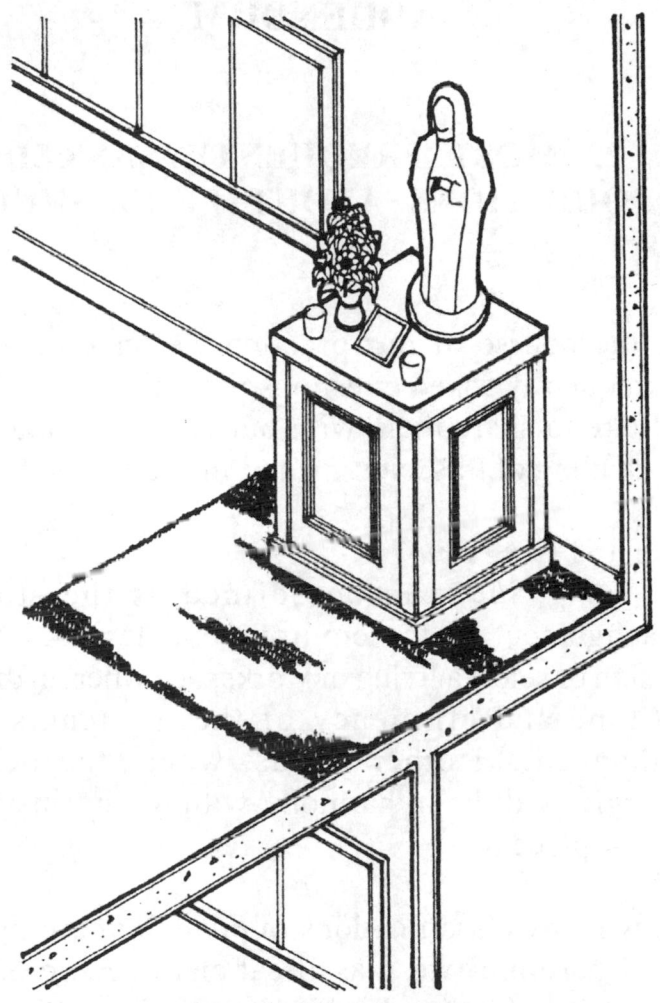

(Fig. 188) An altar on the cantilever section of the house.

ADDENDUM

22 MOST FREQUENTLY ASKED QUESTIONS ABOUT FENG SHUI

In the course of our practice we have encountered some frequently asked questions regarding *Feng Shui*. We would like to share them with our readers to clarify their understanding of this exciting and interesting subject.

1. What is *Feng Shui*?

   Feng Shui can be defined as the study and management of the environment. It enables one to design or select a living or workspace wherein the health, fortune and efficiency of the occupants will be enhanced. In other words, where the occupants energies will be in harmony with the intrinsic energy of the place.

2. How many classifications of *Feng Shui* are there?

   There are two classifications of *Feng Shui: Yin Feng Shui* for the dead and *Yang Feng Shui* for the living, both of which employ the principles of the Form and Compass Schools. Most geomancers agree with the principles underlying the Form School but, differ in their interpretations when it comes to the compass applications as, there are many different Compass Schools.

3. How many schools of *Feng Shui* are there?
Feng Shui is divided into two main schools.
   a) The *Form School* deals with the terrain of the site, e.g., the different shapes and compositions of the mountain or higher ground, as well as the contours of rivers and waterways surrounding the site.
   b) The *Compass School* deals with the juxtaposition of the mountains and rivers vis-a-vis the site in question. In short, how to position the site of either a grave or a house to an exact beneficial degree of the compass. The *Compass School* is divided into many sub-schools.

4. How many *Compass Schools* are there?
   There are at least ten *Compass Schools* but, the more popular are the *Ba-Gua* School, Three Harmony *(San He)*, Three Yuan *(San Yuan)*, Flying Stars (ordinary or single star), *Xuan Kong* Flyng Stars and the highly personalized Four Pillar School which entails mounting the natal chart of the subject to get a more accurate finding of his favorable elements.

5. How do each of these *Feng Shui* Schools differ from each other?

   (a) The most basic is the *'Ba-Gua'* School which does not need a very precise *Lo-pan* or Geomancers Compass to get the orientation. It deals with 8 directions, i.e., 4 cardinal and 4 corner directions to arrive at the favorable placement of the different elements of a house. It does not deal with the occupants on a personal level and is not applicable to *Yin Feng Shui* (*Feng Shui* for the Dead). It is a good starting point to get a solid grasp of the interactions of the 5 elements with the 8 directions and the functions of the different elements of a house.

   (b) The *'San He'* (Three Harmony) School of *Feng Shui* deals with the terrain and the water dragon. This requires an accurate compass and can be used in both *Yin* and *Yang Feng Shui*. It uses the binomial element of the deceased in orienting the grave. It applies the principles of 4-East and 4-West Groups in determining the fortunate orientations for the house. It also deals with problem solving and uses many principles of the 'Four Pillars of Fortune' to provide solutions and personalized house designs.

   (c) The *'San Yuan'* (Three *Yuan*) School of *Feng Shui* cannot operate without an accurate *Lo-pan* which it uses to fine tune the 360 degrees into 384 units.

It deals with the juxtapositioning of a grave or house with different conditions of the terrain. It has very specific interpretations of the effects of both mountain and water dragons. Mastery of this school can enable a geomancer to make or break the future of a person.

(d) The 'Flying (single) Star' School deals with solutions to enhance good fortune not only on a yearly and monthly basis but, even on a daily basis. It lays a good foundation for forecasting events as one can chart the moving energy of the stars. It uses 8 directions like the *Ba-Gua* School.

(e) The *'Xuan Kong* Flying Stars' school deals with the 24 mountains and 360 energy grids over a period of nine cycles. It can accurately predict events and formulate solutions to change the course of one's life. This also requires an accurate *Lo-pan* in order to assess the *Feng Shui* of a site. This is the most popular *Feng Shui* School currently propagated in the West, especially in Europe. It is also called 'The Science of the East.'

(f) The Four Pillars of Fortune School requires expertise in analyzing the occupant's natal charts in order to really personalize the *Feng Shui* and to enhance good fortune. Mastery of Four Pillar Analysis is the gateway to the soul of higher *Feng Shui*.

6. What has *Feng Shui* got to do with superstition and religion?

     Nothing! *Feng Shui* has a very scientific and logical basis. If you understand the system of *Feng Shui* you will be able to neutralize or prevent negative events from occurring and trigger fortunate events to take place. This is when you can say that you are the captain of your life.

     As *Feng Shui* is usually practiced by Taoist and Buddhist monks it tends to be associated with religion. These Taoist priests, for mundane reasons, veiled *Feng Shui* in a mystical way in order to play God to their clients. They rarely explain the principles of *Feng Shui* explicitly but talk about spirits and rituals in order to have leverage to increase their professional fee. They operate on the principle that the less people know about the art the more their service will be needed and the more they will get paid.

     They often prescribed magical paper as a remedy for certain negative *Feng Shui* violations. They claim that they are the only ones who can prescribe these magical writings which command unseen forces that control the spirits connected with the violation.

7. How come different geomancers have different *Feng Shui* analyses and cures?

     It all depends on the degree of training of the geomancer one consults. If the geomancer's knowledge is only up to the Form School then, the cures that he prescribes can be found in the previous chapters of this book. If his training is up to the *Ba-gua* School which deals with 8 directions then his prescriptions or cures will consider the elements of the 8 directions on top of the cures of the Form School. This omits anything personalized about the occupants, e.g. as how to position their beds; the stove in the kitchen, or how to improve the occupant's situation.

The above two levels rely much on the psychology of positive thinking and on the principles that certain changes will happen when you change your environment. This is akin to the ripple effect. Imagine that your environment without change is like the water of a pond that is calm. Changes, like moving furniture around and adding certain items to the environment are like moving some pebbles in the water to create ripples. But after a while the pond will be calm again and everything will be back to normal. This explains why after some changes things seem to improve but, the effect is not dramatic or felt by the occupants.

If the geomancer understands only the 4-East and 4-West or the Eight Mansions principles which is the most popular (but, is still considered layman's knowledge) then, he can fix some of your problems.

If he can correctly apply the water dragon formulae he can greatly improve your situation. But, he should be able to tell you when things will improve and who will be the beneficiary of such changes.

If the geomancer applies the *Xuan Kong* Flying Stars to your property then, he should be able to assess the history of the former occupants and forecast future events that may occur if proper cures are not carried out.

If the geomancer is well-versed in the *San Yuan* School he will be able to prolong the fortune of the property to the optimum level of the energy of the area.

Now you will understand why different geomancers have different cures and why the cures prescribed by some geomancers work and some do not.

8. What about Karma?

It all depends on the karma of the client. If the client has good karma and his luck is going to improve he will probably meet the right geomancer to help him. If the client's fortune is going down he will probably meet a geomancer who may not be thoroughly familiar with the art and who may prescribe the wrong cures. This will further exacerbate the client's condition to jibe with his karma.

If a client is experiencing a reversal of fortune due to bad karma, and he consults a geomancer who does not have a deep understanding of the person's past activities, and who helped him not only to weather through his current misfortune as well as to propel him to a level of success, and if the client after going through the crisis, uses his new found prosperity to engage in more negative or nefarious activities, the geomancer will definitely have a share of the bad karma generated. That's why it is important for the geomancer to charge a professional fee to partly offset this exchange of energy. The geomancer should also do charitable work to offset the karma that is attached to him.

9. What about pieces of mirror, lucky charms and fortune items? Do they really work?

In the Philippines, there is a school with hundreds of trainees going around peddling small pieces of mirror in different shapes. These are pasted on the corners of pillars and on top of door jambs. These pseudo-geomancers claim that the mirrors are to deflect evil spirits who will be scared when they see their own images therein. They even emphasize that the duration of the effect of the mirrors is only for one year and then they have to be replaced in order to recharge the effect of their '*Feng Shui*.' This is not true *Feng Shui* and it does not work!

These things propagate because of the 'band wagon' syndrome. When *Feng Shui* becomes popular there are many charlatans or peddlers of mirrors or lucky charms/items that abound. Their bottom line is to market their goods.

A lot of the so-called 'geomancers' peddle instant cure-all lucky or fortune items and claim that these are especially blessed, implying the authenticity and potency of their items. You will often find temples selling these items.

Most people are gullible and want instant results. They are prodded to purchase quite a number of different items to cure all imaginable mundane problems. Afterwards they find that these do not solve anything and they start to take a negative attitude toward *Feng Shui*. These lucky charm peddler-geomancers are the ones who become fortunate by selling a lot of charms. That's why they call it 'fortune charm' meaning, "you buy the charms and I get your fortune."

These peddlers can give *Feng Shui* a bad name. People should not be superstitious and should strive to learn more about *Feng Shui* themselves by reading more authentic *Feng Shui* books and attending *Feng Shui* conferences or seminars.

There is no substitute for understanding more about the subject yourself in order to be able to discern competent practitioners from spurious ones.

10. What are the modi operandi of these peddler-geomancers?

There are many ways that these 'geomancers' enter the local market especially, if the country is only beginning to catch on to *Feng Shui* fever like the Philippines.

(a) To prop up business, hotels resort to hiring a Chinese as their resident geomancer who claims to be from either Taiwan or Hongkong where *Feng Shui* is widely practiced. This works well with the Filipinos 'colonial mentality'. The geomancer will entertain the hotel guests during Chinese festivals. He usually knows a bit of face reading or hand reading and the basic horoscope compatibilities but, not much about 4-Pillar analysis nor higher *Feng Shui* principles.

The hotel or the geomancer will use the hotel's media connections to come to a business arrangement with some media people who will vigorously mount a press blitz to create an aura of authority around the geomancer's activities. This symbiotic business relationship is orchestrated by the hotel and media to draw in the cafe society crowd who are mostly gullible and superstitious. Their joint effort can create a *Feng Shui* phenomenon or fever to such an extent that the believers in the geomancer become enthralled. That is, until he eventually makes enough wrong pronouncements or forecasts of political or financial issues that proved him to be a false prophet.

A peddler-geomancer always approaches a prospective client by saying he has a fortune object that will bring luck to the buyer. For them to fix a problem, often regarding a wayward spouse, they will offer prayers for a period of time, usually a month, and charge the client handsomely. Many don't even carry a *Lopan* with them when invited to do a *Feng Shui* assessment.

(b) Another type of geomancer will do a free *Feng Shui* assessment provided the client will purchased a life insurance policy worth at least ₱1 million through him. He, of course, will be an accredited agent of the insurance company.

(c) Other geomancers will suggest the furniture should be changed as it does not conform to *Feng Shui* dimensions. They proceed to recommend a specific furniture maker who turns out to be their relative. Needless to say it will cost the client an arm and a leg.

One common trait of these geomancers is their swiftness in analyzing *Feng Shui* and diagnosing the *Feng Shui* cures. And the *Feng Shui* cures are usually available from them.

11. What are the traditional *Feng Shui* cures?
Traditional *Feng Shui* cures make use of the productive and destructive relations of the five elements to neutralize violations. *Feng Shui* violations are due either to conflicting energies of a particular section or *Gua* or a predominance of any of the 5 elements especially Earth *chi*.

The productive relations of the Elements are:
    (a) Metal produces water,
    (b) water produces wood,
    (c) wood produces fire,
    (d) fire produces earth and
    (e) earth produces metal.

The destructive relations of the Elements are:
    (a) Metal destroys wood,
    (b) wood destroys earth,
    (c) earth destroys water,
    (d) water destroys fire and
    (e) fire destroys metal.

For example: if the violation is due to a concentration of earth *chi*, especially of the disastrous or sickly type, then the *Feng Shui* cure can be a metal object which will deplete it because Earth in producing Metal, will be depleted of its energy, just as a mother giving birth to a baby, depletes the energy of her body.

You can either use a 5-tube metallic windchime, a bronze object, a pendulum clock, a piano or a chain of ancient Chinese coins depending on the type of Earth *chi*. These are the cures of the Flyng Star School.

To bring up the *chi* of certain other areas/*guas* you can use plants (Wood element) lights (Fire element) or aquarium or fountain (Water element) or crystal and ceramic jars or vases (Earth element). A rock formation can subdue, block or deplete hidden arrows from outside factors.

You can use the colors that correspond to the five elements to improve or counteract the intrinsic energy of the different *guas*. Colors of the red spectrum correspond to the fire element, blue corresponds to water, green to wood, yellow to earth and silver gray or white to the metal element.

Using corresponding color is an effective way to magnify the different elements. You can place a piece of quartz crystal on a light base with colored cellophane paper to project the particular color needed as crystal can magnify energy. There is a revival of interest in using natural crystals in *Feng Shui* cures.

There is a wide variety of mineral and other inclusions within the crystals. Hence, crystals can be used very effectively in neutralizing many violations such as, the '3 *sha*/killer' *chi* which is determined by the horoscope of the year. It is believed that there is no credible cure for the '3 *sha*' violation except, not having movement or activity in that particular section/ *gua*. But, black tourmaline can be used effectively to neutralize the '3 *sha*' and the five yellow/disastrous Earth *chi*. We will deal with the different *Feng Shui* violations and cures in another book solely devoted to this topic.

12. What are the ill effects of bad *Feng Shui*?

A place with serious *Feng Shui* violations can affect the fortune of the occupants. For instance, a wrong main door placement can affect their health and fortune. Cases of burglary are often connected with this violation.

A wrong stove placement can affect the wealth of the bread winner. It also affects other situations like a wayward spouse, couples desiring to have a baby, the hastening of the recovery of a sick family member, a single person wanting to get married or problems in marriage in general can be solved by adjusting the stove position.

The wrong placement of a water closet can affect the health of a specific family member and can be the cause of a woman who suffers a series of miscarriages. It can also affect the family fortune.

The combined wrong placement of the doors, stove and bed can sometimes prove to be fatal.

Wrong water placements can affect the moral character of the household. Cases of incest and promiscuity are traced to this violation. This is in the realm of the water dragon, which can also affect the following: the quality of learning of students, accidents and mishaps, insubordination or fast turnover of employees, problematic employees, lost opportunities, continuous waves of problems or sickness of family members. Fire incidents are often due to wrong door and stove placements.

13. What are the beneficial effects of good *Feng Shui*?

When everything is in harmony, i.e., the persons staying in the right section of the house with their beds in their favorable directions, the main door and all doors not suffering from *'sha'* (negative *'chi'*) but instead, placed in the peak *'chi'* area and the stove facing the favored direction of the master of the house, things will progress smoothly. Anything the master undertakes will become successful, there will be no bickering in the house, everyone will enjoy good health, problematic employees will resign from their work by their own volition, family solidarity will be reinforced and the warmth of such loving and caring affection will fill the space. In times of disaster, financial or physical, the occupants will be shielded from the impacts of such events.

This is what is known as a lucky house.

14. What is the difference between traditional *Feng Shui* and Modern *Feng Shui*?

In traditional *Feng Shui* the toilets and kitchen are separated from the main house. As China is a big country, houses have more depth than height, i.e., the structures or houses are of single or at most two stories.

In modern day high rise architecture, the principles of *Feng Shui* for multi-tiered houses are applied vertically instead of horizontally, not to mention numerous non-typical toilets and kitchen.

In the olden days, the orientations of houses were easy to determine because the houses usually faced the main gate or the street. Modern day architecture often places the gate and main entrance in different directions and contrives landscapes to further confuse the uninitiated

In traditional *Feng Shui* the reference was usually based on the master of the household, while in modern times, women often are the bigger contributors to the family income. Hence, it is more difficult to assess *Feng Shui* nowadays than during our forefather's time. The modern geomancer has to learn all the main schools of *Feng Shui* in order to arrive at the most accurate assessment of modern design.

15. What is the difference between a master geomancer and an ordinary geomancer?

The Master Geomancer deals with personalized

and specific solutions to the problems at hand. He analyzes the outside factors as thoroughly as the internal structure of a building, especially the roads, electric posts, terrain, bridges, tall trees, water ways and shapes and color of tall structures. He will then analyses the natal chart or eight characters (4-Pillars of Fortune Analysis) of each family member to ascertain their favorable direction in order to place their bedrooms and beds.

But the most important link to make all the *Feng Shui* adjustments work is selecting the auspicious date and time to undertake the renovation or changes.

No matter how good the *Feng Shui* cure is, without a proper date to trigger the cure it is similar to having a nice car without the car key. A wrong renovation date will have a negative effect of at least a hundred days. This could prove fatal to a business that is already having problems.

In order to select the auspicious date, (aside from consulting an almanac) the geomancer should be well-versed in 4-Pillars of Fortune Analysis as it is the basis of the *San He* date selection method . He should also know the Flying Star method of analyzing the energy combination and the *San Yuan* method of selecting the most favored day out of the short-listed dates.

16. Why is it that tenants of some houses that have been assessed by certain geomancers do not experience

improvement but on the contrary their fortune becomes worse?

The fault lies in the incorrect assessment of the geomancers due to their inaccurate procedure of doing a *Feng Shui* job. The correct way is to measure the house/structure and draw it up to scale on a piece of paper and get the correct center of the house prior to analyzing the *Feng Shui*. Another reason is that they were not able to get the correct orientation of the house or unit in question. With high rise building the compass reading from outside the building and inside the building can differ as much as 30 degrees due to the structural steel and electrical wirings of the building. This is exacerbated by the wind and the vehicles either passing or parked in front of the building while taking a reading with the *Lopan*. The most accurate way is to use the technical lot description prepared by a surveyor.

These are the basic things that are tedious to comply with but, they can spell the difference in getting the right information for an accurate assessment.

Ordinary geomancers usually spends little time in getting the correct center of the unit. In getting the position of the main door in relation to the section of the unit, they usually take the compass reading from the center of the living area which is often wrong, except when the unit is small and regular in shape. Sometimes the center of the unit is within the wall of a room which is impossible to determine without having the place drawn to scale. Therefore 90% of *Feng Shui* assessments are wrong because the geomancer bases it on cursory observations.

17. Why are most geomancers not rich if they claim they can improve other's fortune?

When a geomancer becomes popular due to his track record, most of his clients' fortunes improve dramatically. He will not have problems looking for clients. If he does his job correctly with good results, he will certainly be able to command a higher fee than ordinary geomancers who are always in a hurry to finish with a client and catch up with the next. They can only afford to spend an hour or at most two with every client. In their hurried analysis, a lot of mistakes are committed to the detriment of the client. Karma will in due time catch up with them.

In the *Feng Shui* profession or in any occult arts that affect the clients' decisions about their lives there will always be heavy karmic repercussion. If the geomancer offers his opinions without careful analysis, either to show off his mastery of the subject or to dispense with the inquirer, and his 'expert' opinion is taken seriously and executed, he will then have to bear partial karma for the results. In his course of practice the accumulation of these blunders will boomerang on him and deter him from leading a comfortable life.

Successful geomancers can lead a comfortable life but can rarely be extremely rich for there is only so much he can charge for every project he handles. Unlike a manufacturer who can employ thousands of workers to help him accumulate his wealth.

18. Why is China not a powerful or rich country if the Chinese know the true art of *Feng Shui*?

As explained in the preface on *page viii,* the governing class of China wanted to enjoy the art of *Feng Shui* themselves to maintain their control over the populace. Consequently, they banned its propagation outside of the nobility.

During the prosperous *Tang* Dynasty, foreign vassals sent their scholars to China to learn how to improve their fortune. The emperor tasked a monk who was an adept in the esoteric arts to re-invent the principles of *Feng Shui* and teach it to the foreign scholars hoping that this pseudo *Feng Shui* when applied to their countries would cause internal conflict with such disastrous effects that the foreigners would not have the time to invade China.

Unfortunately this pseudo-version of *Feng Shui* was so widely propagated that it trickled down to the Chinese grass roots. The bad karma bore fruit when China's citizens harvested the consequences of practicing the pseudo art and became subservient, stagnant and sickly.

19. How can *Feng Shui* improve the economic status of a country?

If the government can be socially responsible in laying out the road network to auspicious orientations then, all houses built along the roads will, at least, have good orientations. A house or building that has a good orientation is easier to design or adjust to good *Feng Shui* and the effect is more permanent. If the orientation is propitious, most people will be able to imbibe good *Feng Shui*. Their lives or efficiency will improve and this will have an uplifting effect on the entire populace.

This social responsibility should be shouldered by real estate developers. If they do not provide a good *Feng Shui* orientation to their qualified clients they will, in the end, suffer the consequences. After proper credit investigation, the applicants are found to be qualified, i.e., with a secured income and the ability to pay, the units are then turned over to them. But, due to bad *Feng Shui,* the tenants encounter problems related to health and loss of opportunity that drains their income. Sometimes they lose their jobs leading them to become delinquent payers of their monthly amortization. Imagine this to be on a grand scale. The government who paid the developers at the completion of the houses will not be able to collect from the buyers, and in turn, will not be able to pay the developers for the next mass housing project. This results in a huge backlog of housing units.

20. Among the Chinese esoteric arts, which is the most powerful?

The Chinese esoteric arts are comprised of different divination techniques that provide answers to certain issues that need clarification. The *I-Ching, Tai-I* and the 6 Learn Techniques were very useful during the time when telecommunications were not yet invented. People had to act without knowing the opinions or movements of the other party involved. Consequently, they needed a method to know what to do and how to proceed.

Palm and face reading were then, and still are, being used for fortune telling.

4-Pillars of fortune analysis and *Tze Wei* astrology gives people an accurate insight of what's in store for them during their entire life.

Qi-Gong and Chinese medicine deal with the preservation of the life force in order to maintain good health.

Meditation or the art of alchemy deals with magical practice to affect the spiritual plane which in turn has a bearing on the physical plane.

Feng Shui is the art of knowing the interplay of the energies of a site in order to enhance one's fortune and avoid negative consequences.

Aside from *Feng Shui* and medicine the above mentioned techniques deal only with time, people and direction. *Feng Shui* deals with time, people, direction and space. The other techniques can forewarn people about impending disaster or misfortune but, can not come up with an effective way to avoid the situation. It is only with *Feng Shui* that a remedy can be formulated to lessen the impact of what is to happen. Other techniques of divination can anticipate events but, it is only with the manipulation of the Five Elements that you can veer your ship toward a simple side swipe instead of experiencing a head-on collision. Hence*Feng Shui* is the more potent art in enhancing one's position in a specific timeframe. Readers can know more about these in our forthcoming book "The Secrets of Chinese Esoteric Arts Revealed!"

21. Does *Feng Shui* affect the owner of the place or the tenants?

   The tenants. Because they are the one who are living in the place. *Feng Shui* only affects the occupants who have a continuing stay of 60 days or more.

22. How soon will *Feng Shui* start to work when all the cures have been carried out?

   The normal time for *Feng Shui* to work is 60 days or one hexagenary cycle. But, if the geomancer is adept in date selection, then it can have an effect as fast as 9 days!

INDEX

altar 240, 244, 248
apparition 89, 202
aquarium 248
arthritis 211
atrium 165
automobile 235

backing 12, 16, 20,
    63, 186, 216, 244
bamboo 66
basement 147, 235
bed 175, 202, 211, 216,
    222, 229, 248, 252
bedroom 169, 202,
    206, 244, 252
bedroom door 140, 211
building 12, 24, 32,
    60, 63

cabinet, hanging 222
canal 96
ceiling 136, 150
cemetery 4, 93
center of a house 110,
    114, 147, 158,
    165, 179
chi 1, 7, 10, 12, 14, 16,
    36, 41, 45, 49, 54,

57, 60, 63, 66, 69,
    71, 81, 96, 101,
    110, 123, 127,
    136, 144, 147,
    150, 154, 158,
    172, 175, 182,
    206, 211, 248
-dragon 10, 12
-*yang* 4, 33, 66, 69,
    71, 86, 96, 117,
    120, 123, 127,
    136, 198, 229,
    240, 244
-*yin* 4, 7, 66, 86, 89,
    93, 117, 120, 123,
    127, 172, 190,
    198, 202, 229,
    235, 240, 244
chimney stack 76
chiong 45, 81,
    211, 244
creek 24
curtain 216

Devil's Gate 36, 140
door 45, 49, 57, 60,
    71, 76, 86, 89, 123,
    127, 131, 136, 140,

154, 182, 186,
202, 211
dining table 172, 175
divider 211
Dragon 30, 33, 36, 39,
71, 110
driveway 81

earthquake 7
East 33
elders 235

elemental energy 66, 69
electric post 76
electrical substation 54
electrical tower 57
energy grid 158
exhaust 76
exposed beam 136,
150, 190, 194,
222, 248

factor, inside 10, 96
outside 10,
54, 96
factories 57
family room 169
fault line 7

Feng Shui
- Compass School 36
- Form School 10,
30, 71, 140, 172,
182, 198
- *Yang* 1, 4, 117,
123, 235
- *Yin* 235
fire 175, 186, 190, 216
floor 117, 144
flyover 45
fountain 49
funeral parlor 4, 89

gable 76, 127
garage 36, 39, 235
garbage 71, 202
gate 71, 81, 96,
101, 198
Geomancer 1, 76, 127,
131
Gua 162
hexagram Ba-gua 49,
76, 81, 86, 89, 93
hidden arrows 54, 76
hollow 110, 114, 144,
147, 158, 162, 186
hospital 4, 89

house,
    cross-shaped 110
    H-shaped 110
    irregular shaped 165
    L-shaped 114
    old 60
    triangular-shaped
    106, 110
    U-shaped 114

industrial zone 57
inverted T-junction 49

Kirlian photography
    106
kitchen 182, 194

lamp post 81

mirror 123, 216, 222
    concave 49, 211
    convex 49, 60,
    76, 81, 89, 211
Ming Tang 12
mountain 20

nervous 57, 89
north 33, 120

northeast 36, 120
northwest 16

pillar 235
plot, front 20, 30, 106
    rear 20, 24, 30, 106
polarity 4
police station 4, 86
protrusion 110, 114,
    144, 147

refrigerator 190
respiratory 57
ripple effect 106
river 49
roof 60, 101

sewer pipe 194
sha 41, 45, 49
    54, 57,
    71, 76, 81, 86
    93, 127
shapes 106
size 117
skywell 165
slaughter house 4
south 33, 120
southwest 140

stairs 154, 158,
    162, 179, 211, 222,
    244, 248
storage 123
stove 175, 182, 186,
    190, 216, 229, 252
street 41
street sign 81
sunken living room
    144
swimming pool 24,
    120

T-junction 45, 81
temple/church 4,
    89, 93
terrain 10, 30,
    36, 120
Tiger 30, 33, 36, 39,
    71, 110, 120
toilet 127, 131, 136,
    154, 172, 175, 179
topography 10, 12
traffic 45, 49
transmission tower 57
tree 16, 54, 66,
    69, 76

urinary tract infection
    211

venetian blinds 216

walls 96, 101
washing machine 90
water 41, 49, 120,
    172, 186, 190,
    198, 202, 229
water tank 86, 186,
    190
water closet 222,
    244, 248, 252
waterways 10, 12,
    36, 41
well 186, 198, 202
west 33
wind tunnel 57, 60
window 127, 186, 216

Y-junction 49

The **Four Pillars of Fortune for Everybody** contains One Hundred Years Almanac in full color that serves as the basis for the study of Four Pillars of Fortune. It shows you:

- How to convert your birth data, i.e., your year, month, day and hour of birth to eight characters or the Four-Pillar Information which is the equation of your life
- The basis for analyzing the strength of your birthday element to find out what element will balance or enhance your life
- How to use the balancing element of your life equation in Feng Shui to enhance your performance and fortune
- How to determine your fortunate career
- Insights to your inner propensity or character traits
- The trends of your life so that you can effectively program your life to achieve your goals
- How you will fare in your marriage
- Your life expectancy
- The forecast of your fortune and health
- Insight to your past life and future reincarnation based on the writings of General Tzu Ger Liang, a master strategist who was known for his profound knowledge in the art of Divination
- The basis for understanding the soul of Feng Shui - the interaction of Yin and Yang and the five elements

'The Secrets of Chinese Esoteric Arts Revealed' is a compilation of the whole gamut of wisdom of ancient Chinese culture that is applicable to the modern world.

The face reading section discloses the character traits of a person and can be used as a preponderant factor in selecting a mate, an employee or electing public officials to their posts.

The palm analysis will further validate the person's character traits as revealed by a person's facial features. The combination of both the face and palm analyses serves as a solid ground in determining the character profile.

The different tools under the section of divination can provide answers to most people's queries ranging from missing items, weather forecasts, the results of an event, omens, messages from the spiritual plane, personal compatibilities and even the sex of unborn babies.

The Feng Shui section provides a more personalized approach to select the best or most fortunate direction of one's house and office desk to enhance one's performance.

The criteria of diagnosis based on the accumulated experience of Chinese medicine are revealed in the final chapter and can act as a forewarning of a condition of one's health so that immediate medical treatment could be undertaken.

'The Secrets of Chinese Esoteric Arts Revealed' is everybody's essential reference to the journey of life. It unlocks and provides the ancient Chinese wisdom at your finger tips in an easy-to-read format.

FACE READING SERIES

Learn Face Reading in 90 minutes

By Victor L. Dy

In this ever changing world of stiff competition it is an asset if you can decipher the character traits and propensity of action to be taken by people whom you have to interact with. *Learn Face Reading in 90 minutes* outlines step-by-step the most basic ways to read faces to understand the inner character of people so that you can adopt the most appropriate way in dealing with them to obtain the maximum result from your interaction.

This is a must-read book for head hunters, human resource personnel, employers, employees, parents and anybody who would like to avail of the knowledge of the secrets of Chinese face and character reading to have the edge in dealing with their peers.

How to Select Your Mate, Girls! illustrates both the desirable and undesirable features of males whom you will meet in your workplace or schools. It is important to know whom to associate with so as not to be a victim of misassociation. This book reveals the features of males who are:

FACE READING SERIES
How to Select Your Mate, Girls
By VICTOR L. DY

- responsible
- irresponsible
- violent prone - a wife beater
- prone to multiple relationships
- strong sex-drive
- insensitive
- cruel, destructive and a double-crosser
- impulsive
- successful
- generous
- miser
- criminally inclined
- adulterous

and many more features!

FACE READING SERIES

How to Select Your Mate, Guys

By VICTOR L. DY

How to Select Your Mate, Guys! shows both the desirable and undesirable features of females whom you will meet in your workplace or schools. It is important to know how to select your friends. This book reveals the features of females who are:

- sexually accommodating
- liberalized women
- prone to divorce
- talkative persons who cannot keep secrets
- emotional
- nosey
- victims of malicious intent
- spendthrift
- detrimental to their husbands
- successful
- capable of abandoning their families
- better to get married late
- bad wives features
- emotionally unstable
- childless
- promiscuous

and many more features!

Be the Master of your Destiny

And also help improve the lives of others.

Enroll now in Level I of 'APPLIED FENG SHUI FORMODERN LIVING', the world's first Feng Shui correspondence course in English.

Level I:

All lessons are fully illustrated, as in its primer, **'Feng Shui for Everybody'**. The lessons are programmed in step-by-step sequence to assure that every principle of the **Ba-Gua School of Feng Shui** is easy-to-understand and can be immediately applied to improve your present condition.

After finishing Level I of the course, you will be able to fix your own Feng Shui and be your own Geomancer.

Level II:

In Level II of **Applied Feng Shui for Modern Living**, you will learn the Feng Shui for all types of houses and high-rise condiminiums. This course will greatly enhance your career if you are an Architect, an Interior Designer or a Space Planner. Problem-solving will be the core of this level. The **'Three Yuan and Three Harmony'** Schools will be taken up.

After finishing this level, you will achieve the standard of a respected Geomancer from Taiwan. You will also have the opportunity to participate in the world's first course on Feng Shui Date Selection for all activities, e.g., breaking ground, renovation, erecting pillars, installing main doors and gates, installing stoves, altars and beds, digging wells, pools and ponds, transfering to a new place and its procedures. This course is anchored on the **Four Pillars Analysis**, a Chinese system of natal charting that you will also learn.

Knowing the **Four Pillars Analysis** will enable you to personalize Feng Shui and forecast one's future trend - the up and down cycles of life, favorable directions, how to place one's desk and bed, colors that will enhance fortune, fortunate careers. Learning the **Four Pillars Analysis** can also open new career opportunities in counseling.

Level III:

Learn the crux of the **'Moving Stars'** and the **'Xuan Kong Moving Stars' Schools** which are practiced by top Hong Kong Geomancers. You will be able to forecast events and adjust the Feng Shui to either enhance or neutralize them. Thus, you become the Master of Your Destiny! When you conclude this level, you will have attained the standard of a respected Hong Kong Geomancer.

The World's First English Feng Shui Correspondence Course

Applied Feng Shui For Modern Living

*L*evel 1 of Applied Feng Shui for Modern Living is a full year course divided into 12 modules, fully illustrated lessons programmed to lay a comprehensive and solid foundation for the Ba-Gua school of Feng Shui.

This course is also essential for the understanding of other more advanced schools of Feng Shui, e.g., 'The Three Yuan', 'The Three Harmony', 'The Moving Stars', and 'The Xuan Kong Moving Stars' Schools which will be discussed in Levels II and III. All these lessons can be completed at your own pace in the comfort of your home.

The lessons are arranged in step-by-step sequence that will enable you to immediately apply and improve your present condition.

CURRICULUM FOR LEVEL 1:

- The Principle of Yin and Yang - How to create balance and harmony in your environment.
- The Principle of the 5 Elements - How to interpret the Feng Shui of any given house.
- Shape, Orientation and the 5 Elements - How to enhance your fortune. Detailed discussions of the hollows and protrusions in the shape of a structure with interpretations and remedies.
- The 8 Guas and their correspondences - Their effect on the family members.
- Locating and activating the Fortune Spot of your house.

- The correct way of determining the Center of your House - You will be provided with a Feng Shui master guide that aids in determining the root cause affecting the family's health, fortune and harmony.
- The 24 Directions - The basis of Feng Shui analysis. You will learn how to determine the cause of failing health and fortune.
- Garden Feng Shui - What type of plants and trees you should plant.
- The correct placement of your garage - To avoid being accident-prone.
- The proper way to fill up an old well - incorrect procedure can sometimes cause misfortune to your family; determine where to dig a well.
- Factors that increase Fire Risks.
- Determining the factors that cause personality problems of your family and disruption of harmonious relations.

PLUS! Learn how to:
- ◆ Make a husband more responsible.
- ◆ Improve your health.
- ◆ Improve children's grades.
- ◆ Improve human relationships.
- ◆ Be successful in courtship.
- ◆ Improve your business.
- ◆ Identify a house prone to burglary.

These and many more secrets to help you become the Master of Your Destiny.